Psychodynamic Approaches for Treatment of Drug Abuse and Addiction

This book provides clinicians and students with insights on the use of psychodynamic therapy to treat drug abuse and addiction, combining theory with clinical case material.

The perspectives of analysts such as Abraham, Rado, Zimmel, Tibout, Wurmser, Khanzian, Krystal and McDougall are reviewed alongside original and more recent conceptualizations of drug addiction and recovery based on Kleinian, Winnicottian and Kohutian ideas. The case material deals with clinical phenomena that characterize working with this complex population, such as intense projective identification, countertransference difficulties and relapses. The theoretical analysis covers a range of concepts, such as John Steiner's psychic shelters and Betty Joseph's near-death-addiction, which are yet to be fully explored in the context of addiction. Prevalent topics in the addiction field, such as the reward system, the cycle of change and the 12-step program, are also discussed in relation to psychodynamic theory and practice.

Written by an experienced therapist, *Psychodynamic Approaches for Treatment of Drug Abuse and Addiction* is useful reading for anyone looking to understand how psychodynamic thought is applicable in the treatment of drug abuse and addiction. It may also be of some relevance to those working on treating alcohol use disorders and behavioral addictions.

David Potik is a clinical criminologist at the Day-Hospital and at the Dr. Miriam and Sheldon G. Adelson Clinic for Drug Abuse Research and Treatment, both within the division of psychiatry at the Tel-Aviv Sourasky Medical Center, Israel. He also works as a psychotherapist in private practice and is an accredited Eye Movement Desensitization and Reprocessing (EMDR) practitioner. He has published articles on psychoanalytic psychotherapy, psychopathology and drug addiction.

"David Potik's *Psychodynamic Approaches for Treatment of Drug Abuse and Addiction* is an excellent introduction to the psychoanalytic literature on addiction theory and treatment. His specific application of object relations theory to a broad range of treatment settings is an invaluable contribution that many will find enlightening as well as useful".

Psychodynamic Approaches for Treatment of Drug Abuse and Addiction

Theory and Treatment

David Potik

Routledge
Taylor & Francis Group

LONDON AND NEW YORK

First published 2021
by Routledge
2 Park Square, Milton Park, Abingdon, Oxon OX14 4RN

and by Routledge
52 Vanderbilt Avenue, New York, NY 10017

Routledge is an imprint of the Taylor & Francis Group, an informa business

© 2021 David Potik

Chapter 3: © 2018 Springer Nature
Chapter 7: © 2010 John Wiley and Sons

British Library Cataloguing-in-Publication Data
A catalogue record for this book is available from the British Library

Library of Congress Cataloging-in-Publication Data
A catalog record has been requested for this book

ISBN: 978-0-367-08701-2 (hbk)
ISBN: 978-0-367-08702-9 (pbk)
ISBN: 978-0-429-02389-7 (ebk)

Typeset in Times New Roman
by codeMantra

I dedicate this book to my dear father who sadly did not live to see its publication.

Contents

Acknowledgments

This book is the result of accumulating psychotherapeutic work with individuals coping with drug abuse and addiction, psychoanalytic thinking, findings of empirical research, supervision and consultations with colleagues. The Adelson Clinic for Drug Abuse Treatment and Research has been a place for learning and I am acknowledging my indebtedness to the clinic's staff and to Dr. Miriam Adelson throughout the years. My deepest gratitude is to Dr. Eli Elbaz for the supervision, and Marsha Weinstein for the interesting and fertile discussions about therapeutic issues and effective treatment for this challenging population. I thank the nursing staff and the psychosocial staff at the clinic: Yali Abramsohn, Nir Caspi, Yael Ishay, Hannah Israel, Zehavit Mendelson and Smadar Yavor-Naim.

I would like to extend my gratitude to professor Shaul Schreiber, the director of the psychiatric division at the Tel-Aviv Sourasky Medical Center, and Oren Avitan, the director of the Adelson Clinic. I thank Anat Sason, a research assistant in the clinic, and Dr. Einat Peles for the guidance and assistance in conducting empirical research and the opportunity to examine clinical assumptions scientifically. Two inspiring physicians, with whom I had the honor to work with are Dr. Vera Rados and Dr. Zila Gitman of blessed memory, who combine miraculously in their personality humaneness and professionalism.

I also would like to thank patients, therapists and supervisors for their agreement to share the clinical material with other professionals and allow mutual learning from experience. All personal details had been changed in order to protect patients' confidentiality. And, very last, my deepest gratitude to my family for the love and the support.

Introduction

The usage of psychoactive drugs is a phenomenon that accompanies humanity from earlier ages. Over the years, the rates of individuals who experiment in drugs either alone or together with other individuals are only rising, and so does the public discourse over various drugs and their influences. Drug abuse and addiction have economic, moral, political, religious and social aspects that affect our lives. Amphetamines, benzodiazepines, cannabis, cocaine, opioid pain killers and designer drugs are terms that professionals in both the addiction and the mental health field hear either in their work or in their social milieu. The legalization of medical cannabis, the decriminalization of its use for recreational purposes, the consequences of the opioid epidemic and the renewed scientific interest in hallucinogenic drugs for treatment of mental disorders have brought the issue of drug abuse and addiction straight into the social, political and the economic agenda. Today, unlike in the past, almost every patient who seeks therapy either in the private sector or in the public one probably has used some drug.

In the last decades, technological developments in neuroscience enabled discovering the biochemical mechanisms which stand at the basis of drug addiction. Thanks to science, we know about the reward system, the ruinous consequences of prolonged drug abuse on the human brain, and there are even attempts to develop vaccines for the treatment of cocaine addiction. Simultaneously, there are treatment and counseling methods designed to assist patients who suffer from drug abuse and addiction, when most of them focus on eliciting motivation, changing thinking patterns and developing skills for not starting to abuse drugs again after periods of drug abstinence.

However, biological and cognitive approaches do not provide convincing answers to the complex therapeutic issues which arise during treatment. The therapeutic encounter with this population reveals not only an intense desire for consciousness-altering drugs but also a disturbed matrix of interpersonal and intrapersonal relations, damaged sense of self and mental pain. Different psychoanalytic schools of thought deal extensively with these issues, and therefore clinical work based on these paradigms could prove useful in investigating the mental areas in which unconscious forces influence the individual's behavior.

The psychoanalytic approach on its various schools of thought provides a comprehensive perspective of the addiction phenomenon and addresses etiology, personality construct, object relations, anxieties, defences and behaviors. An additional advantage is that every psychoanalytic school of thought suggests different theoretical conceptualization and different therapeutic approach. From the rise of psychoanalysis, drug abusers and drug-addicted individuals have been considered not appropriate population for psychoanalysis or psychoanalytic treatment. However, throughout the last century, some psychoanalysts rowed against the stream and provided substantial contributions for those who did try to work with this unique population.

The main aim of this book is to offer new knowledge about psychodynamic psychotherapy of drug abuse and addiction. It is written mostly for clinicians and it presents many challenges and questions which arise during treatment, such as how to treat patients who relapse? How to cope with intense projective identification? When to support a patient who wants to come off opioid maintenance treatment? Can therapists treat patients who continue to abuse drugs?

Therapists who work within the psychodynamic approach and students in therapeutic professions will find here rich clinical and theoretical material. Although this book focuses on drug abuse and addiction, the theoretical ideas and the therapeutic approaches presented here have relevance also for therapists working with behavioral addictions and alcohol use disorders. The ideas in the book may also be of interest to therapists and counselors working in this field within different schools of thought and for professionals in the mental health field who have interest or encounter patients who abuse drugs.

The first two chapters provide a comprehensive historical review of different psychoanalytic perspectives of drug abuse and addiction. The purpose of this review is to present the main theoretical conceptualizations and therapeutic approaches of psychoanalysts who dealt with the addiction phenomenon from the early days of psychoanalysis until these days. The next chapters rely on the ideas of Melanie Klein and her followers. A theoretical framework for understanding drug addiction, which is based on Klein's developmental theory, is presented in the third chapter. Its main premise is that Klein's paranoid-schizoid position has many similarities to active drug addiction and that drug addicts use the same defence mechanisms as infants in coping with the anxieties that characterize this position.

The next chapter continues this theoretical framework for understanding drug addiction, as it pertains to primary mental states. Its main premise is that Klein's depressive position has many similarities to recovery from drug addiction. During recovery, patients experience mourning and reparation processes as infants who cope with the anxieties arising from their struggle with depressive anxiety. The fifth chapter deals with one of the main difficulties in treatment of drug abuse – relapses. The chapter begins with a review of one of the leading models used by professionals in this field for understanding this phenomenon, the wheel of change, and continues with Kleinian and Neo-Kleinian conceptualizations of relapse, which are based on the works of John Steiner and Herbert Rosenfeld.

The destructive self-administration of drugs, the overwhelming projective identification and the difficulties in managing countertransference are the main issues of the sixth chapter. By discussing some of Freud's, Kernberg's and Betty Joseph's ideas, I try to shed light on those complex issues and offer therapeutic interventions. The theoretical material in this chapter, and throughout the book, is illustrated by clinical case material.

The seventh chapter presents Winnicottian conceptualization of drug addiction and recovery among patients in methadone maintenance treatment (MMT) and discusses the role of psychodynamic psychotherapy among drug addicts, by focusing on the processes which patients undergo during treatment. The main premise is that treatment in MMT programs is accompanied by changes in patients' life-styles and behavior, which are parallel to transitional phenomena.

The next chapter continues the previous one and completes the Winnicottian conceptualization of drug addiction and recovery among patients in opioid maintenance treatment, as it deals with an issue which does not receive much attention in the professional literature – detoxification and coming off opioid maintenance treatment. Chapter 9 presents drug abuse and addiction according to the self psychology school of thought. The ideas of Heinz Kohut and his followers regarding treatment of drug abusers are reviewed, and a case material of a young patient who used cannabis, cocaine and MDMA is presented.

The last chapter focuses on the 12-step program, a recovery program that evolved from the experience of people who coped with addiction. This program is not mostly learned in academic institutions and the main aim of this chapter is to present it for professionals who received an academic education (therapists, counselors, psychiatrists, nurses). Empirical studies about this program's efficacy are reviewed, and the interfaces between the 12-step program and different psychoanalytic schools of thought are discussed.

The premise that drug abusers are not an appropriate population for psychoanalytic treatment has prevailed in psychoanalytic literature and practice for years. In this respect, this contribution constitutes an attempt to disprove this assumption and to continue the work of inspiring figures, such as Bion, Winnicott and Searles, who treated difficult patients who for years have not been considered the classic patients for either psychoanalysis or psychoanalytic psychotherapy. I believe that psychoanalysts who will read this book should remember Britton's (1998) comment about the demanded patience required for onward development of psychoanalytic ideas.

Finally, this book promotes and supports psychoanalytic thought in a period that is quite dominated by neuroscientific developments and treatment methods that do not pay much attention to unconscious processes. The therapeutic work in the addiction field is often integrative, and therefore, there are references to other knowledge bodies and treatment methods. For example, in the third chapter, there is a short explanation about the reward system, and in the fifth chapter, I discuss how the wheel of change and other approaches (cognitive-behavioral, motivational interviewing) relate to relapses. In the seventh chapter I explain the treatment in therapeutic communities. I hope that this integration will encourage professional dialogue from which both patients and professionals will benefit.

Reference

Britton, R. (1998). *Belief and imagination: Explorations in psychoanalysis*. Routledge.

Chapter 1

An historical overview of psychoanalytic perspectives on drug abuse and addiction – Part I

"I have carried out experiments and studied, in myself and others, the effect of coca on the healthy human body".

(Freud, 1884\1975, p. 58)

The addiction field is situated in the edges of psychoanalytic thought and practice from its earliest days. For more than a century, analysts dealt with complex mental conditions, such as psychoses, severe personality disorders and regressive states (Bion, 1967; Kernberg, 1984; Searles, 1979; Winnicott, 1955), whereas the status of the addiction field was of a stepbrother or a stepsister who is never considered part of the family. Perhaps this status has become fixated because of Freud's assertion that drug abusers are not appropriate candidates for analysis since difficulties which will appear during the treatment will lead to further abuse (Loose, 2000).

During his life, Freud presented several ideas about drug abuse and addictions. He saw addiction as a substitute for the primary addiction – masturbation and noted that oral fixations have a central role in the development of behaviors, such as drinking alcohol or smoking nicotine (Freud, 1905/1975). In "Civilization and Its Discontents" (Freud, 1930/1961), he claimed that alcohol and drug use enable relief for the suffering of law-abiding people who obey society's laws and restrictions. In a certain sense, this argument is heard today by many law-abiding people who view cannabis use as a natural escape from the daily grind.

Freud investigated the influences of cocaine toward the end of the 19th century in a period in which pharmaceutical companies tried to promote this drug as a panacea for mental and physical malaises (Markel, 2011). The reports on self-experiencing with cocaine reveal that he felt sexual arousal, vitality and vigor, and Gay (1988) suggests that Freud used it for coping with depressive moods. Following the death of one of his friends after prolonged cocaine abuse, Freud changed his mind about the beneficial use of cocaine (Markel, 2011), and turned to other research directions. At that stage of his life, Freud saw his future career as studying the medical uses of cocaine

(Volkan, 1994), and perhaps had it not been for his friend's death, things would have turned out differently for psychoanalysis.

Loose (2000) provides a comprehensive review of a few significant articles about psychoanalytic thinking and addictions, which were published until Freud's death. He terms this period as the drive theory period because the impetus of most of the contributions was on the libido and on the psychosexual stages theory (Loose, 2000). Loose does not mention additional periods in psychoanalytic writing about addictions, and, in my opinion, there are additional periods that are characterized by the emergence of different ideas concerning theory and treatment of drug abuse and addiction. Those ideas appeared against a background, of scientific, social and historical changes.

The first period – from the emergence of psychoanalysis to World War II

The first article in the psychoanalytic literature which focused on addiction is that of Carl Abraham, in which he argued that alcohol use influences on sexual impulses because it removes defences and inhibitions and causes increased sexual activity. This article was not based on analysis of patients with alcohol use disorders but on observation of men's behavior in pubs. There, Abraham saw men falling on each other's necks and exhibiting emotion, and, consequently, he deduced that alcohol use enables inhibitions release, which causes the rise of latent homosexual impulses to the conscious (1908/1979). According to this claim, alcohol use is the result of an oral conflict as alcoholism represents a regressive oral tendency (Volkan, 1994). Among individuals who are not homosexuals, the homosexual component of the sexual instinct had undergone sublimation by the influence of education and the society. In contrast, among addicted individuals, alcohol becomes a substitution for genital intercourse, and so alcohol becomes associated with perversion (cited in Levin, 1987).

Abraham did not claim that all men have homosexual identity, but rather that latent homosexual impulses that exist among males tend to appear during drunkenness (Loose, 2000). Lack of sexual activity or abstinence from it leads to a search for sexual gratification, which belongs to an earlier stage of infantile sexual development (Abraham, 1908/1979). Therefore, individuals who suffer from drug use disorders and addiction look for drugs and alcohol because of an oral fixation, as the substances are used as substitutions for the gratification of infantile sexual wishes. According to drive theory, those individuals cannot contain any frustration and demand immediate gratification, and even prefer it to the gratification obtained from interpersonal interactions (Loose, 2000).

Besides emphasizing the idea that alcohol is a psychoactive substance which temporarily neutralizes the repression mechanism and allows repressed material to arrive to the conscious, Abraham also notes that external factors such as genetics and the environment do not provide a convincing explanation for alcoholism, and there is a personality factor which should be explored (Abraham, 1908/1979). An interesting conclusion which arises from this article is that already at the beginning of the 20th century, prevailed the stereotypic gender that manhood is associated with drinking large amounts of alcohol.

Sandor Rado is the next significant analyst who wrote several articles about addiction in different periods. In the beginning, he assumed that addiction is a substitute for sexual activity since it enables immediate gratification, which bypasses the erogenous zones (Rado, 1926). Meaning, drug abuse creates sexualization of the body since it provides a certain orgasm, and people become addicted since they can gain oral sexual gratification whenever they desire. Rado termed this process alimentary orgasm and noted that this orgasm is experienced by the baby during breastfeeding in pre-genital stages.

In his next articles, he introduced elements that in later years will be attributed to ego psychology (Loose, 2000), and self psychology (Ulman & Paul, 2006). First, he argued that an individual does not become a drug addict because he uses drugs but because he has an urge to use them. The main factor of addiction is craving, and addicts can switch among different types of drugs and go from using one drug to another (Rado, 1933). Second, Rado distinguished between two main drug categories according to their influence: hypnotic, which ameliorate pain and stimulants, and sedative drugs, which provide euphoria and pleasure. Third, he provided a psychological explanation for the specific choice of drug abusers in specific drugs and added that those who suffer from depression would search for stimulant drugs, which will provide to the ego a high self-value (Rado, 1928).

Fourth, he related to drug addiction as pharmacothymia and described a process in which the ego is captured by a pharmacothymic regime that destroys the natural ego organization (Rado, 1933). Reality's frustrations hurt the ego's omnipotence, and narcotic drug addiction allows the ego to regain elation, omnipotence and "its original narcissistic stature" (Rado, 1933, p. 8). Besides, Rado described a personality factor which he termed the 'action self', and which represented the individual's image of himself. The action self is nourished from pleasures and successes, and when one cannot gain them in his daily activities, he turns to drug abuse (Rado, 1969).

Rado never relinquished the drive model and noted that addiction is rooted in attempts to gratify archaic oral cravings, but simultaneously he noted that those cravings are associated with the need for safety and preservation of self-value. In his last article on this subject, Rado (1957) offered a general theory about the etiology of addiction and noted that it constitutes an inferior substitution for sexual gratification, as addicted individuals are characterized with ego deficits and recurrent self-regulation attempts as a malignant form of reparation.

Rado did not present with a clear and organized theory of addiction, but rather diverse ideas which are associated with different psychoanalytic schools of thought. Rado's contribution, as well as that of most of the psychoanalytic writers in this period, is mostly theoretical yet highly significant. During four decades, he offered analysts different ideas to use in the treatment of individuals who suffer from drug abuse and addiction. In addition, Rado aspired to create bridges between the psychoanalytical world and the scientific world and was one of the most prominent figures who promoted an adaptational psychodynamic approach.

To summarize his contributions, first, he noted that drugs do not only affect the erogenous zones but also the entire body and added that there are neural operating systems (Rado, 1969). Those assumptions appeared a few decades before the rise of neuroscience. Most impressing, in one of his later contributions, he noted that addiction is associated with regulation, reward and punishment (Rado, 1957). Three years before the publication of this article, Olds and Milner (1954) implanted electrodes in different areas of rats' brains and managed to discover a system whose unique function is creating a rewarding effect on behavior.

Second, his ideas correspond with the concept of addiction as a disorder that is characterized by a recurrent search for gratification despite the destructive consequences is the accepted view of this disorder in the scientific world today (Volkow, Koob, & McLellan, 2016). Third, Rado was also one of the first analysts who offered a distinction of drug types according to their mental effects. Although Loose (2000) argues that this distinction is quite simplistic since it is based on the pleasure principle (searching for pleasure and avoiding pain), in my opinion, Rado laid the foundations of self-medication theory, which will be delineated years later by another analyst. Fourth, the idea that drug abuse assists in boosting self-esteem was also ahead of its time and will be elaborated in the future by ego and self psychology analysts. Unfortunately, Rado, one of the most conspicuous analysts that Budapest produced (Gay, 1988), did not receive enough recognition for his contributions to the addiction field.

The addiction phenomenon received attention also on the other side of the continent. Edward Glover, a British psychiatrist and psychoanalyst who was also one of the pioneers of forensic psychiatry, published a few articles on the aetiology of drug addiction. The subject of his first article was alcohol addiction and he claimed that alcohol abuse and addiction enable the addicted individual infantile impulse gratification (Glover, 1928). Concerning drug addiction, Glover (1928) noted that some addictions originate in early developmental stages, whereas the origin of other addictions is in the oedipal drama. He thought that individuals use drugs progressively for both controlling and releasing aggressive impulses, and conceptualized the drug as an object with sadistic qualities which lives both in the external reality and in the body of the user.

There are clear associations between aggression and addiction. The internal world of drug addicts contains much aggression, and they live on the verge of psychosis (Glover, 1932). Drugs assist drug addicts in coping with paranoid and sadistic impulses (Glover, 1932), and ease the existence in a chaotic reality. In the phantasy world of drug addicts, drugs could kill, punish or cure bad internal objects, as they have a simultaneous effect on objects projected to the external world.

Although, one of her bitter opponents in later years, the resemblance to Melanie Klein's ideas is quite evident. In addition, the link between Kleinian ideas and ego psychology ideas is also evident in these conceptualizations, as Glover is one of the first analysts who claimed that drugs assist in ameliorating or avoiding mental pain. In other words, he points on the ability of drugs to regulate internal and external aggression, and suggests (as Rado did) that addiction is not an attempt to escape from reality but more of the ego's attempt to defend the individual's psyche. Although Glover did not treat drug abusers, he noticed that addiction has a unique course that is situated in the transition stage between neurosis and psychosis. Actually, this important contribution which linked addictions and borderline mental conditions (Glover, 1932), was a head of its time, and years later Krystal and Kernberg would present similar ideas.

Otto Fenichel, an Austrian analyst, referred to addictions in his comprehensive book about the psychoanalysis of neurosis (Fenichel, 1945). He hypothesized that understanding of the addictions' etiology requires an examination of the psychological structure of the addicted individual, and especially of his premorbid personality (Fenichel, 1945). Loyal to Freud's ideas, he viewed drug abuse as an attempt to gratify archaic oral cravings and added that drug abusers long for safety. However, the idea that drugs have an essential role as a last defensive line before depressive breakdown (Fenichel, 1945) corresponds with ego psychology.

Ernst Simmel opened a sanatorium in Berlin that provided treatment for a population that suffered from diverse mental morbidity. Simmel, an analyst and a neurologist with an extensive social awareness, aspired to provide free psychoanalytic treatment for every patient (Mackie, 2016). Unlike today, when there is not enough integration between mental health and addiction services, this facility provided treatment for individuals who suffered from neuroses, psychoses and drug use disorders. Simmel (1929) presented with an interesting formulation, according to which the drug abuser tries to poison the internal object that tries to destroy him, meaning the mother. He noted that the addicted individual is a depressive individual who poisoned his superego with the poison with which he killed the object.

Simmel also viewed addiction as a psychological phenomenon that provides abusers different functions according to their psychic needs. Meaning, drug addicts seek for gratification of oral cravings, but they mostly look for certain experiences that their ego cannot create or provide (Simmel, 1929). For example, alcohol provides a sanctuary for individuals struggling with internal conflict and simultaneously enables others to feel control (Simmel, 1948). Therefore, clinicians should not only focus on the biochemical effect of alcohol but strive to understand its psychological influence on the ego.

Simmel was a multifaceted analyst who also wrote on gambling addiction and treated traumatized veterans following World War I. He had believed that the number of people who will use psychoactive substances would rise in the next years, and he was indeed right. Due to financial difficulties, the unique Berlinian sanatorium had been closed in 1931, and with the rise of Nazism in Germany, Simmel, like other Jewish analysts (Rado, Fenichel), left Europe and immigrated to the United States, where he opened another sanatorium.

Alfred Gross, Simmel's first associate in the Berlinian Tegel Sanatorium, published in 1935 an article which did not receive much attention throughout the years (Loose, 2000), in which he called to investigate the toxic effects of drugs on the human psyche. Gross rejected the traditional distinction for drug classes to pleasure inducing or pain sedating since individuals react differently to drugs. He noted that drugs differ by their effect and added that individuals react differently after using the same drug. Meaning an individual who continually uses the same drug may react differently after several uses of it and using different drug dosages may affect differentially on the psyche (Gross, 1935). Intense anxiety states and psychotic episodes following cannabis or hallucinogens abuse among either individuals who use these drugs for the first time or those who abuse them frequently are examples for this argument.

Although Glover and Rado had noted that drugs serve as mental functions, Gross's contribution is so important since it was the first time a suggestion was made to focus on the interaction between the individual and the drug. More specifically, Gross addressed the interface between intrapsychic and personality factors, different dosages of drugs and the way of administration. Further elaboration of similar ideas would appear about 50 years later when another analyst suggested that understanding of the addict's experience requires attention not only to the interaction between the individual and the drug but also to the physical and social environment (Zinberg, 1984).

Psychoanalytic formulations of alcoholism and drug abuse, and addiction in the United States

The analytic writing on addictions in Europe dealt with both alcohol and drugs, whereas on the other side of the ocean, analysts dealt mostly with alcoholism. In 1920, entered the 18th amendment, which prohibited the manufacture, sale or transportation of alcoholic beverages. This amendment, which also prohibited the importation of alcoholic beverages to the United States, signifies the beginning of the prohibition period. The rates of alcohol consumption had declined significantly in the first years, which followed this amendment, but after a few years, a sharp incline, which achieved 60%–70% of the initial numbers, had occurred (Miron & Zwiebel, 1991). Following the repeal of the 18th amendment in 1933, a high incline in the alcohol consumption rates did not occur, but the psychiatric establishment encountered a growing number of patients who suffered from alcoholism.

Karl Menninger, an American psychiatrist, adopted Freud's ideas about the association between the death instinct and addiction and viewed alcoholism as a chronic suicide (Menninger, 1938). Robert Knight, a psychiatrist and a psychoanalyst, noticed that family matters influence the development of addiction and added that alcoholism is more of a symptom than a disease (Knight, 1937a). His vast clinical experience with individuals who suffered from alcoholism led him to important conclusions about the etiology and the characteristics of this disease. For example, he found that inadequate parenting, emotional problems and alcohol use in puberty constitute risk factors that contribute to the development of personality disorders and alcoholism in adulthood (Knight, 1937b). One of the significant conclusions which arises from Knight's writings is that traumatic experiences play a significant role in the etiology of addictions.

Paul Schilder, an Austrian psychiatrist who was also one of Freud's students, relied on case studies to indicate the association between family malfunction and ego deficits among individuals who suffered from alcoholism (Schilder, 1941). He found some significant risk factors, such as insecurity feeling, emotional abuse, physical abuse and parental neglect during childhood, which had associations with alcohol addiction in adulthood (Schilder, 1941). Years later, these conclusions, which derived from clinical practice, would receive empirical support (Schwandt, Heilig, Hommer, George, & Ramchandani, 2013).

From the beginning of the 1940s, Harry Tiebout, an American psychiatrist, intensively promoted the recognition of 'Alcoholics Anonymous' among his colleagues and the public. Tiebout found in the history of individuals who suffered from alcohol abuse inadequate parenting in the form of overindulgence or severe rigidity. Consequently, their childhood was characterized by constant frustration, difficulties in self-expression and mostly rejection of any attempt of imposing authority. Therefore, he recommended that the therapeutic treatment should focus on learning to cope with restrictions (Tiebout, 1947).

Tiebout was one of the first clinicians who addressed the relationship between narcissistic disorders and alcohol abuse. He mentioned a few personality characteristics of alcohol abusers, such as unconscious need to stand out, a feeling of isolation, perfectionism and labile self-esteem (Tiebout, 1945).

Individuals with narcissistic disorders may use alcohol or drugs as a primary means for fueling their pathological grandiosity and reassure omnipotence when the environment does not provide admiration and gratification (Tiebout, 1944). These ideas correspond clearly with self psychology, and in a study conducted among adolescents in the United States, narcissistic traits were indeed associated with low altruism level and also with substance abuse (Carter, Johnson, Exline, Post, & Pagano, 2012).

Concluding remarks

Analysts in the 1930s and the 1940s of the previous century still mentioned Freud's ideas about the relationship between addiction and masturbation but simultaneously developed independent ideas which have been focused on the individual's inability to cope with negative emotional states and on the possibility that drugs replace functions of mental agencies. A few analysts even suggested an association between drug abuse and self-value. In the next years, the main analytic contributions to the addictions field, as well as most of the empirical research, will arrive from the United States, where ego psychology began to rise with the arrival of analysts such as Ernst Kris, Rudolph Lowenstein, David Rappaport, Rene Spitz and Edith Jacobson.

In the war itself, both allied and the axis powers used amphetamines and methamphetamines massively for vigor, performance enhancement and for battling combat fatigue (Defalque & Wright, 2011; Rasmussen, 2011). In the following years, this trend will grow as many countries will invest large amounts of money in studying the influences of various synthetic drugs on the human mind and human behavior.

References

Abraham, K. (1908/1979). The psychological relations between sexuality and alcoholism. In *Selected papers on psychoanalysis* (pp. 80–90). Brunner/Mazel. (Original published in 1908).

Bion, W. R. (1967). *Second thoughts*. William Heinemann Medical Books Ltd.

Carter, R. R., Johnson, S. M., Exline, J. J., Post, S. G., & Pagano, M. E. (2012). Addiction and "generation me": Narcissistic and prosocial behaviors of adolescents with substance dependency disorder in comparison to normative adolescents. *Alcoholism Treatment Quarterly, 30*(2), 163–178.

Defalque, R. J., & Wright, A. J. (2011). Methamphetamine for Hitler's Germany: 1937 to 1945. *Bulletin of Anesthesia History, 29*(2), 21–24.

Fenichel, O. (1945). *The psychoanalytic theory of neurosis*. Norton.

Freud, S. (1884/1975). On coca. In R. Byck (Ed.), *Cocaine papers* (pp. 47–74). Stonehill Publishing Co.

Freud, S. (1905/1975). *Three essays on the theory of sexuality*. Basic Books. (Original work published 1905).

Freud, S. (1930/1961). Civilization and its discontents. In J. Strachey (Ed. & Trans.), *The standard edition of the complete psychological works of Sigmund Freud* (Vol. 21, pp. 64–148). Hogarth Press. (Original work published 1930).

Gay, P. (1988). *Freud: A life for our time.* J. M. Dent & Sons Ltd.

Glover, E. (1928). The aetiology of alcoholism. In *On the early development of mind* (pp. 81–90). Imago Publishing Co., 1956.

Glover, E. (1932). On the aetiology of drug addiction. *International Journal of Psychoanalysis, 53,* 63–73.

Gross, A. (1935). The psychic effects of toxic and toxoid substance. *The International Journal of Psychoanalysis, 16,* 425–438.

Kernberg, O. F. (1984). *Severe personality disorders: Psychotherapeutic strategies.* Yale University Press.

Knight, R. P. (1937a). The dynamics and treatment of chronic alcohol addiction. *Bulletin of the Menninger Clinic, 1*(7), 233–250.

Knight, R. P. (1937b). The psychodynamics of chronic alcoholism. *The Journal of Nervous and Mental Disease, 86*(5), 538–548.

Levin, J. D. (1987). *Treatment of alcoholism and other addictions: A self-psychology approach.* Jason Aronson.

Loose, R. (2000). The addicted subject caught between the ego and the drive: The post-Freudian reduction and simplification of a complex clinical problem. *Psychoanalytische Perspectieven, 41/42,* 55–81.

Mackie, B. S. (2016). *Treating people with psychosis in institutions: A psychoanalytic perspective.* Karnac.

Markel, H. (2011). *An anatomy of addiction: Sigmund Freud, William Halsted, and the miracle drug cocaine.* Pantheon.

Menninger, K. (1938). *Man against himself.* Harcourt, Brace & Co.

Miron, J., & Zwiebel, J. (1991). Alcohol consumption during prohibition. *American Economic Review, 81*(2), 242–247.

Olds, J., & Milner, P. (1954). Positive reinforcement produced by electrical stimulation of septal area and other regions of rat brain. *Journal of Comparative and Physiological Psychology, 47*(6), 419–427.

Rado, S. (1926). The psychic effects of intoxicants: An attempt to evolve a psychoanalytic theory of morbid cravings. *International Journal of Psychoanalysis, 7,* 396–413.

Rado, S. (1928). The psychical effects of intoxication: Attempt at a psycho-analytical theory of drug-addiction. *International Journal of Psychoanalysis, 9,* 301–317.

Rado, S. (1933). The psychoanalysis of pharmacothymia (drug addiction). *The Psychoanalytic Quarterly, 2*(1), 1–23.

Rado, S. (1957). Narcotic bondage: A general theory of the dependence on narcotic drugs. *American Journal of Psychiatry, 114*(2), 165–170.

Rado, S. (1969). *Adaptional psychodynamics: Motivation and control.* Science House.

Rasmussen, N. (2011). Medical science and the military: The allies' use of amphetamine during World War II. *Journal of Interdisciplinary History, 42*(2), 205–233.

Schilder, P. (1941). The psychogenesis of alcoholism. *Quarterly Journal of Studies on Alcohol, 2,* 277–292.

Schwandt, M. L., Heilig, M., Hommer, D. W., George, D. T., & Ramchandani, V. A. (2013). Childhood trauma exposure and alcohol dependence severity in adulthood: Mediation by emotional abuse severity and neuroticism. *Alcoholism: Clinical and Experimental Research, 37*(6), 984–992.

Searles, H. F. (1979). *Countertransference and related subjects: Selected papers.* International Universities Press.

Simmel, E. (1929). Psychoanalytic treatment in a sanatorium. *International Journal of Psychoanalysis, 10,* 70–89.

Simmel, E. (1948). Alcoholism and addiction. *The Psychoanalytic Quarterly, 17,* 6–31.

Tiebout, H. M. (1944). Therapeutic mechanisms of Alcoholics Anonymous. *American Journal of Psychiatry, 100*(4), 468–473.

Tiebout, H. M. (1945). The syndrome of alcohol addiction. *Quarterly Journal of Studies on Alcohol, 5*(4), 533–546.

Tiebout, H.M. (1947). The problem of gaining cooperation from the alcoholic patient. *Quarterly Journal of Studies on Alcohol, 8*(1), 47–54.

Ulman, R. B., & Paul, H. (2006). *The self psychology of addiction and its treatment: Narcissus in wonderland.* Routledge.

Volkan, K. (1994). *Dancing among the maenads: The psychology of compulsive drug use.* Peter Lang.

Volkow, N. D., Koob, G. F., & McLellan, T. A. (2016). Neurobiologic advances from the brain disease model of addiction. *New England Journal of Medicine, 374*(4), 363–371.

Winnicott, D. W. (1955). Metapsychological and clinical aspects of regression within the psycho-analytical set-up. *International Journal of Psychoanalysis, 36,* 16–26.

Zinberg, N. E. (1984). *Drug, set, and setting: The basis for controlled intoxicant use.* Yale University Press.

Chapter 2

An historical overview of psychoanalytic perspectives on drug abuse and addiction – Part 2

"Certainly, one might wonder how addiction could possibly be seen as an attempt to relieve suffering when there is so much of it as a consequence of drug use".

(Khantzian, 2013, p. 668)

The second period – from the end of World War II to the 1990s

A higher number of publications about drug abuse and addiction appeared in the second period than in the previous decades. In my opinion, this incline stemmed from social and political processes that took place in the world and caused drugs to become an integral part of the society's daily discourse and the lifestyle of various society layers. First, the cultural revolution in the United States occurred as a direct reaction to the dark period of World War II (McFarlane, 2007). The hippie counterculture, which had begun as a youth movement in San Francisco, spread across America, carrying with it new ideas about love, freedom, sexuality, equality and nature conservation (McFarlane, 2007).

In a period in which the United States was sinking in the Vietnamese mud, the flower children offered their country and the whole world new existence modalities, which included music and drug use. Cannabis and LSD are the most identified drugs with this period (Davis & Munoz, 1968; Smith, Raswyck, & Davidson, 2014), but young people also used stimulants and opioids (DeGrandpre, 2006; Mold, 2007; Rasmussen, 2008).

Second, drug abuse has become an integral part of the lifestyle of artists and musicians. The names of famous musicians, such as Elvis Presley, Jim Morrison, Brian Jones, Jimmy Hendrix and Janis Joplin have been associated with either drug addiction or overdose (Amburn, 1992; Davis, 2005; Thompson II & Cole, 1990; Tyranka, 2014). Third, scientific advancements led to discoveries of new drugs that became a focus of attraction for many people. Alexander Shulgin investigated MDMA (Shulgin & Shulgin, 1997), and a pharmaceutical company that searched for an anesthetic agent with analgesic properties discovered ketamine (Mion, 2017).

The experiencing in hallucinogenic drugs as a potential gate for other consciousness levels raised curiosity among academics, such as Timothy Leary who used psilocybin and LSD, and even suggested it as a treatment for alcoholics and offenders (Penner, 2014). The rates of phencyclidine (PCP) were on the rise since its discovery (Bush, 2013), and cocaine abuse gained renewed popularity (Das, 2013). In this time, the American public and the rest of the world also discovered the addictive and devastating potential of pain killers and barbiturates (Lopez-Munoz, Ucha-Udabe, & Alamo, 2005). Out of the public's eye, the US intelligence services allegedly examined the effects of drugs on people and communities (Albarelli, 2009).

In the 1960s, drug abuse has become an integral part of the lifestyle of hippies, and in the 1970s, it has become one of the characteristics of the developing clubs' culture. Cocaine and Quaalude gained enormous popularity as party drugs, and studies began to indicate the association between drug abuse rates and crime rates (Davis, Baum, & Graham, 1991; Grogger & Willis, 2000). In conclusion, in previous years, drug abuse prevailed among war veterans who experienced traumatic events, or among individuals who were considered as the margins of society and searched for drugs to cope either with mental distress or with existential difficulties. In the last four decades of the 20th century, drug abuse has become an integral part of young people's lifestyles, a focus of attraction for the curious ones, and probably also an integral part of those in the music and entertainment business.

Additional significant events in this period include the introduction of methadone for treatment of heroin addiction (Dole & Nyswander, 1967) and the establishment of the National Institute on Drug Abuse (NIDA) in 1974. The growth in the abusers' number led to the need to conduct descriptive epidemiological studies concerning the incidence of drug abuse and to identify determinants and risk factors for drug abuse (O'donel, Voss, Clayton, Slatin, & Room, 1976). Following the increase in drug abuse rates, the medical establishment and the social services encountered more and more people who abused drugs or suffered from drug-induced psychopathology.

Mostly, the drug abuse treatment models after World War II were based on Alcoholics Anonymous philosophy, total abstinence, behavioral changes and acupuncture (Cui, Wu, & Luo, 2008; McElrath, 1997; White, 1998). In 1977, NIDA published a monograph that focused solely on psychodynamic treatment of drug abuse and addiction (Blaine & Julius, 1977). Heinz Kohut wrote the preface and other psychoanalysts offered theoretical and clinical contributions, which provided clinicians new ideas for treating this growing population.

The publishing of this monograph has importance since, at that period, research had dealt mostly either with pharmacokinetics or with epidemiology. However, the attempt to look beyond the cellular level into the psychodynamics of drug dependence will not have any significant continuity because of the rapid developments of neuroscience and the view of addiction as a brain disease (Volkow, Koob, & McLellan, 2016).

Almost two decades ago, Morgenstern and Leeds (1993) presented contemporary psychoanalytic theories of substance abuse. Their article includes review of ideas of four analysts, and in retrospect, in my opinion, these analysts provided the most significant contributions during the five decades of the second period. Most of the theoretical and clinical contributions to the addiction field at this period came from relatively a small number of analysts who treated drug abusers for years and updated their theoretical ideas and their recommendations about the analytic technique. Their works appeared in psychoanalytic journals and reminded the psychoanalytic establishment about the existence of an outcast population segment that does not receive enough attention. In the next lines, I will elaborate on their work.

Leon Wurmser

In my opinion, the central character that symbolizes the transition into the second period is Leon Wurmser, a psychiatrist and psychoanalyst with a classical analytic training who published many works on alcohol and drug addiction. Wurmser is a prolific writer with more than 350 scientific publications and 15 books in different subjects, such as shame, masochism and neuroses. He is the first to write widely on psychopathology and psychotherapy of addictions based on clinical experience. Wurmser also differs from most of the earlier analysts because he was the first analyst who ran drug rehabilitation centers and managed academic training for therapists.

Beginning with the 1970s, Wurmser had published articles in psychoanalytic journals, which dealt with psychoanalytic treatment of drug abusers. From this perspective, he is one of the pioneers in providing an unwelcomed population with some accessibility to a professional community that was elitist and conservative. His theoretical writing and his case illustrations enabled the analytic community to understand that alcohol and drug abusers are people who suffer from mental malaises just as neurotic people, and that unlike the prevailing stereotype, they constitute a population that can benefit from psychoanalytic treatment.

In his writing on addictions, Wurmser (1985, 1987) uses terms related to the drive model, yet he relinquishes the idea of libidinal gratification as the primary etiological factor for the development of addiction. Instead, he deals with the patients' personality and especially with their self-value and the effect of psychological trauma on their lives. Loyal to the classical analytic theory, he argues that the intrapsychic conflict is the heart of the addiction problem, and therefore, its solution will lead to the solution of the addiction problem. But, he also notes that drug abuse results from a narcissistic crisis in which the value of the self is threatened. Such crises are the result of a conflict between different psychic agencies. He focuses on the superego and claims that the merit of drug abuse is that it causes a temporary overthrow of the drug abuser's harsh superego (Wurmser, 1987).

Morgenstern and Leeds (1993) emphasize that despite the use of the terms self-value or narcissistic crisis, Wurmser does not note that addiction stems from deficits in the self-structure or in developmental arrests as do self psychology analysts (Kohut, 1977; Ulman & Paul, 2006). Wurmser had noted what many studies among drug-abusing populations would show in the next years, meaning, that the etiology of addictions lays in childhood traumatic experiences. He explains that real (and not fantasized) trauma is the origin of addiction and especially experiences of abandonment, sexual seduction, violence or parental invasiveness (Wurmser, 1984a). Children exposed to such situations grow up with anger and aggression, which is projected toward authoritative figures in life as well as in drug treatment programs. Therefore, acts of rebelliousness and lack of obedience toward the therapeutic setting are actually transferences of earlier traumatic childhood experiences.

In Wurmser's conceptualizations, the superego, an agency that did not receive much attention in other analysts' writings on addictions, has a central role. The superego is developed in a distorted way when children experience loyalty conflicts in their families (Wurmser & Zients, 1982). For example, a loyalty conflict may occur during immigration to a new country, when the family values and those of the environment sometimes clash. Growing in a house where parents adhere to orthodox values, while school and society promote liberalism, may cause some confusion and pose the child in unbearable situations.

Such loyalty conflicts or values crises have a few effects. First, the child cannot cope with this situation and does not internalize a clear and organized values system. Second, to deal with the emotional magnitude of those conflicts, the child must shut out parts of the overwhelming experience, and this split is the basis for identity problems or the creation of a false self among drug abusers. Although Wurmser notes that children vanish emotionally or shut out emotional contents associated with traumatic childhood experiences, he does not use the term dissociation.

Not only drug abuse enables coping with the impact of such experiences, but it also enables coping with separation anxiety and provides psychopharmacological liberation from the threatening and overwhelming conflict (Wurmser, 1974). Drug abuse assists the ego to deal with the superego in a few ways. First, it enables a temporary release from the superego since it neutralizes this agency's effect on the psyche. Second, it cancels the reasonable considerations and the reality's limitations. However, the growing severance of the superego during drug addiction damages other functions, such as the "ego ideal", self-introspection capacity and acknowledgment of the boundaries of external reality (Wurmser, 1984b).

According to Wurmser (1984a), drug abusers are characterized by different pathologies in different superego facets. Among some of them, this function is missing while among others, it is unstable or distorted, or it is not strong enough to control painful emotional contents. Drug abusers suffer from the return of the repressed material associated with the intrapsychic conflict, and every abuse of the drug enables to avoid the painful encounter with the repressed material (Wurmser, 1984a). Because of superego deficits, drug abusers do not feel positive emotions, high self-value or well-being, which stem from personal achievements and interactions with others. Drug abuse does provide such experiences since it is actually a chemical manipulation on emotions and a regressive mean for wish fulfillment. In this sense, drug abuse is quite like hallucination and imagination, which are the earliest forms of wish fulfillment (Morgenstern & Leeds, 1993).

Wurmser (1974, 1985) notes that drug abusers try to avoid archaic emotions that flood the psyche, such as anxiety, pain and shame. He uses the term 'psychophobia' to describe this fear and adds that drug abusers scorn any internal introspection and display contempt to emotional expressions (Wurmser, 1987). Wurmser's drug abuser is a skeptic individual who is anxious about his self-value and feels an inability to match his ideal ego. He is flooded with chronic feelings of shame and ambiguous guilt (Morgenstern & Leeds, 1993). Consequently, he searches for emotional detachment since any interaction with the external world is too embarrassing, frightening or painful. Drug abuse enables temporary relief from this flood of an overwhelming bill of emotions, but the emotional life shrinks as the addiction becomes severer. Since the emotional life becomes quite limited, even good experiences are experienced as very suspicious.

Wurmser's therapeutic approach

Wurmser notes that in some instances, drug abusers will need a referral to detoxification centers (Wurmser, 1985), but analysis will have a central role in treatment. He sees drug abuse as a severe neurosis that requires analysis of defence mechanisms and the superego (Wurmser, 1987). At the beginning of analysis, the patient appears with a specific symptom, such as panic attack, and as long as analysis continues, the addiction will be the focus of the treatment until the therapy arrives to the neurotic process and to the fundamental conflict that stands in the addiction's core (Wurmser, 1984a).

Concerning the therapeutic stance, he notes that moralistic attitude toward the patient's resistance and his impulsive behaviors will not prove useful since the problem is not an absence of a superego but rather a harsh one. Acting out during analysis and in the abusers' daily encounters with other people are examples of coping difficulties, which originate during loyalty conflicts in childhood. Therefore, one of the central aims of analysis is to assist the patient in examining his superego during transference relations. Wurmser (1985) recommends analysts to provide the patient strong emotional presence next to an attitude of kindness, warmness and flexibility during the analytic process. Additional therapeutic recommendations include multi-systematic interventions, such as medications, family guidance, self-help or 12-step groups. He sees in such groups simplistic yet necessary solution because they provide an external substitute for a damaged superego (Wurmser, 1985). However, unlike 12-step programs, analysis will not inspire to inherit the function of a robust inner agency but instead would inspire to assist the patient in developing one.

Henry Krystal

Another prominent figure who acted in this period is Henry Krystal, a psychiatrist and psychoanalyst who survived the horrors of the holocaust as a youngster. Krystal immigrated to the United States and wrote extensively on the impact of emotional trauma on the survivors. He is also well known for his writings on affects and alexithymia (Krystal & Krystal, 1988). According to Krystal (1978, 1982), drug abusers are characterized by severe psychopathology of their object relations and suffer from significant disorders in emotional functioning. Actually, he is one of the first who described emotional regulation difficulties among this population and especially their inability to identify and describe emotional states (Krystal, 1978; Krystal & Raskin, 1970).

Krystal (1982) uses the term alexithymia to describe a condition in which individuals have difficulties identifying and labeling their own emotions and notes that such patients may feel confusion, shock and numbness and may act out when aroused. These difficulties appear not only among drug abusers, but also among individuals with psychosomatic disorders and those who experienced traumatic experiences (Krystal, 1979, 1982). Next to the emotional dysfunction, alexithymia also has a cognitive aspect that relates to the inability of those patients to explain to themselves why they feel this way or to give feelings a meaning.

Individuals with alexithymia experience their emotions as physiological states. They are not capable of saying if they are angry, sad or tired, and therefore, feelings of irritation or sadness might be experienced as physical stress or pain. Incapacity to identify and verbalize emotions leads to problems in identifying emotional states and difficulties in self-caring (Morgenstern & Leeds, 1993). Dysfunctional emotional tolerance is also a major personality characteristic of drug abusers who cope poorly with both negative and positive emotions. These characteristics constitute robust issues in the patients' daily lives, and therapists are not always aware of it. For example, some drug abstinent patients report that they went to a wedding or another happy event and used cocaine. They negate any craving involved, but they say they did feel good and did not understand the nature of those feelings. Such patients report that they were confused because they felt pleasant physical sensations and that the available drug was a means to deal with this confusion.

During healthy emotional development, individuals learn to identify and verbalize emotional states. In alexithymia, any emotional arousal is not pleasant or containable, and there is a need to get rid of it quickly through sedation or impulsive acting out (Krystal, 1977). This idea corresponds with similar ideas in previous decades about the association between the ego's inability to cope with emotions and drug abuse. In this context, Krystal and Raskin (1970) noted that the personality construct of individuals with drug use disorders is characterized by damaged stimulus barrier, and drug abuse allows them managing intense affects. Yet, alexithymia is not a dimension, but rather a continuum, and people can work on their emotional abilities and learn to better express themselves.

The optimistic derivative of this premise is that drug use rates may be reduced once individuals with drug use disorders will learn to identify their emotions and cope with emotional arousal in adaptive ways. Morgenstern and Leeds (1993) note that Krystal's contribution is implemented in cognitive-behavioral treatment (CBT), when patients learn to identify emotional states and adopt coping strategies as part of relapse prevention skills (Marlatt & Gordon, 1985). Vast research has indeed suggested that alexithymia is quite common among drug-abusing patients (Nehra, Kumar, Sharma, & Nehra, 2014; Torrado, Ouakinin, & Bacelar-Nicolau, 2013).

Besides alexithymia, individuals with drug use disorders are characterized with disturbed object relations whose origin is in the separation-individuation process (Krystal, 1978). A successful resolution of this process is achieved after experiencing both omnipotence over independence and acknowledgment upon the mother. Like individuals with a borderline personality disorder, those with drug use disorders crave to merge with their ideal object but simultaneously dread it (Krystal, 1977). This ambivalence also appears in the external object relations when others are idealized and conceived as an absolute source for nutrition and support, but when they do not stand up to the expectations, they are devalued and attacked with furious rage.

The conflict with the drug, which represents the primary maternal object, is also acted-out when it is introjected during intoxication and when the individual separates from it during the withdrawal stage (Krystal, 1977). Some of these ideas overlap Kernberg's (1975) ideas about internal and external object relations of individuals with borderline personality organization.

Krystal's therapeutic approach

Krystal (1977) acknowledges the difficulties in treating patients with disturbed object relations and those with poor affect tolerance. Like Freud, he notes that some drug abusers would rather turn to drug abuse to solve their problems than to come for therapy. For patients with alexithymia, he offers modifications in the analytic technique and negates usage of interpretations and interventions, such as "*you do not allow yourself to experience affection (or anger) toward me*". Instead, he offers a stage that precedes the psychoanalytic treatment and focuses on psychoeducation and includes explanation about the essence of alexithymia, recognition of various affects and verbalization. The second phase includes skill training, which enables the patient practicing and acquiring new capacities (Krystal, 1982).

Krystal is also skeptical about conducting psychoanalysis with drug abusers disorders who are characterized with disturbed object relations. The extreme rage and the intense projective identification consist significant difficulties for analyzing transference relations (Morgenstern & Leeds, 1993). He notes that psychoanalysis or psychoanalytic psychotherapy is an appropriate form of treatment for only a small group of drug abusers and recommends a more comprehensive treatment for most of the patients. It seems that Krystal describes the characteristics of many heroin and cocaine abusers, and his approach is more realistic than that of other analysts who offered full analysis for drug abusers.

Following treatment in a comprehensive treatment facility, the intensity of projective identification will be reduced, but the therapist will have to cope with the patient's primitive and raw aggression. If the patient understands that his search for drugs is actually a search for the ideal mother, he will gradually give up his omnipotent demands. The insight the patient will gain will help him in accepting his traumatic past and starting to develop a more realistic view of himself and the world. Krystal's conceptualizations about drug abuse and addiction etiology emphasize the importance of joint exploration of the patients' fantasy world because it provides a comprehensive explanation of their disturbed object relations. Clinicians who encounter destructive behavior, unstable personal relations and difficulties in self-care, actually, witness the enactments of early infantile drama (Krystal, 1978).

Many of Krystal's therapeutic recommendations differ from the views of his contemporaries. Although his theoretical writing is sometimes unclear, his therapeutic approach is holistic and down-to-earth. He notes that, in many cases, alcohol and drug abusers will need a certain period of detoxification and physiological balance before analytic treatment. Krytsal supports treatment at detoxification centers and therapeutic communities, which are facilities that provide physiological and behavioral stabilization. Second, his recommended treatment for alexithymic patients corresponds with CBT, and a study found that alexithymia can change significantly over the course of a year following CBT (Spek, Nyklicek, Cuijpers, & Pop, 2008). Following such treatment, patients may have more capabilities of introspection and internalization, which are vital for psychoanalytic treatment.

It should be noted that a few of these recommendations were ahead of its time since currently many drug abuse and addiction programs include developing skill training and emotional regulation capacities. Neuroimaging studies suggest that there is a link between alexithymia and neural correlates of reward and loss processing among drug abusers (Li & Sinha, 2006; Morie et al., 2016).

Edward J. Khantzian

Another pioneer in the second period is Edward Khantzian. Khantzian has a central role in developing addiction medicine and integrating the treatment of addictions into the academic and psychiatric world in the United States.

His book "treating addiction as human process" emphasized that addiction is motivated by suffering rather by hedonism or sensation-seeking (Khantzian, 1999). Probably, Khantzian's most significant contribution to this field is the self-medication hypothesis, which has become one of the major theories that describe the etiology of drug abuse and addiction. The core assumptions about the etiology of addictive disorders are that addictive disorders stem from suffering rather from seeking pleasure or self-destructive impulse and that individuals abuse drugs because of their inability to cope with this suffering (Khantzian, 1997, 2015). Patients experiment with various classes of drugs, and in a process of trial and error, discover which specific drug helps them to cope the best with their emotional pain.

Khantzian (1997) notes that terms such as "drug of choice" (Weider & Kaplan, 1969) and "preferential use of drugs" (Milkman & Frosch, 1973) already appeared in the writings of clinicians in the 1970s, who had noticed that patients selectively choose their drugs of use. The empirical support for this premise is not robust (Arendt et al., 2007; Suh, Ruffins, Robins, Albanese, & Khantzian, 2008), but the clinical experience does show that drug-abusing patients do have a favorite drug and that different drugs appeal to different individuals because of their pharmacological traits.

Opioids are well known for their calming effect, but they also help in attenuating intense and rageful affect. Opioids can help individuals to cope with internal rage as well as with its disruptive effect on interpersonal relations (Khantzian, 1985, 1997). Alcohol, barbiturates and benzodiazepines have a rapid onset of action, which brings a temporary feeling of relief (Khantzian, 1985, 1997). Individuals who use these drugs feel isolation, emptiness and anxiety, which mask fear of closeness and dependency. In addition, those who use these substances have a predisposition for depression (1985, 1997). Stimulants, such as amphetamines and cocaine, are so appealing because they provide solutions for different varieties of distress. They provide elation and energy boosts for de-energized, bored and depressed people, and they act as augmentators for hypomanic individuals, or for those who suffer from bipolar disorder. Stimulants can act paradoxically and counteract emotional liability and hyperactivity, and therefore, those with attention-deficit/ hyperactivity disorder may use them (Khantzian, 1985, 1997).

Over the years, one of the major lines of criticism of this theory concerned the fact that many people experiment with different drugs but do not become addicted. Khantzian's answer was that drug abusers are characterized with disturbances and vulnerabilities in many aspects of their intrapersonal and interpersonal world, which predispose them to develop addiction. Once they find a drug that provides better mental relief than other drugs, the chances for developing addiction will rise (Khantzian, 2012, 2015). Khantzian's answer is a significant pillar in his conceptualization of addiction. Meaning, the premise that addiction is a self-regulation disorder and that suffering is a consequence of the addicted individuals' inability to regulate emotions, behavior, relationships, self-esteem and, especially, self-care (Khantzian, 2012).

The notion of addiction as a self-regulation disorder is supported by empirical studies that showed that drug abusers have difficulties in emotional and behavioral regulation (Blatt et al., 1984; Shedler & Block, 1990). Early traumatic experiences lead to coping inability with negative emotions and create vulnerability to addiction. Consequently, individuals experience their affects either as extremely and overwhelmingly or they are cut off from their emotions and cannot verbalize their feelings. The emotional life of such individuals is characterized by intense fluctuations between rage, ambiguous dysphoria and even alexithymia (Khantzian, 1985, 1997, 2012). At this point, there is an overlap between Khantzian's ideas and those of other analysts (Krystal & Raskin, 1970; McDougall, 1984), and Khantzian (2015) indeed acknowledges their contributions and uses their ideas to articulate the associations between pathological development of affects and addiction. Trauma has an essential role in Khantzian's conceptualization of addiction, and although he does not use the term dissociation in most of his writings, he notes that drug abuse is significantly associated with the effects of early trauma on affects and personality development (Khantzian, 2012, 2015). In such cases, drug abuse constitutes an attempt to solve painful states, which are not always conscious and lack symbolic representation (Khantzian, 1997).

Khantzian relies on Kohut's contributions (1971, 1977) to explain self-esteem regulation difficulties of drug addicts. He notes that drug abusers experience periodic or chronic feelings of helplessness, shame and low sense of self-worth because of the impoverished self-structure. Drug abusers have difficulties in coping with such overwhelming feelings and may exhibit omnipotence and bravado, which mask emptiness, inadequacy and rage (Khantzian, 2012). The troubled sense of self and the traumatic life history are a few of the reasons for the difficulties of drug abusers to interact with others. Drug abusers do need other people for comfort and emotional intimacy, but they either cannot express themselves or afraid of expressing their needs and find themselves dependent (Khantzian, 2012). Consequently, they remain aloof and often have the experience that no one understands them.

Addiction is a failed attempt of self-regulation, which only enhances the suffering if the individual continues to adhere to this solution (Khantzian & Albanese, 2008). Drug abuse becomes drug addiction when the recurrent attempts to alleviate mental suffering lead only to its intensification and to the appearance of physical suffering (withdrawal symptoms). The self-regulating skills, which were deficient already from the beginning, are lessened more because the addicted individual does not use them. The developmental deficiencies also cause self-care deficits, which interfere with the ability to anticipate danger or harm (Khantzian, 1997, 2012). Lack of self-care skills or deficient self-care skills causes drug addicts to find themselves in risky situations, when family members and therapists wonder where the anxiety or the fear that should prevent such behaviors. Methadone maintenance treatment (MMT) patients who continue injecting drugs and share needles and syringes despite the risk of infectious diseases consist an excellent example.

Khantzian is one of a very few analysts who related to the issue of dual diagnosis. He notes that high rates of comorbidity exist because patients with psychiatric illness discover that drugs relieve a wide range of painful feelings associated with their mental illness. These patients, like other people, experiment with different drug classes until they find the one that best relieves the painful affects that predominate with their mental Illness (Khantzian, 2003). However, unlike drug abusers and addicts without psychiatric illness, dually diagnosed patients also abuse drugs to ease the distress associated with antipsychotic medications (Khantzian, 2003). Dually diagnosed patients, like drug abusers without psychiatric illness, are individuals who "wittingly and unwittingly substitute the suffering which they perpetuate and control with use for the suffering they do not understand or control" (Khantzian, 2015, p. 814).

The self-medication theory has been trivialized and dismissed since its introduction. Lembke (2012) claims that it does not provide, as initially intended, a useful rationale for guiding treatment and instead has led to under-recognition and under-treatment of drug abuse. Over the years, Khantzian updated and revised the self-medication hypothesis, and he still argues that this theory is relevant today as ever before because it derives from clinical evaluation and treatment of thousands of patients (practice-based evidence) during five decades (Khantzian, 2017). He notes that the view of addiction as a disease and the understandings of brain pathways that explain the physiological bases for addiction and relapse does not explain why 10%–20% of users become addicted (Khantzian, 2017). Khantzian is a medical doctor in his basic training, and it is quite unusual today, at least at the addiction field, that a physician does not strictly adhere to the disease model.

Khantzian's therapeutic approach

Khantzian is an enthusiastic advocate of psychodynamic treatment for individuals suffering from drug use disorders. He believes that addiction stems from human suffering, and therefore, it should be the focus of therapy. The first stage of therapy includes understating of the patient's psychic vulnerability, which stands at the addiction's core. When patients feel confused or report that they do not know what they feel, therapists should not interpret it as resistance or as a denial. Patients will benefit more when they learn how to recognize their emotions and name them. In this context, he notes that mentalization-based therapy (Allen, Fonagy & Bateman, 2008) is recommended for drug-abusing patients with such difficulties (Khantzian, 2012).

There is also another group of patients that is characterized with emotional regulation difficulties and the therapist may find himself a target for their rage. Khantzian (2018) recommends using validations in the treatment of such traumatized patients who frequently feel rage and to combine it with medications. As therapy will progress, the therapist will be able to examine with the patient how drugs were conceived as a possible solution during hard times. In later stages, the patient will understand why he chose certain drugs and the emotional states he wrestled with during his addiction (Khantzian, 2013, 2018). The therapist should be ready for the appearance of omnipotence and rage throughout the entire therapy and should keep a therapeutic stance of empathy, support and understanding that the patient masks low self-value and vulnerability.

The classic psychoanalytic stance, which includes distancing, passivity and interpreting, is not recommended because it can increase the patient's confusion, shame and estrangement (Khantzian, 2018). The therapist has an active role during treatment, and he does not deal only with the patient's inner world, but also encourages the patient to avoid risky situations, acquiring skills for naming emotions and for emotional regulation. Khantzian supports the usage of confrontations only when the patient endangers himself and does not use them regularly because patients experience them as a threat to their self-worth. At the end of a long psychodynamic treatment, the patient will learn to understand the developmental and environmental roots of his problems, but the treatment will not deal only with the past but also with transference relations. In other words, like his theoretical ideas, Khantzian's therapeutic approach includes a fusion of different schools of thought and psychotherapy methods.

Khantzian supports the integration of group psychotherapy and the 12-step program for the treatment of drug abuse and addiction. Group psychotherapy is a recommended treatment for alexithymic patents because they can be influenced by patients with disruptive behaviors. Group psychotherapy is also significant because it includes opportunities for therapeutic work on self-value and the creation of interpersonal relations for drug abusers who usually avoid interactions (Khantzian, 2008, 2015).

Joyce McDougall

Another prominent analyst who acted in this period is Joyce McDougall. McDougall was born and raised in New Zealand and, in her 20s, moved with her family to London to pursue analytic training. Later, she settled down in France where she wrote her books, which deal with addictions, creativity, sexuality, psychosomatics and perversions. In her writing, there is mixture of tongues between French psychoanalysis, American psychoanalysis and the British object relations school of thought.

Unlike, Wurmser, Krystal and Khantzian, she had treated patients with a wide array of behavioral addictions or compulsive behaviors, such as compulsive sexual behavior, overeating, workaholism and addictive relationship (McDougall, 1982, 1989). According to her, the main effect of drugs and behavioral addictions is the ability to relieve pain and provide temporary anesthesia of the consciousness. Addiction has a defensive function that allows avoidance from underlying fears associated with independence, existence and selfhood (McDougall, 1982, 1989).

According to McDougall (1982), the theater is a metaphor for the psychic reality and the plays may be performed in our own minds or bodies, or may take place in the external world, when the psychic plays may be played using other people's minds and bodies. Relating to addictions, she relies on Winnicott's ideas and notes that the intermediate area of experience of drug addicts is restricted and replete with pathological activities such as pursuit of addictions. Addiction constitutes a transitional theater that includes actions whose main aim is tension discharge and stress, which raise pain through endless action. In this theater, the players are being restricted to inanimate objects, which represent the mother's breast (McDougall, 1982).

In the first act, the drug is conceived as good and sought of, whereas in the second act, it is conceived as a bad prosecuting mother. In the third act, the addicted individual promises both himself and his environment that he will not use drugs again. This scenario is driven by a perception of the addicted object as good, and the fantasy of stealing the mother's breast and using it without fear of punishment. Then, the object is conceived as bad, and in the third act, there is a promise to the punishing father or the detoxification institution not to use drugs again (McDougall, 1982). While genuine transitional objects represent the mother's soothing presence, drugs, which are pathological transitional objects, cannot be introjected and do not create psychic change (McDougall, 1982). Consequently, the drama or, more accurately, the tragedy continues with an endless search after drugs in the external world.

McDougall (1989) suggests additional theoretical conceptualization for the development of addictions, in which she views addiction as a psychosomatic attempt to cope with conflicts by temporarily blurring the awareness of their existence. In this definition, she actually attributes the addictions to the psychosomatic disorders, meaning to conditions of physical illness or impaired physical health in which psychological factors play an important role (McDougall, 1984, 1989). Psychosomatic disorders and addictions are defensive formations of coping with distress, which are common to all people and do not characterize only addicted individuals.

We all may fall ill, overeat, overwork or drink more alcohol in certain life periods when these behaviors "protect" us from awareness to anxiety, anger or guilt (Morgenstern & Leeds, 1993). The difference is that individuals who are vulnerable to develop psychosomatic or addictive disorders use these coping methods routinely. Most people would think of such behaviors or their consequences as dangerous, but addicted individuals conceive them as routine events and are not aware of the negative aspects of their actions (McDougall, 1989; Morgenstern & Leeds, 1993). For example, individuals with heroin or cocaine addiction describe quite indifferently situations of violence with other addicted individuals or the police. During therapy, they recall them and their possible harmful consequences, and relate to their behavior as insanity.

In healthy development, individuals develop internal defence mechanisms to deal with anxiety and overstimulation. Internal conflicts take the form of symbolic representations and appear in neuroses, dreams and fantasies (McDougall, 1989). These symbolic representations act as buffers between the individual and the painful feelings and also allow to contemplate the painful feelings. Those who fail in developing this reflective ability may suffer from neurotic inhibitions. Meaning, such individuals may have difficulties in controlling and externalizing emotions, and addicted individuals constitute an example for such population.

The development of internal and symbolic means for dealing with affects helps us in adulthood to cope with stressful situations. However, addicted individuals do not have such symbolic means, and therefore, they simply discharge or externalize emotions from the psyche in a raw manner.

These individuals use a method she terms "discharge-in-action", in which feelings are discharged or externalized outward away from the psyche without any awareness. This "discharge in action" helps them not to feel mental pain, and simultaneously they are not capable of therapeutic work if the addiction continues. McDougall (1982) states that some individuals never develop internal and symbolic means of dealing with affects. Morgenstern and Leeds (1993) emphasize that this description does not relate to impulsivity and that McDougall (1982) noted that this mode of defence also characterizes individuals with psychosomatic illness and personality disorders as well as drug abusers.

The origin of this mode of defence is in failures in early interaction between the child and his mother that create vulnerability and damage the development of the child's capabilities to cope with internal conflicts (McDougall, 1982). Consequently, in the lack of symbolic capacities, the child and later the adult must rely on external means to cope with mental distress. McDougall (1989) adds that from an early age, such children are characterized with dependent relations with their mother or other caregivers who sometimes do not allow the child to develop independence. They grow up with an understanding that physical and mental separation is impossible and that they cannot have independent desires, fantasies or emotions. Such anxieties are prevalent among drug abusers and they nourish fear from independence and independent existence.

From this aspect, McDougall's ideas about the inability of drug abusers to tolerate affects are quite similar to those of Krystal's, because she also believes that drug abusers have specific problems in affect tolerance and recognition of emotions. However, Morgenstern and Leeds (1993) note that there are also differences and while McDougall sees addiction as a primary defence against affects, Krystal notes that drug abusers' major problems are associated with ambivalence, aggression and object relations. Second, Krystal views alexithymia as a complex condition that is a product of impaired development, whereas according to McDougall, alexithymia is a defence against psychotic anxieties. The question whether alexithymia is a deficit or defence is important (Morgenstern & Leeds, 1993), because it has implications for psychoanalytic technique.

McDougall's therapeutic approach

McDougall's conception of psychoanalysis for individuals with drug addiction is very realistic. She notes that the treatment depends on a few factors, such as the level of suffering, the patient's introspection ability and the readiness to ask for help (McDougall, 1982, 1989). Besides, the treatment has many difficulties and may lengthen because of the rigid defences and the stormy lifestyle of drug addicts that appear during therapy. However, the therapist should bear in mind that the curtain conceals psychic deadness and lack of authentic identity. During the therapeutic journey, the patient and the therapist will also discover feelings of boredom, despair, dissatisfaction with life and difficulties in finding happiness without drugs (McDougall, 1982, 1989).

The third period – from the 1990s until the present

In my opinion, the third period has begun toward the end of the second millennium and lingers until this time. In this period, there are clear trends of drug abuse and addiction to different drugs in different society layers. The first one concerns the prevalence of cannabis (for further elaboration on the effects of cannabis abuse, see Chapter). In the past two decades, there is growing societal and medical acceptance of cannabis and a national and global expansion of the legal cannabis market. Second, the opioid epidemic is mostly identified with the United States in which this phenomenon has been declared as a national public health emergency. However, the opioid crisis continues to devastate communities and families across Canada and in other countries around the world (Government of Canada, 2019; Martins & Ghandour, 2017).

Third, there is an increase in nonmedical prescription drug use. This term relates to the taking of prescription drugs, whether obtained by prescription or otherwise, other than in the manner or for the reasons or time period prescribed, or by a person for whom the drug was not prescribed. The prevalent use of methylphenidate for academic performance enhancement is a typical example (Bogle & Smith, 2009; Steyn, 2016). Fourth, recently, there is a renewed medical interest in hallucinogens, such as MDMA, psilocybin and ketamine, for treatment of depression and post-traumatic stress disorder (Begola & Schillerstrom, 2019; Domany et al., 2019). Finally, drug use has become a legitimate component of the leisure culture of many people's lifestyle, whether it is an individual at the suburbs who smokes marijuana in hand-rolled cigarette (joint) at the end of the day or curious young adults who use amphetamines and synthetic cannabinoids (Cooper, 2016; Radfar & Rawson, 2014). However, in the growing discourse on the decriminalization of certain drugs, their harmful impacts on mental health are sometimes ignored or forgotten.

Despite the rising rates of drug abuse, there are significantly fewer publications concerning psychoanalytic treatment of drug abuse in comparison to the previous period. After more than a century in which psychoanalysts wrote on drug abuse and addiction, finally, a book in the series of essential psychoanalytic papers that dealt solely with addiction was published (Yalisove, 1997). This is a significant event because it represents an acknowledgment in the existence of a unique variation of mental pain and also an understanding that drug abusers can benefit from psychoanalytic treatment. The book is a compilation of past and present contributions that deal with alcoholism, recovery and modifications in psychoanalytic technique (Yalisove, 1997).

However, in the last three decades, there are not any analysts such as Wurmser and Krystal who wrote extensively on addictions, but more humble contributions of psychoanalysts and therapists who use psychodynamic conceptualizations in their work with drug abusers. Hagman, a psychoanalyst who worked with MMT patients, provided very useful articles for therapists, who are either making their first steps in the addiction field or for those who try to integrate psychoanalytic conceptualization in their work with drug abusers and addicted individuals. In one article, he describes elaborately the components and principles of methadone maintenance counseling (Hagman, 1994), and in another article, he provides a psychoanalytic conceptualization of MMT and examines problems of resistance and transference relations (Hagman, 1995). Jerry (1997) presented an object relations approach based on Winnicott's ideas and demonstrated its relevance in treating a patient using cocaine. Waska (2006) used some of Klein's ideas to examine the deeper object relational issues that lie behind the addictive process and to analyze the dynamics of the patients' transference relations.

Lance Dodes, a psychiatrist and a psychoanalyst with extensive clinical experience, notes that the heart of addiction is helplessness and that drugs are particularly apt for altering this feeling (Dodes, 2002). Every addictive act, whether it is calling a dealer to buy drugs or entering a casino is preceded by helplessness or powerlessness, when this behavior aims to restore a feeling of control and empowerment (Dodes, 2002). All people have periods in their life when they feel uncertainty and lack of control. Nevertheless, such feelings raise emotional issues, which drug-addicted individuals cannot tolerate because of psychological vulnerability.

Dodes relies on some of Kohut's ideas to explain the second significant factor behind addiction. Kohut noted that "narcissistic rage enslaves the ego and allows it to function only as its tool and rationalizer" (1972, p. 387), whereas in chronic narcissistic rage "conscious and preconscious ideation, in particular as it concerns the aims and goals of the personality, becomes more and more subservient to the pervasive rage" (p. 396). According to Dodes (1990), replacing the word "addiction" for the term "narcissistic rage" in these lines creates an immaculate description of acute and chronic addictive states. The third aspect is that all addictions are actually displacements or substitutes for other actions to respond to helplessness. Every addiction results from a redirection of energy to a displaced effort because the direct action is not considered permissible (Dodes, 2002).

In therapy, the therapist should help the patient to recognize the "key moment" that leads to drug abuse (Dodes, 2011). These are moments when the thought of using drugs first came to the patient's mind, but patients do not always recognize them because of defence mechanisms such as rationalization. Teaching patients to recognize the emotional situations that precipitate helplessness, such as interpersonal conflicts, may help them in relapse prevention.

With the rise of drug abuse and addiction rates, the number of patients who suffer from drug use disorders increased with the need for treatment facilities. This trend also led to the demand of therapists, counselors and other professionals in the mental health field to acquire professional knowledge about addictions treatment. Currently, there are designated programs in many academic institutions, which provide appropriate knowledge and training. In the last decade, in one of psychoanalysis's fortresses, the New York University, post-doctoral program in psychoanalysis and psychotherapy, a course that focused on psychodynamic treatment of addiction, was being taught. It seems that after more than a century, the subject of drug abuse and addiction moves from offstage toward the onstage of psychoanalytic theory and treatment.

In this context, another sign for the relocation of the addictions issue in the psychoanalytic world is the publication of articles that deal with drug abuse in the journal, which is most identified with the relational school of thought (Burton, 2005; Director, 2002, 2005). Rothschild (2007) suggests an integration of the relational approach with the harm reduction approach and notes that both approaches promote a context of mutuality and a collaboration between two fully functioning participants. Thombs and Osborne (2013) note that the relational writing on drug abuse represents an effort of forces from within the psychoanalytic community to show that psychodynamic conceptualization is still relevant for treatment of drug abusers. I believe that the relational discourse is valuable because of the traumatic life history of the patients and the focus on dissociated self-states, which contribute to the patients' self-defeating behavior.

Director (2002) is one of the prominent advocates for working within this analytic school of thought with drug abusers. She relies on the transition in the psychoanalytic world from insight and interpretation as the major tools for achieving therapeutic change toward the analyst's ability to participate in the patient's dynamics. An approach in which enactments are the central medium of the work is tailor-made for a population that is characterized with acting rather on reflecting on inner experience (Boesky, 1982; Director, 2002). According to this approach, unresolved standoffs between such forces as dependency and defiance, domination and submission drive chronic drug addiction, and these standoffs are embodied in patients' relationships to drugs (Director, 2002).

In relational psychotherapy, there is an effort to trace self-states that appear at the basis of the addiction and appear as enactments during therapy (Director, 2002). From this aspect, therapists can receive plenty of therapeutic material in every meeting because drug-abusing patients are characterized by emotional regulation difficulties in interpersonal relations. Director suggests using "therapeutic dissociation" (Davies, 1996) and inviting a dissociated aspect of the experience to the transference relations for revealing "both its historical roots and its present-day interpersonal influence within the safe confines of the therapeutic relationship" (1996, p. 567). Director demonstrates it in a description of a patient who used cocaine during analysis and made her feel irrelevant and unimportant. In such moments, she felt quasi dissociative state and experienced the patient's helplessness while the patient felt omnipotence. As analysis progressed, both patient and therapist found out that cocaine use was always with other people and allowed feeling unity between the patient and the object that was missing earlier in her childhood.

Director's case illustration includes deviation from the classical psychoanalytic setting in a few aspects. First, she allows telephonic availability beyond therapy hours and answers the patient's phone call when the latter is distressed. Second, when a patient tells Director that she imagines them both using cocaine in a bar, Director does not interpret but asks her to continue describing the fantasy. Third, when the patient hugs her, Director chooses not to adhere to the classic technique.

Actually, psychotherapists working within the dynamic thought allow some drug-abusing patients to call them in specific terms and in specific times. It should be noted that such intervention is anchored in the therapeutic contract, and it is used after much consideration only with some of the patients. The rationale for this move is to serve as auxiliary ego for patients with severe ego deficits that lack basic relapse prevention skills. In addition, the patient starts to perceive both the therapist and therapy as consistent objects in his life. Perhaps the significant innovation is that a psychoanalyst legitimizes important therapeutic components that characterize the psychoanalytic treatment of drug abuse and addiction. In other words, Director actually supports changes in the technique and in the setting for analysts who treat individuals with drug abuse problems.

However, the gap between Director's ideas and those of psychoanalysts who adhere to the classic technique is quite large. When some of my colleagues presented the issue of telephonic availability to a few supervising psychoanalysts it seemed that it was as a thorn in their flesh. One of the interpretations which a colleague therapist received when he presented a case of an addicted individual was *"when you talk to a patient beyond sessions, you are fulfilling his wish to have sex with you"*. The case which was presented was that of a patient who was already three years into therapy and had never shown any romantic or sexual interest toward his male therapist. No fantasies or dreams of latent homosexual content had appeared during therapy. When the therapist tried to explain this to the supervising analyst, she said, *"I know addicts well. I know that they look for a fix. I don't understand why you have to break the boundaries of therapy"*.

Hoffman (2009, p. 621) notes that the

> psychoanalytic arrangement lends itself to that kind of empathic identification with another person's struggle *to be* a person in the face of devastating hardship, the hardship of particular *unnecessary* traumas superimposed on the inevitable, *necessary* traumas of the human condition.

He (Hoffman, 2009, p. 631) also adds that "so much is mistakenly and reflexively blocked before it could possibly get off the ground by the question: But is that really psychoanalytic?"

References

Albarelli, H. A. (2009). *Terrible mistake: The murder of Frank Olson and the CIA's secret cold war experiments.* Trine Day.

Allen, J. G., Fonagy, P., & Bateman, A. W. (2008). Mentalizing in clinical practice. American Psychiatric Publishing, Inc.

Amburn, E. (1992). *Pearl: The obsessions and passions of Janis Joplin.* Warner Books.

Arendt, M., Rosenberg, R., Fjordback, L., Brandholdt, J., Foldager, L., Sher, L., & Munk-Jorgensen, P. (2007). Testing the self-medication hypothesis of depression and aggression in cannabis-dependent subjects. *Psychological Medicine, 37*(7), 935–945.

Begola, M. J., & Schillerstrom, J. E. (2019). Hallucinogens and their therapeutic use: A literature review. *Journal of Psychiatric Practice, 25*(5), 334–346.

Blaine, J., & Julius, D. (Eds.). (1977). *Psychodynamics of drug dependence*. NIDA Research monograph no. 12. National Institute on Drug Abuse.

Blatt, S. J., Berman, W., Bloom-Feshbach, S., Sugarman, A., Wilber, C., & Kleber, H. D. (1984). Psychological assessment of psychopathology in opiate addicts. *Journal of Nervous and Mental Diseases, 172*(3), 156–165.

Boesky, D. (1982). Acting out: A reconsideration of the concept. *The International Journal of Psychoanalysis, 63*(1), 39–55.

Bogle, K. E., & Smith, B. H. (2009). Illicit methylphenidate use: A review of prevalence, availability, pharmacology, and consequences. *Current Drug Abuse Reviews, 2*(2), 157–176.

Burton, N. (2005). Finding the lost girls: Multiplicity and dissociation in the treatment of addictions. *Psychoanalytic Dialogues, 15*(4), 587–612.

Bush, D. M. (2013). *Emergency department visits involving phencyclidine (PCP): The CBHSQ Report*. Substance Abuse and Mental Health Services Administration.

Cooper, Z. D. (2016). Adverse effects of synthetic cannabinoids: Management of acute toxicity and withdrawal. *Current Psychiatry Reports, 18*(5), 52.

Cui, C. L., Wu, L. Z., & Luo, F. (2008). Acupuncture for the treatment of drug addiction. *Neurochemical Research, 33*(10), 2013–2022.

Das, G. (2013). Cocaine abuse in North America: A milestone in history. *Journal of Clinical Pharmacology, 33*(4), 296–310.

Davies, J. M. (1996). Linking the "pre-analytic" with the postclassical: Integration, dissociation, and the multiplicity of unconscious process. *Contemporary Psychoanalysis, 32*(4), 553–576.

Davis, F., & Munoz, L. (1968). Heads and freaks: Patterns and meanings of drug use among hippies. *Journal of Health and Social Behavior, 9*(2), 156–164.

Davis, H., Baum, C., & Graham, D. J. (1991). Indices of drug misuse for prescription drugs. *The International Journal of the Addictions, 26*(7), 777–795.

Davis, S. (2005). *Jim Morrison: Life, death, legend*. Gotham Books.

DeGrandpre, R. (2006). *The cult of pharmacology: How America became the world's most troubled drug culture*. Duke University Press.

Director, L. (2002). The value of relational psychoanalysis in the treatment of chronic drug and alcohol use. *Psychoanalytic Dialogues, 12*(4), 551–580.

Director, L. (2005). Encounters with omnipotence in the psychoanalysis of substance users. *Psychoanalytic Dialogues, 15*(4), 567–586.

Dodes, L. M. (1990). Addiction, helplessness, and narcissistic rage. *Psychoanalysis Quarterly, 59*(3), 398–419.

Dodes, L. M. (2002). *The heart of addiction: A new approach to understanding and managing alcoholism and other addictive behaviors*. HarperCollins.

Dodes, L. M. (2011). *Breaking addiction: A 7-step handbook for ending any addiction*. HarperCollins.

Dole, V. P., & Nyswander, M. E. (1967). Heroin addiction – A metabolic disease. *Archives of Internal Medicine, 120*(1), 19–24.

Domany, Y., Bleich-Cohen, M., Tarrasch, R., Meidan, R., Litvak-Lazar, O., Stoppleman, N., Schreiber, S., Bloch, M., Hendler, T., & Sharon, H. (2019). Repeated oral ketamine for out-patient treatment of resistant depression: randomised, double-blind, placebo-controlled, proof-of-concept study. *The British journal of psychiatry: the journal of mental science, 214*(1), 20–26.

Government of Canada. (2019, 17 September). Opioid-related harms and deaths in Canada. Retrieved from https://www.canada.ca/en/health canada/services/substance-use/problematic-prescription-drug-use/opioids/data-surveillance-research/harms-deaths.

Grogger, J., & Willis, M. (2000). The emergence of crack cocaine and the rise in urban crime rates. *The Review of Economics and Statistics, 82*(4), 519–529.

Hagman, G. (1994). Methadone maintenance counseling: Definition, principles, components. *Journal of Substance Abuse Treatment, 11*(5), 405–413.

Hagman, G. (1995). A psychoanalyst in methadonia. *Journal of Substance Abuse Treatment, 12*(3), 167–179.

Hoffman, I. Z. (2009). Therapeutic passion in the Countertransference. *Psychoanalytic Dialogues, 19*(5), 617–637.

Jerry, P. A. (1997). Psychodynamic psychotherapy of the intravenous cocaine abuser. *Journal of Substance Abuse Treatment, 14*(4), 319–332.

Kernberg, O. F. (1975). *Borderline conditions and pathological narcissism.* Jason Aronson.

Khantzian, E. J. (1985). The self-medication hypothesis of addictive disorders. *American Journal of Psychiatry, 142*(11), 1259–1264.

Khantzian, E. J. (1997). The self-medication hypothesis of substance use disorders: Reconsideration and recent applications. *Harvard Review of Psychiatry, 4*(5), 231–244.

Khantzian, E. J. (1999). *Treating addiction as a human process.* Jason Aronson.

Khantzian, E. J. (2003). The self-medication hypothesis revisited: The dually diagnosed patient. *Primary Psychiatry, 10*(9), 47–54.

Khantzian, E. J. (2008). Supportive psychotherapy: The nature of the connection to patients. *American Journal of Psychiatry, 165*(10), 1355.

Khantzian, E. J. (2012). Reflections on treating addictive disorders: A psychodynamic perspective. *American Journal on Addictions, 21*(3), 274–279.

Khantzian, E. J. (2013). Addiction as a self-regulation disorder and the role of self-medication. *Addiction, 108*(4), 668–669.

Khantzian, E. J. (2015). Psychodynamic psychotherapy for the treatment of substance use disorders. In N. el-Guebaly, G. Carrà, & M. Galanter (Eds.), *Textbook of addiction treatment: International perspectives* (pp. 811–819). Springer-Verlag.

Khantzian, E. J. (2017). The theory of self-medication and addiction. *Psychiatric Times, 34*, 2.

Khantzian, E. J. (2018). *Treating addiction: Beyond the pain.* Rowman & Littlefield.

Khantzian, E. J., & Albanese, M. J. (2008). *Understanding addiction as self medication: Finding hope behind the pain.* Rowman & Littlefield.

Kohut, H. (1971). *The analysis of the self.* International Universities Press.

Kohut, H. (1972). Thoughts on narcissism and narcissistic rage. *The Psychoanalytic Study of the Child, 27*, 360–400.

Kohut, H. (1977). Preface. In D. Blaine & D. A. Julius (Eds.), *Psychodynamics of drug dependence.* Research Monograph 12 (pp. vii–ix). National Institute on Drug Abuse.

Krystal, H. (1977). Self- and object- representation in alcoholism and other drug dependence: Implications for therapy. In J. D. Blaine & A. Julius (Eds.), *Psychodynamics of drug dependence*. Research Monograph 12 (pp. 88–100). National Institute on Drug Abuse.

Krystal, H. (1978). Self-representation and the capacity for self-care. *Annual of Psychoanalysis, 6*, 209–246.

Krystal, H. (1979). Alexithymia and psychotherapy. *American Journal of Psychotherapy, 33*(1), 17–31.

Krystal, H. (1982). Alexithymia and the effectiveness of psychoanalytic treatment. *International Journal of Psychoanalytic Psychotherapy, 9*, 353–378.

Krystal, H., & Krystal, J. H. (1988). *Integration and self-healing: Affect, trauma, alexithymia*. Analytic Press.

Krystal, H., & Raskin, H. A. (1970). *Drug dependence: Aspects of ego function*. Wayne State University Press.

Lembke, A. (2012). Time to abandon the self-medication hypothesis in patients with psychiatric disorders. *The American Journal of Drug and Alcohol Abuse, 38*(6), 524–529.

Li, C. S., & Sinha, R. (2006). Alexithymia and stress-induced brain activation in cocaine-dependent men and women. *Journal of psychiatry & neuroscience: JPN, 31*(2), 115–121.

Lopez-Munoz, F., Ucha-Udabe, R., & Alamo, C. (2005) The history of barbiturates a century after their clinical introduction. *Neuropsychiatric Disease and Treatment, 1*(4), 329–343.

Marlatt, G. A., & Gordon, J. R. (1985). *Relapse prevention: Maintenance strategies in the treatment of addictive behaviors*. Guilford Press.

Martins, S. S., & Ghandour, L. A. (2017). Nonmedical use of prescription drugs in adolescents and young adults: Not just a Western phenomenon. *World Psychiatry: Official Journal of the World Psychiatric Association (WPA), 16*(1), 102–104.

McDougall, J. (1982). *Theaters of the mind: Illusion and truth on psychoanalytic stage*. Free Associations Books.

McDougall, J. (1984). The 'dis-affected' patient: Reflections on affect pathology. *Psychoanalytic Quarterly, 53*(3), 386–409.

McDougall, J. (1989). *Theatres of the body: A psychoanalytic approach to psychosomatic illness*. Karnac Books.

McElrath, D. (1997). The Minnesota model. *Journal of Psychoactive Drugs, 29*(2), 141–144.

McFarlane, S. (2007). *The hippie narrative: A literary perspective on the counterculture*. McFarland Publications.

Milkman, H., & Frosch, W. A. (1973). On the preferential abuse of heroin and amphetamine. *Journal of Nervous and Mental Disease, 156*, 242–248.

Mion, G. (2017). History of anaesthesia: The ketamine story – past, present and future. *European Journal of Anaesthesiology, 34*(9), 571–575.

Mold, A. (2007). Illicit drugs and the rise of epidemiology during the 1960s. *Journal of Epidemiology and Community Health, 61*(4), 278–281.

Morgenstern, J., & Leeds, J. (1993). Contemporary psychoanalytic theories of substance abuse: A disorder in search of a paradigm. *Psychotherapy: Theory, Research, Practice, Training, 30*(2), 194–206.

Morie, K. P., Yip, S. W., Nich, C., Hunkele, K., Carroll, K. M., & Potenza, M. N. (2016). Alexithymia and addiction: A review and preliminary data suggesting neurobiological links to reward/loss processing. *Current Addiction Reports, 3*(2), 239–248.

Nehra, D. K., Kumar, P., Sharma, V., & Nehra, S. (2014). Alexithymia and emotional intelligence among people with cannabis dependence and healthy control: A comparative study. *Dysphrenia, 5,* 49–55.

O'donel, J. A., Voss, H. L., Clayton, R. R., Slatin, G. T., & Room, R. G. W. (1976). *Young men and drugs – A nationwide survey.* Research Monograph No. 5. National Institute on Drug Abuse.

Penner, J. (2014). *Timothy Leary: The Harvard years.* Park Street Press.

Radfar, S. R., & Rawson, R. A. (2014). Current research on methamphetamine: Epidemiology, medical and psychiatric effects, treatment, and harm reduction efforts. *Addiction and Health, 6*(3–4), 146–154.

Rasmussen N. (2008). America's first amphetamine epidemic 1929–1971. A quantitative and qualitative retrospective with implications for the present. *American Journal of Public Health, 98,* 974–985.

Rothschild, D. (2007). Bringing the pieces together: Relational psychoanalysis, harm reduction therapy and substance abuse treatment. *Psychoanalytic Perspectives, 5*(1), 69–94.

Shedler, J., & Block, J. (1990). Adolescent drug use and psychological health. *American Psychologist, 45*(5), 612–630.

Shulgin, A., & Shulgin, A. (1997). *TIHKAL: The continuation.* Transform Press.

Smith, D. E., Raswyck, G. E., & Davidson, L. D. (2014). From Hofmann to the Haight Ashbury, and into the future: The past and potential of lysergic acid diethlyamide. *Journal of Psychoactive Drugs, 46*(1), 3–10.

Spek, V., Nyklicek, I., Cuijpers, P., & Pop, V. (2008). Alexithymia and cognitive behaviour therapy outcome for subthreshold depression. *Acta Psychiatrica Scandivica, 118*(2), 164–167.

Steyn, F. (2016). Methylphenidate use and poly-substance use among undergraduate students attending a South African university. *South African Journal of Psychiatry, 22*(1), a760.

Suh, J. J., Ruffins, S., Robins, C. E., Albanese, M. J., & Khantzian, E. J. (2008). Self-medication hypothesis: Connecting affective experience and drug choice. *Psychoanalytic Psychology, 25*(3), 518–532.

Thombs, D. L., & Osborn, C. J. (2013). *Introduction to addictive behaviors (4th ed.).* The Guilford Press.

Thompson II, C. C., & Cole, J. P. (1990). *The death of Elvis: What really happened.* Delacorte Press.

Torrado, M. V., Ouakinin, S. S., & Bacelar-Nicolau, L. (2013). Alexithymia, emotional awareness and perceived dysfunctional parental behaviors in heroin dependents. *International Journal of Mental Health and Addiction, 11*(6), 703–718.

Tyranka, P. (2014). *Brian Jones: The making of the Rolling Stones.* Viking.

Ulman, R. B., & Paul, H. (2006). *The self psychology of addiction and its treatment: Narcissus in wonderland.* Routledge.

Volkow, N. D., Koob, G. F., & McLellan, T. A. (2016). Neurobiologic advances from the brain disease model of addiction. *New England Journal of Medicine, 374*(4), 363–371.

Waska, R. (2006). Addictions and the quest to control the object. *Journal of the American Psychoanalytic Association, 66*(1), 43–62.

Weider, H., & Kaplan, E. (1969). Drug use in adolescents. *Psychoanalytic Study of the Child, 24*(1), 399–431.

White, W. (1998). *Slaying the dragon: The history of addiction treatment and recovery in America.* Chestnut Health Systems.

Wurmser, L. (1974). Psychoanalytic considerations of the etiology of compulsive drug use. *Journal of the American Psychoanalytic Association, 22*(4), 820–843.

Wurmser, L. (1984a). More respect for the neurotic process. *Journal of the Substance Abuse Treatment, 1*(1), 37–45.

Wurmser, L. (1984b). The role of superego conflicts in substance abuse and their treatment. *International Journal of Psychoanalytic Psychotherapy, 10*, 227–258.

Wurmser, L. (1985). Denial and split identity: Timely issues in the psychoanalytic psychotherapy of compulsive drug users. *Journal of Substance Abuse Treatment, 2*(2), 89–96.

Wurmser, L. (1987). Flight from conscience: Experiences with the psychoanalytic treatment of compulsive drug abusers: II. Dynamic and therapeutic conclusions from the experiences with psychoanalysis of drug users. *Journal of Substance Abuse Treatment, 4*(3–4), 169–179.

Wurmser, L., & Zients, A. (1982). The return of the denied superego. *Psychoanalytic Inquiry, 2*(4), 539–580.

Yalisove, D. L. (Ed.). (1997). *Essential papers in psychoanalysis. Essential papers on addiction.* New York University Press.

Chapter 3

Drug addiction ≈ the paranoid-schizoid position*

> "Pleasure is experienced also when the warm stream of milk runs down the throat and fills the stomach".
>
> Melanie Klein (1936, p. 290)

Drug addicts do not constitute a "classic" population for psychoanalytic treatment. Lack of motivation for personal change, poor ego control and the need for constant assistance with daily challenges are only a few of the difficulties cited by analysts as major barriers to analytic treatment (Leeds & Morgenstern, 1996). However, as many have correctly noted, there is confusion between the psychoanalytic understanding of addiction and the psychoanalytic treatment of the disorder (Leeds & Morgenstern, 1996). During active drug abuse, there is little that therapists can contribute to the addict, but, when in recovery, patients may be more accessible. In my opinion, because psychoanalytic treatment indeed stems from psychoanalytic theory, the stereotype of addicts or abusers as inaccessible to psychoanalytic treatment (Wurmser, 1974) may stem from an insufficiency of theory, as a result of which the subjective experience of the addict or, more importantly, their suffering has not been conveyed to the analytic community.

The psychoanalytic understanding of addiction can help therapists to see that their addicted patients aren't merely interested in mind-altering drugs, but rather have intense desires and a rich inner world. Clinical work with this population teaches that the drug is an object of paramount importance to the addict's daily existence, with which the addicted individual has unique object relations. Hence, ideas emanating from the object relations school of thought may provide an authentic experience-near conceptualization of the complex phenomenon of addiction.

---

* This chapter was previously published as a journal article: Potik, D. (2018), Kleinian conceptualization of heroin addiction, Part 1: the paranoid-schizoid position. *Clinical Social Work Journal*, 45, 34–41. © 2018 Springer Nature, reprinted by permission.

The object relations school of thought viewed addiction as the result of a failure in the separation-individuation process (Graham & Glickauf-Hughes, 1992). According to this premise, individuals who cannot differentiate themselves from the mother during this process turn to an external object whose pharmacological properties assist in coping with mental distress (Graham & Glickauf-Hughes, 1992). In other words, drug addicts do not achieve independence through the separation-individuation process and so search for an external object that will help them in affect regulation and mastery of conflicts (Graham & Glickauf-Hughes, 1992). According to Krystal and Raskin (1970), addicts have problems with self and object representation because their early relations with the loved object were characterized by ambivalence. The loved object was experienced as either seductive or aggressive; as a result, in adulthood, their object representations become rigid. They are not sure how external objects (people) feel toward them and demand constant reassurance. The drug is experienced as was the mother during the child's infancy (Krystal & Raskin, 1970).

Although these object relations theories constitute a significant contribution to the psychoanalytic understanding of the addiction phenomenon, they do not relate specifically to heroin addiction. Additionally, these object relations theories do not discuss major contents of the addict's daily life, nor do they explain the subjective experience of the patient as he is trapped in the vicious cycle of addiction, which includes a great deal of mental suffering and involvement in crime. A more comprehensive object relations framework, which relies on Winnicott's developmental theory, sees heroin addiction as a regressive response to deprivation and the object of addiction as a transitional phenomenon (Potik, Adelson, & Schreiber, 2007; Winnicott, 1971). This conceptualization relates to the subjective experience of heroin addicts, such as the withdrawal state, and to the therapeutic challenges facing the methadone maintenance clinic therapists and counselors treating these patients. However, this Winnicottian conceptualization does not take into consideration the importance of aggression and primitive defence mechanisms in the heroin addict's subjective experience or his relations with family members.

In this chapter and the next one, I would like to present yet another theoretical framework, based on object relations, for understanding drug addiction and recovery. Many sessions of psychodynamic treatment and listening to patients' subjective experience of their daily struggles while using heroin, alongside the guilt and will for reparation that appear during recovery, have helped me to understand the relevance of Klein's ideas to the addictions field. Waska (2006) also used some of Klein's ideas in his discussion of the internal and external object relations of drug addicts. He found that his addicted patients were characterized by a dread of abandonment and persecution from a narcissistic object as well as a phantasy of harming their object (Waska, 2006).

Waska's ideas help therapists to understand transference relations, but he does not relate specifically to heroin addiction, and I believe that a psychoanalytic theoretical conceptualization is still required to better understand the inner world of individuals struggling with heroin addiction.

By using Melanie Klein's developmental theory regarding primary mental states, I will describe the similarity between the conflicts that characterize a drug addict's mental life and the dramas that characterize the infant's internal world during his early mental development, which is characterized by a constant struggle between life and death. This chapter focuses on the similarities between the paranoid-schizoid position and heroin addiction. My main premise in this chapter is that the paranoid-schizoid position has many similarities to drug addiction and that heroin addicts use the same defence mechanisms as do infants in coping with the (same) anxieties that arise during their struggle with a persecutory internal and external reality. The chapter is theoretical in nature and relies on my extensive experience working with drug addicts and patients with behavioral addictions. The vignettes that appear in the text are taken from psychoanalytic psychotherapy sessions with patients who have used heroin and cocaine for many years.

Drug addiction ≈ the paranoid-schizoid position

Primary object relations

Drug addiction is defined as repeated use of a psychoactive substance or substances to the extent that the user is chronically or periodically intoxicated, shows a compulsion to take the preferred substance, has great difficulty voluntarily ceasing or modifying his substance use and exhibits determination to obtain psychoactive substances by almost any means (World Health Organization, 1994). I have chosen to use the word "addiction" here, although the latest edition of the diagnostic and statistical manual of mental disorders (DSM) does not use this word, but rather suggests using the term "substance use disorder" (American Psychiatric Association, 2013), since the word "addiction" better describes the situation in which an individual is totally absorbed by and in an external object to the point that nothing else interests him or her.

The DSM-5 criteria for substance use disorder include symptoms such as craving, failure to fulfill major role obligations at work, school or home and giving up or reducing important social, occupational or recreational activities because of the substance use (APA, 2013). The DSM-5's criteria and the WHO's definition imply the existence of physical and mental dependence on an external object or, more precisely, on objects with certain unique features. Whether it is heroin's pleasurable "rush" or cocaine's euphoria that the addict seeks, he or she is ready to incorporate these drugs into his body to receive pleasant sensations and positive emotions. According to Klein, the infant also yearns to receive pleasure from an external object – in his case, mother's milk – to the extent that his mental life is characterized by constant craving for that milk.

There are many similarities between mental activity at the beginning of life and the inner world of the drug addict. Throughout her work, Klein (1957) ascribed much importance to the infant's first object relation to the breast, which the infant perceives instinctively as a source of nourishment, and in a deeper sense, the source of life itself. The infant's mental and physical proximity to the breast provides him with a sense of prenatal unity (Klein, 1957). Similarly, drug-addicted individuals describe the use of heroin as a pleasurable and worriless experience. Some of them report that their first experience of heroin was the very best; for ever after, they try unsuccessfully to repeat this experience. Similarly, Klein (1957) cites a universal yearning to return to a prenatal state, which gives rise to a longing for an ever-present breast with an inexhaustible supply of milk. The infant's ultimate phantasy – to remain suspended in a state of constant breastfeeding – is quite similar to the addicted individual's phantasy to sustain continuous use of the drug (or, as one patient told me, "*my dream is to sit on an endless mountain of cocaine*").

This sentence implies that drug addiction is encoded in the brain as pleasurable – as is proximity to the breast during feeding. Drugs activate pathways in the brain that are responsible for reward-seeking behaviors. Major structures of the reward pathways include the ventral tegmental area (VTA), the nucleus accumbens and the prefrontal cortex (Koob & Simon, 2009). The VTA is connected to both the nucleus accumbens and the prefrontal cortex through this pathway, and it sends information to these structures through its neurons. The neurons of the VTA contain dopamine, a neurotransmitter, which is released both in the nucleus accumbens and in the prefrontal cortex when the individual is involved in pleasurable activities or when he or she is using drugs (Koob & Simon, 2009).

Whether smoked, snorted or injected, heroin reaches the brain and is converted to morphine by enzymes. Then, the morphine binds to opiate receptors that are concentrated in areas within the reward pathway (the VTA, nucleus accumbens and cortex), bringing a euphoric rush and a sense of security. In addition, the binding of morphine to areas in the pain pathway leads to a loss of pain (analgesia) and to warm feelings of relaxation, pleasure and satisfaction (Seecof & Tennant, 1986). The craving for a direct, magic link to the source of gratification is a central component of the phantasy life of both infants and drug addicts. Of course, such a link is not possible, since reality invades the pleasant experience and causes frustration and hatred, also intensifying the inborn conflict between life and death. These unavoidable grievances, together with pleasant experiences, result in a feeling that both a bad object and a good object exist. According to Klein (1957), early emotional life is characterized by a feeling of losing and regaining the good object. Both breastfeeding and drug use provide feelings of satiation and fullness, but once they have passed, both the infant and the addict will try to both get the good object and to control it.

Allegedly, mother's milk is a healthy food important to growth and development, whereas drugs are perceived as being poisonous and not contributing a thing to the life of the addicted individual. However, once the therapist understands that the drug is actually like milk and, moreover, is (often) the only meaningful object in the patient's world, the comparison seems less strange. The following vignette illustrates this point.

At a conference on drug addiction, an experienced therapist described a session with a recovered patient. The therapist asked, *"What did the drug mean to you?"* The patient replied, *"For me, the drug was a source of life, just like milk"*. The therapist pondered this comment. He had studied philosophy and comparative religions before changing careers to social work, and his first associations were of life as related to water, since he had learned that in many religions, water is a symbol of the creative force of life (Brüsch, 2011). He then said to the patient that for him, water was the source of life – and not milk. But the patient continued insisting that the drug was just like milk for him.

This vignette also implies how deeply rooted addiction is in the addict's consciousness. Consequently, it also suggests the mental territory in which treatment should occur: that is, the territory where somatic sensations create mental experiences that are in turn interpreted as relations with the object that causes the sensations. The object is either loved or hated by the subject, depending on the object's "intention" to do good or to cause harm, as imputed to it by the subject (Hinshelwood, 1991). Somatic sensations of hunger and satiation are quite similar to the sensations of craving and using a drug; in both instances, the object is perceived completely differently before and after ingestion. An external object that provides an experience of proper treatment and gratification is experienced as a good object and is loved. Hunger, gas and physical pain are experienced simultaneously as threatening attacks internally and externally, and the object that "causes" them is therefore perceived as persecutory and frustrating, and as being able to provide for the infant's (or addict's) needs, but as refusing to do so (Klein, 1946).

During the earliest periods of life, the infant does not attribute his experiences to any one source, nor does he understand that both his negative and his positive experiences are related to the same breast. Similarly, the splitting that arises during such primary object relations also characterizes the drug addict's perception of the people and things around her. This is reflected in her behavior toward these "objects", who (or which) are perceived differently according to whether they meet or frustrate the addict's need.

For example, the dynamic between a drug addict and her family changes constantly, in accordance with the family's changing response to the addict's needs; this response then determines the quality of the addict's introjected experience. Drug addicts see their family members as partial objects that can be used according to their idiosyncratic needs. Family members and other people are perceived as a breast full of goods, as the addicted individual does not see these others' concern regarding his own behavior. Rather, the addict perceives others merely as a means to an end; he or she initiates goal-directed, short, one-dimensional object relations with others in order to win the chance to be alone with the "milk". When family members agree to provide money for drugs, the addict feels loved by the breast and preserves an omnipotent feeling of controlling the object. But when family members refuse to support the addict's destructive habit, they become an object for the addict's projection of his or her aggressive impulses, because he knows they have the ability to provide the money that will stop their suffering but refuse to do so.

At such times, the addicted individual experiences an internal attack (exemplified by the withdrawal state), to which he responds with an external attack on his frustrating family members. For example, the addicted individual may shout, swear or even hit family members, as the aim of this external attack is to punish the hated object for its continuing refusal to provide the desired milk. When the addicted individual turns to criminal activity to get the money he needs to buy drugs, the innocent people he tries to rob may become the object of his projected sadistic impulses, if they refuse to give up their money.

The addict's use of projection and splitting is similar to that of the infant during the early months of life, when these defences predominate. The absence of milk gives rise to oral-sadistic impulses in the infant, who yearns not only to feed at the breast, but also to bite the frustrating object. When perceived as preventing the longed-for gratification, the breast becomes the object of the infant's sadistic oral, anal and urethral impulses (Klein, 1946), just as the addict's family changes, in seconds, from a loved object to a hated object. One parent of an addicted patient described the situation thus:

> When he's not in withdrawal, he's a good son. He talks to me normally. But when he needs money for drugs, it's awful. It's like he's not my son... he turns into a different person. He can ask nicely and promise he'll go to rehab, but if I refuse to give him any money, he can start cursing and breaking the furniture in the house. I would never have believed that my own son would steal money from me.

The withdrawal state ≈ disintegration anxiety

Withdrawal is a state characterized by certain physical and psychological symptoms, which commence upon the cessation of or reduction in the use of a psychoactive substance that has been taken repeatedly, usually for a prolonged period and at high doses (WHO, 1994). The course of the with-drawal syndrome changes depending on the type of substance being used and the dose that was taken immediately before the cessation or reduction of use (WHO, 1994). Opioid (heroin) withdrawal is accompanied by aching muscles, chills, muscle and abdominal cramps, excessive tear formation and drug-seeking behavior (World Health Organization, 1994). It is experienced as a violent attack from the insides of the body and the psyche, and it is quite similar to the disintegration anxiety aroused in the infant's psyche by hunger and the absence of the good breast (Klein, 1946).

As disintegration anxiety intensifies, the infant responds by crying, screaming and with psychomotor agitation. Like the infant's disintegra-tion anxiety, the addicted individual's anxiety when he or she is in with-drawal corresponds to a feeling of ego fragmentation and a loss of control of the body. One patient described the withdrawal state thus: "*My biggest fear is withdrawal. I could tolerate anything except that. [When you're in withdrawal], you don't know what's wrong with your body...it's like your bones are twisting...it's [such] excruciating pain that you feel you're going to die*". Some patients say that the only way to cope with this anxiety is to prepare drugs in advance:

> I always had drugs ready for the morning. If I'd used drugs the night before, I'd always save some for the morning. I did not want to wake up in withdrawal...it's the worst thing...to wake up in withdrawal in the middle of the night when your body hurts and to have to start looking for drugs...to start thinking where to look for them...when you're in withdrawal, nothing interests you, since you just want it to be over.

The craving for milk – or for drugs – is like an internal attack of the body on itself and on the ego. This craving causes psychic restlessness and motivates the addicted individual to seek drugs, just as the craving for milk during times of hunger motivates the infant to scream. According to Kleinian the-ory, the infant's physical universe constitutes a matrix for the consolidation of his mental experience, and the body of the Kleinian infant is the stormy environment in which this occurs. Meticulous observation of the internal and external management of drug addicts reveals that the physical sensations that appear during drug abuse and withdrawal have enormous influence on the organization of mental experiences. In both cases, there is intensive pre-occupation with primary life actions (incorporation and expulsion), as the matrix of experience is composed of impulses related to the mother's milk (the drug). The drug, like the milk, is perceived as necessary to existence, as a substance without which life cannot exist. Therapists have difficulty understanding that the drug is an object of love, no less than is the primary good object. In the words of one addict, "*I love drugs. When I used drugs, they were like my father, my mother – my everything*". Therefore, addicted individuals no less than infants feel physically and mentally fragmented until their next "feed", which provides the essential feeling of aliveness.

From an objective perspective, analysts might conceive of the drug as sour milk, because of the intense harm it causes. However, we should remember that the addicted individual idealizes the source of her pleasure, without thinking about its negative aspects or impact. Sometimes, the addict's "milk" is indeed "sour" because it is quite rare for heroin to be pure and more common for it to be mixed with various chemicals. When a drug addict uses a "tainted" drug, he or she again experiences an internal attack, for the poisoned and poisonous milk may bring physical malaise, and the addicted individual cannot incorporate any other substances. But, despite the bad experience, the addict is not likely to sustain abstinence. Like the other states experienced in the paranoid-schizoid position, the individual will again encounter the frustration and internal attack (in the form of withdrawal), which will spur the search for milk to stop the ensuing disintegration anxiety.

Thus, the addicted individual experiences withdrawal and craves the positive effects of the drug. He turns to the loved object, the mother, for money, but she refuses; within minutes (or moments), she turns into a hated object, which could stop the suffering but refuses to do so. Still disappointed by the good object that refused to breastfeed him, the individual leaves home, feeling exposed, vulnerable and desperate for the money that will enable him to buy the drugs that will end his hunger and frustration. He sees other addicts who have drugs and hopes that the longed-for satisfaction is near. When other addicts refuse to share the desired milk, the addict immediately perceives them as bad and frustrating objects. Such a situation is reminiscent of the infant's inner world, when he perceives the breast as hoarding its wonderful substance for itself and enjoying its power over the infant (Mitchell & Black, 1995).

According to Klein (1935, 1940), the paranoid-schizoid position exists from birth to three-four months of life. This period is characterized by a specific constellation of anxieties, defences and internal and external object relations. An ego structure reliant on these defences constitutes severe personality pathology (Summers, 1994), and the drug addict's ego structure implies the existence of such pathology. The movement between the paranoid-schizoid and depressive positions occurs both through development and during an individual's life (Joseph, 1978). However, the depressive position requires an integrative perception of the external object and the self, the regulation of aggressive drives and the ability to cope with guilt and responsibility. The drug addict's ego does not have the capacity to deal with such issues, and therefore, any psychic equilibrium between the positions is not possible.

The constant search for the idealized object (the drug) that would enable a magical transformation both stands in contrast to, and prevents any normal psychosocial functioning. Not only does the use of primitive defence mechanisms creates difficulties in external object relations, but it also causes difficulties in coping with life's challenges. Once the abuser starts to prioritize the drug, his interest and involvement in former relationships diminishes. Profound psychosocial regression also occurs in additional areas of life, resulting in job loss, homelessness and an inability to fulfill basic obligations. Additional characteristics of the psychosocial regression of heroin abusers include involvement in criminal activity and exposure to infectious diseases (McKenzie, Macalino, Mclung, Shield, & Rich, 2005; Willner-Reid, Belendiuk, Epstein, Schmittner, & Preston, 2008).

Projective identification and envy

The powerful anxieties experienced in the paranoid-schizoid position drive the ego to develop specific defence mechanisms, and a relatively violent one of which is projective identification (Klein, 1946). Projective identification arises from the infant's wish to be rid of the negative parts of his or her own ego, by vomiting or expelling them into the mother's body. The phantasmatic projection of the negative parts of the self, and of the attendant death instinct, reduces the infant's annihilation anxiety. The aim of this projection is not just to expel these poisonous elements, but also to gain control of the object (Klein, 1946), and turn it into an extension of the self (Klein, 1952).

As previously noted, during withdrawal, a drug abuser may turn to his or her parents for financial aid, and if the parents refuse to provide it, they may become the object of the abuser's aggressive impulses. The abuser may then try to steal various family belongings regardless of the consequences, as an expression of greed, or she may try to control her parents, so as to ensure a continuous flow of money. One patient in recovery described an exchange between him and a parent who refused to give him money:

> I already told you I'd go to rehab. Come on...today's the last time I'll ask you for money...what kind of a parent are you anyway? Can't you see that I'm in withdrawal...I'm suffering but you won't help me...you don't care...you enjoy seeing me suffer...what kind of mother can see her son suffer and not help him? What kind of mother are you? You are a shitty mother!.

Such scenes occur when the user's muscles ache, when he's sweating and his eyes are tearing, when he is suffering from diarrhea, agitation and anxiety. Now, he experiences his mother as a source of evil and a persecutory object. The addict who is in the throes of such an internal attack will expel his oral and anal aggressive impulses along with other aggressive split-off ego parts, projecting his own guilt, shame and humiliation onto his mother in an attempt to control her. If she identifies with these negative emotions and gives the user the money he desires, then the user has succeeded in gaining control over the object. Bell (2001) notes that in every interaction that involves projective identification a new object relation is perpetuated.

Projective identification also involves the projection of good parts of the self onto the object. In fact, it is essential to ego integration and healthy object relations (Klein, 1946). Unfortunately, during drug abuse, the projection onto the object of good parts of the self and other identifications with the good object are quite rare. The drug abuser considers experiences to be "good" only if they satisfy his selfish needs, and rarely does he identify with the good object. If his mother agrees to provide money, his gratitude is usually momentary and shallow, as he lacks the ability to identify with her sorrow or introject it. As a rule, the drug addict's introjection of good objects is temporary and without mental processing, and it occurs when the parents are ready to meet the addict's pressing needs (e.g., to pay bail when he has been arrested). In such situations, the good object saves the user from internal attack (withdrawal) and from imprisonment by the bad, persecutory object (the police), until the next time.

But satiation is only temporary. The heroin abuser can experience euphoria for a few moments only, and just like the infant, he needs feeding every four hours. Alongside this similarity, there are significant differences between the drug abuser's life and the infant's mental world. Unlike milk, drugs do not contribute to the developmental process. In fact, no physical or mental maturation or growth can take place while an individual abuses drugs. The infant enjoys the mother's touch and the proximity to her body, and as his pleasant experiences accrue, the infant learns that when he cries or fusses, his mother will appear. The drug abuser's moments of joy are brief and end when he has finished preparing the drug for abuse, using it and experiencing its effect. He knows that no matter how much he cries or shouts, the good object will not reappear to meet his needs. If he wants another pleasant experience, he must find the strength to fight his daily existential war for more milk.

Envy is another characteristic of the paranoid-schizoid position. Envy is the desire not only to possess the contents of the good object but also to spoil it or take it away from others (Klein, 1957). Envy is an expression of pure aggression, which aims to leave both the object and the infant without the "goods". It is actually an attempt to "scorch the earth" so that no one (else) will be able to enjoy the desirable contents of the good object. Envy is a significant feature of the object relations of drug addicts; it tends to manifest itself when a particular object appears to have special qualities. The following vignette is taken from a session with a patient who sought psychoanalytic psychotherapy while attending a day-care center for the treatment of drug abuse, which provided drug abuse counseling and weekly urinalysis to detect drug use. The patient sought therapy from me after one year of treatment at the day-care center, and although he was no longer using drugs, he felt stuck in his life.

PATIENT: I wanted to tell you about something that happened this week. When I was on my way to the day-care center, I saw some patients who were still using drugs even though they're in treatment. I knew some of them, since I used to use drugs with them in the past. But now, I'm embarrassed to pass by them. They shout, curse and ask people for money. They told me I looked good and that I'd gained weight since the last time they saw me. I told them that I was working now and that I have a girlfriend. They offered me a line of cocaine.

THERAPIST: Do you mean they offered you drugs for free?

PATIENT: Yes. That's how it goes when you're "clean". If they think you're clean, other abusers might offer you a pill or a line of cocaine. When you're in withdrawal, no one gives you a thing.

THERAPIST: How do you explain that?

PATIENT: This happens a lot among addicts, and I've seen it many times. When patients at the day-care center see someone who looks good, who's dressed neatly and who's working, they know that he's recovered and they're jealous. Inside, they also want to stop abusing drugs like him, but they can't do it, so they want to ruin his life. They want to see him abuse drugs and lose everything he has. I've seen it many times…they're jealous of his achievements and offer him drugs for free since they hope to ruin his recovery attempts. It is easier to bring someone down than to go to rehab.

THERAPIST: It sounds to me like you have to tolerate a lot of pressure in such situations.

PATIENT: Yes. And don't think that it's easy. If you refuse their offer, they suddenly change their tone and say: "What's the matter with you? You think you're better than us? You forgot where you came from? You became arrogant? If that doesn't work, they may curse you or tell you that you're a nobody".

This interaction lucidly demonstrates the reality of the paranoid-schizoid position experienced by the abuser, whose behavior abounds with the mechanisms that characterize this position. Although in this vignette, the patient used the word "jealous" to describe the other drug abusers' behavior, it is really envy that constitutes their will to spoil the patient's achievements. If the patient had indeed accepted their offer, his urine tests would show that he had used drugs; the staff of the day-care center might reproach him, he might feel disappointment and failure, abuse drugs again and start missing days at work. The other users know this and hence aim to "level the playing field" by causing the recovered patient's reality to conform to their own, thereby obviating their guilt and sense of responsibility for their condition. When the patient refused their offer, they attacked him, devaluing him and attempting to project their negative parts onto him in an effort to instill in him unpleasant feelings and cause him to return to the vicious cycle of drug addiction.

Concluding remarks

In this chapter, I have tried to demonstrate how Klein's developmental theory provides a fascinating phenomenological explanation of the experience
of drug addiction, a dreadful phenomenon that annihilates the willpower
of the drug abuser, enslaving him to destructive desires and estranging him
from society. His craving for drugs and his experience of internal violence
and readiness to harm external objects are often not understood by therapists or by his family, both of whom believe that going into rehabilitation is
"just a matter of willpower", of making a decision. They fail to understand
that the cycle of addiction is quite lacking in elation and euphoria but rather
is brimming over with suffering and pain for the drug abuser, who feels that
he is fighting an endless war to survive.

Heroin addicts almost always enter treatment under a certain pressure.
It may be the pressure to manage mental or physical problems or external
pressure exerted by the family or the criminal justice system (Gerstein &
Lewin, 1990). Consequently, they display a great deal of ambivalence or
reluctance about entering or remaining in treatment, and since both detoxification and psychotherapy are demanding, the rates of retention in
treatment are not high (Gerstein & Lewin, 1990). During the initial stage
of treatment, heroin addicts have to cope with physical withdrawal, psychological craving and feelings of emptiness and frustration. Coping with
or processing these negative emotions is not possible unless the addict acknowledges that the source of his gratification is also the source of his
destruction. The craving for a euphoric rush, the envy and greed and the
inability to accept responsibility and commit to a therapeutic process that
demands introspection, all indicate that the addicted individual is coping
with issues that are characteristic of the paranoid-schizoid position. Psychotherapeutic treatment is definitely possible with addicted patients in
this position, but it requires recognition of the destructive power of drugs
and the magnitude of their impact as well as a readiness to proceed with
treatment despite the difficulties. In other words, psychotherapeutic treatment can take place only when there has been some movement toward the
depressive position.

In the next chapter, I will focus on the similarities between the depressive
position and the mental processes which patients undergo during recovery
from heroin addiction by using clinical data from psychodynamic treatment
of such patients to illustrate such a progression and demonstrate the clinical relevance of the Kleinian technique. Acquiring new knowledge about
and new perspectives on addiction is essential to psychotherapists who may
encounter drug abusers and their families, especially in light of reports of a
growing "heroin epidemic" across the United States (Corcoran, & Cohen,
2014; Wolfson, 2014).

References

American Psychiatric Association. (2013). *Diagnostic and statistical manual of mental disorders* (5th ed.). American Psychiatric Publishing.

Bell, D. (2001). *Projective* identification. In C. Bronstein (Ed.), *Kleinian theory: A Contemporary perspective* (pp. 125–147). Whurr Publishers.

Brüsch, P. (2011). *Water – Its significance in science, in nature and culture, in world religions and in the universe.* Swiss Federal Institute of Technology.

Corcoran, T., & Cohen, S. (2014). Heroin epidemic plagues N.Y. suburbs. *USA Today.* Retrieved from http://www.usatoday.com/story/news/nation/2014/01/31/heroin-epidemic-plagues-ny-suburbs/5096813/.

Gerstein, D. R., & Lewin, L. S. (1990). Treating drug problems. *New England Journal of Medicine, 323*(12), 844–848.

Graham, A., & Glickauf-Hughes, C. (1992). Object relations and addiction: The role of "transmuting externalizations". *Journal of Contemporary Psychotherapy, 22*(1), 21–33.

Hinshelwood, R. D. (1991). *A dictionary of Kleinian thought.* Free Association Books.

Joseph, B. (1987). Projective Identification: Clinical aspects. In J. Sandler (Ed.), *Projection, identification, projective identification* (pp. 65–76). International Universities Press.

Klein, M. (1935). A contribution to the psychogenesis of manic-depressive states. In *Love, guilt & reparation, 1921–1945* (pp. 262–289). Free Press, 1975.

Klein, M. (1936). Weaning. In *Love, guilt & reparation, 1921–1945* (pp. 290–305). Free Press, 1975.

Klein, M. (1940). Mourning and its relation to manic-depressive states. *International Journal of Psychoanalysis, 21,* 125–153.

Klein, M. (1946). Notes on some schizoid mechanisms. *International Journal of Psychoanalysis, 27,* 99–110.

Klein, M. (1952). Some theoretical conclusions regarding the emotional life of the infant. In *Envy and gratitude and other works 1946–1963* (pp. 61–93). Vintage, 1997.

Klein, M. (1957). Envy and gratitude. In *Envy and gratitude and other works 1946–1963* (pp. 176–235). Vintage, 1997.

Koob, G. F., & Simon, J. E. (2009). The neurobiology of addiction: Where we have been and where we are going. *Journal of Drug Issues, 39*(1), 115–132.

Krystal, H., & Raskin, H. (1970). *Drug dependence: Aspects of ego functions.* Wayne State University Press.

Leeds, J., & Morgenstern, J. (1996). Psychoanalytic theories of substance abuse. In F. Rotgers, D. S. Keller & J. Morgenstern (Eds.), *Treating substance abuse: Theory and technique* (pp. 68–83). Guilford.

McKenzie, M., Macalino, G., McLung, C., Shield, D. C., & Rich, J. D. (2005). Opiate replacement therapy at time of release from incarceration: Project MOD, a pilot program. *Journal of Opioid Management, 1*(3), 147–151.

Mitchell, S. M., & Black, M. (1995). Melanie Klein and contemporary Kleinian theory. In *Freud and beyond: A history of modern psychoanalytic thought* (pp. 85–111). Basic Books.

Potik, D., Adelson, M., & Schreiber, S. (2007). Drug addiction from a psychodynamic perspective: Methadone maintenance treatment (MMT) as transitional phenomena. *Psychology and Psychotherapy: Theory, Research and Practice, 80*(2), 311–325.

Seecof, R., & Tennant, F. S. Jr. (1986). Subjective perceptions to the intravenous "rush" of heroin and cocaine in opioid addicts. *American Journal of Drug and Alcohol Abuse, 12*(1–2), 79–87.

Summers, F. (1994). The work of Melanie Klein. In *Object relations theories and psychopathology—a comprehensive text* (pp. 73–136). The Analytic Press.

Waska, R. (2006). Addictions and the quest to control the object. *Journal of the American Psychoanalytic Association, 66*(1), 43–62.

Willner-Reid, J., Belendiuk, K. A., Epstein, D. H., Schmittner, J., & Preston, K. L. (2008). Hepatitis C and human immunodeficiency virus risk behaviors in polydrug users on methadone maintenance. *Journal of Substance Abuse Treatment, 35*(1), 78–86.

Winnicott, D. W. (1971). *Playing and reality.* Tavistock Publications.

Wolfson, E. (2014). Prescription drugs have pushed heroin into the suburbs. *Newsweek.* Retrieved from http://www.newsweek.com/prescription-drugs-have-pushed-heroin-suburbs-252625.

World Health Organization. (1994). *Lexicon of alcohol and drug terms.* World Health Organization.

Wurmser, L. (1974). Psychoanalytic considerations of the etiology of compulsive drug use. *Journal of the American Psychoanalytic Association, 22*(4), 820–843.

Chapter 4

Recovery and reparation ≈ the depressive position

"From them springs the desire to restore which expresses itself in numerous phantasies of saving her and making all kinds of reparation".

(Klein, 1936, p. 294)

Detoxification is a set of interventions aimed at managing acute intoxication and withdrawal (Center for Substance Abuse Treatment, 1995). In this prolonged process, there is a release from physical and psychological dependence via total cessation of the substance or in a gradual process of reducing drug doses until the body does not react with withdrawal symptoms. In Kleinian thinking, the physical and mental symptoms which appear during detoxification (detox) are attacks on the body. During such periods, patients cope not only with these attacks but also with a craving for a drug, which is conceived as a magical rescue source which could stop the painful attacks. Sometimes, the phantasy about the desired milk (the drug) is so intense that they may leave drug rehabilitation centers and return to abuse drugs.

Sometimes, family members lock an addicted family member in an isolated house for a month without any access to drugs. They hope that this action would end the pursuit after drugs, but their attempts are doomed to failure. Cases, in which family members try to force the addicted family member to enter rehabilitation also tend to end the same. The family's attempts stem from powerlessness and difficulty to see how their *good and talented son or daughter* turned *bad* and ruin everything around them. Families of drug addicts have much hope when the addicted family member agrees to turn for help, and it is indeed a significant step in the movement toward the depressive position.

However, only if the addicted person will experience a loss or develop a minimal awareness toward the bad sides of the good object (the drug), an internal process of change will begin. The following sayings imply on such processes: "*I injected drugs with someone in the evening, but in the morning, I woke up alone*", "*I am not as young as I used to be, how much will I have to suffer to obtain drugs?*" "*A week ago, I left everything and found myself driving an hour to find drugs, I did not find a thing... I thought to myself how I had deteriorated...I got out of the car and I simply started crying*".

These examples indicate an acknowledgment in the destructive power of drugs and the magnitude of their impact. Therapists who hear such sayings should feel encouraged since the patient neither creates splitting of the drug in his internal world, nor describes the drug solely as an ideal and satisfying object. The staying in rehabilitation centers provides both physical distancing and a feeling of primary separateness from the drug. This feeling intensifies with every day of drug abstinence, and patients become more and more aware that they did not control their addiction and that the addiction controlled their life.

Additional painful discovery is that they have been enslaved to the drugs ("*I was a slave to the drug. All my actions were done under its influence. Like a king that commends you to go and use drugs again and again…you do everything to obtain it*"). Gradually, during the treatment, the drug, which was conceived as a good and satisfying object, is revealed as an object with annihilating functions. In this position, the infant is more aware that he does not control the good object but needs it and yearns for it during its absence (Temperley, 2001). Both the infant and the person who try to remain drug abstinent cope with new anxieties and with sensational discoveries concerning the essence of the objects in their life. With the maturation of the perception mechanism, the ability of the infant to modify phantasys by comparing them with reality reduces the anxiety, and the internalization of good experiences reassures him concerning his internal state (Temperley, 2001).

The internal world contains less dangerous internal objects, and therefore, there is a reduction in the need either to attack external objects or to fear the reaction of persecutory objects. The cyclical pursuit after the milk stops and the maturation allows conceiving the reality in other colors besides black and white. As the body contains less poisonous substances, distorted perceptions decrease, and there is not any need to live in a dichotomous and persecutory world in which one embodies both the persecutor and the persecuted. The encounter with the post schizoid-paranoid position helps both the drug abstinent patient and the Kleinian infant in dissipating the anxiety, and consequently, the need to use projection, projective identification and envy diminishes (Klein, 1958).

Losses and grief

One of the central developmental achievements of the depressive position is the mutual integration of both objects and the self. The analytic setting strives toward such integration when the therapist encourages the patient to examine the consequences of his addiction. During this process, the patient discovers that the beloved drug, which provided him with pleasure, comfort and sanctuary, had also severe impact not only on his psyche and his physical health but also on the lives of his close ones. This process is like the maturation that occurs in the depressive position and leads the infant to the discovery that the bad mother, who is the target for the projection of negative feelings, is also the beloved mother (Klein, 1935, 1940).

The mental reality of the depressive position is bounded with painful discoveries. Patients discover that their world is meager with external objects since they no longer socialize with other addicts and because they do not have any contact with people who do not use drugs. When patients look at people who do not use drugs, they may feel jealousy, which stems from profound self-examination. In contrast to envy, this is not a desire to rob the goods that others possess, but an intense desire to enjoy life as other people who do not use drugs. An example of such jealousy appears when patients discover that their former partner is in a relationship with a person who does not use drugs, as a patient said about his previous partner:

> I would like to be with her again, now that I do not abuse drugs...but I'm happy that she is satisfied with her man. he works in a steady job, not like me...of course I would like to be in his place...its healthy jealousy.

The jealousy of the infant to the breast is jealousy without the desire to hurt and annihilate. It is jealousy of other objects that have healthy object relations with the breast and enjoy its qualities. In both cases, there is oedipal jealousy in the virtues of the opponent or the third object (Klein, 1957), and fear concerning the loss of an object relation with the loved object. This example also illustrates that the resolution of the Oedipus complex is inextricably intertwined with the working through of the depressive position and vice versa (Britton, 1998). Klein (1936, 1940) notes that the depressive position begins in a real loss, which is the loss of the breast during weaning. It is an external loss but also an internal loss of omnipotence and of object relation of pleasant union with the ideal breast or the ideal mother. Among patients in recovery, the acknowledgment that their omnipotence has originated in an external object, which provided an illusion, appears slowly.

The depressive position holds many discoveries when every discovery concerning the new world is bounded with mental pain. Analytic treatment strives toward integration of the self by shedding light on annihilating parts of the patient's self that were dominant during the paranoid-schizoid position (addiction). These discoveries are painful since patients understand that during that period, verbal and physical attacks such as evacuation of the house from its good contents (stealing) had hurt the mother and caused her much pain. Similarly the infant feels that his aggression had hurt the loved mother (Klein, 1940). The recognition in the impact of aggression raises depressive anxiety concerning the faith of internal and external objects, in light of the phantasized destruction that was created by the infant's aggression (Temperley, 2001). In this position, the infant imagines his world as viciously and poorly populated and his insides as emptied.

During the recovery process, such experiences correspond with the reality, since the destruction is indeed real, and both the internal and external worlds lack any objects. As one patient described:

"Now that I returned from rehab, I don't have anyone to talk to. I'm not hanging out with drug addicts anymore and I don't know any people who are not addicted either. What can I do? I'm at home all day...I did not study...I don't have any profession".

Therapists who work within Klein's framework of understanding can understand that such losses indicate movement toward the depressive position. During abstinence, the analytic work leads the patient to encounter his deepest anxieties and fears (*"I'm afraid to live without any drugs, they are with me for so many years, like a part of me"*), to moving discoveries (*"now I understand that I never really lived or felt something authentic"*) and also to hurting acknowledgments (*"I did not see how my addiction had affected my family, I wasn't there when my children grew up"*).

Additional indication for significant progress toward the depressive position is the emergence of guilt. In the following example, a patient who used drugs for many years was treated successfully in a rehabilitation center and went back to live with his family. However, he encountered new situations, as he described in one of the sessions:

"A few days ago, I saw my teenaged daughter dressed provocatively for a date. I was shocked since, in the old days, girls did not dress this way. Therefore, I made her a remark. She answered me: what makes you think you can comment on my behavior? Where were you all these years? You weren't home. You just came for money and left. Do you really think that now you can suddenly arrive and say something and the whole family will obey you? At the beginning, I was angry, who the hell is she to talk to me this way? I wanted to slap her because she annoyed me. But I do not want to hurt her again...I try to talk to her again after a long time that I wasn't home. I thought about what she said, and she is right. Indeed, what kind of parent am I?! Where was I all those years? Their mother had raised them alone without my help".

In this example, the daughter's behavior raises much frustration when she refuses the patient's request, and the desire to hurt her intensifies. But on the other hand, arises fear that the destructive attack will hurt her and harm the relations with her. The horror, which stems from the possible loss of the good object and the phantasized damage of the destruction of the frustrating object, elicits depressive anxiety, and patients struggle to contain this complex reality. The same drama occurs in the infant's world, as loved objects cause pain and frustration, but an attack on these objects may annihilate them. Sometimes, the intensity of the emotional pain is so high that the death instinct drives toward destruction and comforting regression to the paranoid-schizoid position. An example for such situation appears in the words of another patient who reacted differently to a conflict with his teenaged daughter:

"I slapped her (his daughter) because of her words! Who the hell she thinks she is to talk to me like that?! I'm an adult and she's just a girl. So, my wife threw me out of the house, so what?! No one will talk to me like that".

One of the characteristics of the mental reality of the depressive position is the frequent encounter with negative feelings. The lessening of paranoia indeed alleviates the existence, but the loss of omnipotence may lead to drug abuse. Movement toward the paranoid-schizoid position may also appear when there is not any minimal ability to contain any ambivalence toward the drug.

On the other hand, when patients acknowledge their responsibility to their aggression and experience guilt regarding their destructiveness, there is progress in the mourning process. Typical sayings during therapy that imply a mourning process are: "*I look on people who grew up with me and they have family and kids. Some work, some have their own house. Where am I and where are they?*", or "*when I used drugs, I did not see a thing. Now I understand that time did not stop, and the world did not wait for me. The world carried on and I stayed behind*".

During the recovery process, patients mourn on many losses, including loss of family relations, physical health, mental health, promising career and other opportunities. When the family is ready to accept the patient, he can find comfort, safety and love in the good object. However, if the patient has no family, the grief may be more acute due to the bitter loneliness and the absence of good objects. Such situations of loneliness and absence of good internalized objects have many similarities to the infant's feeling of loss of good objects after the imagined destruction of the good mother.

Processing grief is complicated since in the latent level, the sorrow rivers storm, and the patient stands before a tangled forest of feelings and internal object relations, as he wonders where to turn. In this process, when the patient repeatedly faces the consequences of his aggression, there is growing recognition in the devastating power of drug addiction ("*this drug which made me feel so good, also ruined so many things in my life*") and acknowledgement that the source of gratification is also the source of destruction.

The temporary anchorage in the depressive position has many complexities for patients since they encounter difficult situations which raise guilt, frustration and sorrow without sufficient containment capacity. In this position, there are unconscious phantasies concerning the destruction of the good mother because of the infant's greed and internal aggression. Among patients, the unconscious phantasies concerning the destruction of the good object do correspond with painful external reality ("*my addiction ruined the family*", "*my wife left me because of the drugs, I made her suffer*", "*my mother was always healthy, she got cancer because of my drug abuse*"). One patient described the re-encounter with the consequences of his greedy desire in the following way:

Now that I am home, I think of the times that I stole from the house, we have a new television now. I sold the old one to get money for drugs.

I stole money from my parents. I'm embarrassed to talk about it. My mother told me to stop so many times. My father was ready to take me to any rehab center, but I wanted more and more drugs. I've gotten in troubles, I stole, I got arrested but nothing had stopped me.

Clinical vignette

In the next lines, I will present a clinical vignette which deals with the delicate balance that characterizes the depressive position. This vignette is taken from treatment of a 32-year-old patient who abused heroin and cocaine for two years. The patient was successfully treated in a detoxification center for a month and continued treatment in a day-care center in his hometown. The treatment there included counseling, group therapy and urine drug testing. After his return from detox, his parents looked for additional treatment with his consent, and we started to meet once a week. This is a part of a session that focused on dreams and anxieties. This session helped me to grasp the mental reality of such patients because it mostly dealt with the internal world of an individual who experiences a renewed encounter with the consequences of his destructive impulses, and on the other hand, tries to repair.

THERAPIST: "I want to commend you on your efforts in the last months. You look much better than three months ago, when we first met. Do you feel the difference?"

PATIENT: "Sure, I gained weight. I already wear a different size".

THERAPIST: "Do people around you say something about the change?"

PATIENT: "My mother says that I'm more at home. She says that in the past, I came home only to ask for money and left quickly. Now I see her more often".

THERAPIST: "What exactly does she tell you?"

PATIENT: "She says that she can actually talk to me now. She asks for small home repairs at home and I help her".

THERAPIST: "The sayings of the family indicate that the change is visible, and that people around you are thankful. Do you feel that there is a change?"

PATIENT: "Yes, it's not only the family. The police do not stop me anymore when I go out. You know, I'm glad that I have a family. I see other patients in the day-care center that served long times in jail and they do not have any family. Other patients got infectious diseases when they injected drugs. Thanks god that I did not catch any disease. I talked to an HIV patient and he told me he regrets all the times he injected drugs, but that's it. He has a disease. He is also an immigrant and lives alone. Poor guy, I don't know how one can live this way. When I abused drugs, I always knew that I could approach my family".

THERAPIST: "I hear that you are busy in internal and external introspection and you also think about the past. On what you lost and what you have now".

PATIENT: "I think a lot…especially at nights".

THERAPIST: "Do you have any dreams?"

PATIENT: "Yes. I have strange dreams. They confuse me. When I abused drugs, I did not have any dreams. Since I returned from rehab, I have strange dreams".

THERAPIST: "Can you describe a recent dream?"

PATIENT: "I do not remember everything. I dreamt once that I try to inject drugs and the needle does not enter the vein, and one time I searched relentlessly for drugs. I looked everywhere but I did not find anything. Then, I woke up. But in most of the dreams, I try to inject but fail. Once I do succeed, I don't get high".

THERAPIST: "How did you wake up?"

PATIENT: "With fear. I was glad it was just a dream. But it was creepy. I feared that I relapsed again and now I'll have to search again for money and drugs, get to fights, get arrested by the police. Everything all over again. At last my mother is happy that I got off drugs and started therapy, and now a relapse again".

THERAPIST: "I feel that you fear damaging or destroying your achievements in the last months".

PATIENT: "Yes, I'm afraid of it".

A silence of a few seconds.

THERAPIST: "At the beginning of the session, you said that you get well without drugs, but perhaps you want to abuse drugs".

PATIENT: "Why do you think so?"

THERAPIST: "I think that your dream implies that you have a craving for drugs but you're very afraid of this craving and its consequences, especially in light of your achievements. You are afraid that if you will abuse drugs, you will not only ruin your achievements, but you will also hurt the people you love. And you're afraid you will not be able to handle it".

A silence of a few seconds

PATIENT: "You know. I don't talk to anyone about it. My family thinks that this thing with drugs is over and that I can carry on with my life as nothing happened. But I won't lie to you, there is craving, it's hard, despite the support, especially when I'm not busy, a thought about drugs or a robbery may come. There are days when I work from morning till night. I never worked like this. A few years ago, I had much money without working. Now, I hang around in my hood, and guys who are still involved in robberies ask me to join them. Sometimes, I think to myself that maybe I will participate in one last hit (robbery) and then I would be able to live better financially for the next years".

THERAPIST: "I think that your dream reflects a struggle between a will to stay abstinent and between a will to abuse drugs and achieve a state in which you do not have to worry any longer. But as you can see when you look on other patients in the day-care center, such place doesn't exist. It's just an illusion. Abusing drugs again has many risks. You may neglect yourself, and you may get infected with contagious diseases or end up in jail for years if you follow temptations. Your actions affect both you and your family".

PATIENT: "I'm also afraid that something bad will happen to my mother. I see that she takes medications for hypertension and heart disease. It's because the troubles I caused her. If I will start abusing again, I don't know if she would survive".

This session started with my acknowledgment in the patient's attempts to detach from persecutory and disastrous lifestyle. I examined whether the change is felt by others, since I wanted to see if the patient can understand how he is perceived by the objects around him. The aim of my mirroring attempts was to strengthen the anchoring in the depressive position by indicating the good things achieved when the patient remains drug abstinent. The patient showed a high awareness level and understanding that his life in the past (paranoid-schizoid position) was characterized with consecutive dangers. He described clearly the drama of the first position in which he hurt other people while searching for gratification, and simultaneously, being threatened by internal and external reality.

The dream reflects the internal struggle between creation and destruction as well as the anxiety that the bad can annihilate the good. This is the mental reality of abstinent patients who cope with external and internal conflicts between life and death instincts, as the death instinct strives toward annihilation and the life instinct tries to prevent it. The death instinct appears as old-new craving, which pushes toward an unperturbed oceanic merger. This craving comes from the depth of the unconscious and accompanied by splitting of the frightening aspects of the objects. It aims to present the paranoid-schizoid position as paradise lost. The search for drugs is a search for an omnipotent reality that does not require any coping with the challenges of the depressive position. In the dream, when the patient finds drugs or injects them, the death instinct overcomes the life instinct and the patient wakes up with flooding depressive anxiety concerning the faith of the good object.

Patients report that they wake up from such dreams with anxiety whether they abused drugs and what will be with their urine tests ("*I woke up thinking about my urine tests. I thought I ruined it, I was already clean for months*"). Patients fear that they have hurt additional good objects, meaning their family members ("*since I returned from detox, I try to be sincere with everyone. I tell my wife everything. When I woke up, I thought, how I will tell her that I relapsed. What will be now?*"). There is similarity between such sayings and the infant's feeling that he lost everything because of uncontrollable and greedy impulses concerning the mother's breast. This depressive anxiety toward the faith of the loved objects motivates both the infant and the patient to reparation attempts of damaged objects that had been hurt by their aggressive impulses. The depressive pain, which contains guilt and yearning for internal and external reconstruction, drafts reparation wishes and phantasy for rehabilitation of the good object (Klein, 1940).

In psychodynamic treatment of drug abusers, such dreams are prevalent in the first months after detoxification and drug abstinence, and it is of high importance to directly address dreams that deal with craving and annihilation. The Kleinian technique, which focuses on analysis of anxieties and defences, may prove very useful in therapy of individuals whose mental life is characterized by raw aggression, persecution, guilt and fear of hurting good objects. Direct interpretations help the patient to see the true nature of the paranoid-schizoid position and acknowledge the inner conflict. According to Dorban (2002), the immediate interpretation of anxiety, when it is in its climax, stems from the presumption that the patient experiences significant difficulties in coping with his anxieties and extricates him from annihilating circles. The direct interpretation invites the patient to a mutual observation of the struggling forces in his intrapersonal ring and enables him to meet internal personality part, which asks to spoil and sabotage the recovery process.

According to Ogden (2004, p. 860), the nightmare "is a dream in which the individual's emotional pain is subjected (to a significant degree) to unconscious psychological work that issues in psychological growth". The mental growth can occur through a direct interpretation of the anxieties that stand at the basis of the dream, and prevention of a chain reaction, which can occur if the death instinct will reach its aim. Hence, the immediate interpretation is necessary also for relapse prevention. If the therapist chooses not to provide with a direct interpretation, the disturbing dreams may continue for many nights, and the patient will not understand why such contents appear, especially when he started a healthier lifestyle. The appearance of such dreams may even lead the patient to abuse drugs as a mean of dissipating anxiety.

The annihilation anxiety is also embodied in the figure of the HIV patient, which is conceived as a doomed person. In this symbolization process, the anxiety is projected through projective identification and part of the patient's ego becomes identified with the object (Segal, 2001). Consequently, the symbol is identified with the symbolized, and the HIV patient is identified with the annihilation anxiety. Symbolization is an achievement of the depressive position, and the annihilation anxiety indeed receives visual representation. However, it is important to verbalize it and not to leave it as a nameless dread, since at heart, patients fear that returning to active drug addiction will end in total annihilation (*"I know that if I will relapse again, it will be the end, and nothing will stop me now"*).

Some patients need that the therapist will know and tell them what they are afraid of. They know that they are afraid, but the thing is that the therapist must know and say it loud. Direct interpretation of craving dreams sheds light on the patient's internal world, reflects the struggling forces and relates directly to the anxieties that characterize the different positions.

Ogden (2004) notes that patients turn for analysis following an unbeknownst emotional pain, which embodies in the inability to dream (inability to do unconscious psychological work) or in disrupted dreams. He adds that the psychoanalytic situation is designed to generate conditions in which the patient (with the therapist's participation) may become able to dream his undreamt and interrupted dreams (Ogden, 2004).

One of the substantial differences between psychodynamic treatment of drug abuse and between drug counseling is dream analysis and the readiness to explore unconscious material that appears in dreams. Dream analysis and interpretation of anxieties and defences constitute a Bionian investigation toward a dark territory, and the patient learns that the therapist is neither afraid to pace in an unknown land and address threatening material, nor is he afraid of the patient's aggression. Such processes help the patients to establish new relations with external objects and feel safety.

Guilt and responsibility in psychotherapy of drug abusers

The attempts to establish new object relations with external objects are associated with aggression toward them. During recovery, patients face either temptations or emotional crises concerning abusing drugs, which are accompanied by different levels of anxiety. Some patients may abuse drugs impulsively without much thought of future consequences, whereas others may have intense conflicts that involve guilt. Patients report that in times of craving before drug abuse, they think about their closest people and imagine what would happen if their drug abuse will be revealed. They understand that they will disappoint their loved ones and will lose a significant amount of trust. Sometimes, the phantasy about the consequences of the patient's aggression and the possible harm to the external object may help to cope with the craving and avoid drug abuse.

Bion had remarked that there is no sense of an absent good object, and the infant is either in the presence of a good object or in the presence of a bad object in the mother's emotional or physical absence (Bion in Temperley, 2001). In times of distress, the understanding of the patient that he does not possess the good object, meaning human objects, sharpens and powerlessness intensifies. In such times, the patient is frustrated since people cannot immediately come and comfort him or to be with him until the tempest passes. He may feel impotence and anger toward the objects and desire to harm them, but there is also fear of losing them. In such times, the yearning for a mind-altering object that can be quickly incorporated into the body and expel negative feelings grows. The patient misses it but concomitantly is aware of its destructive potential, and the mourning focuses on the good experiences that the drug has provided.

Mourning processes help patients acknowledging that drugs are partial objects whereas people and interpersonal relations are more complex.

Readiness to separate from the drug and depend on human objects who may sometimes fail and may not always be available signifies that the patient struggles with the contents of the depressive position. In this position, the patient encounters his desires and faces his aggression when the therapeutic setting is a suitable place for mitigating the transitions between the positions. During the sessions and between them, the patient has time to think and imagine what would happen to his beloved objects or himself if he would abuse drugs and will conceal it.

Before relapses, some patients contemplate whether their action will harm the therapeutic process. Patients may talk elaborately and openly about drug cravings or anxieties of returning to intensive drug abuse, but they may not be so candid and report drug abuse during therapy. In rehabilitative drug programs, when patients are required to provide with urine tests, sometimes the drug abuse is revealed, and patients are summoned to their therapists for clarification. In private practice, the therapist does not always know about the patient's drug abuse, and he depends on the patient's reliability. Patients who had admitted drug abuse during times of drug abstinence reported that they had decided to come forward after thinking about the dissonance of paying for therapy and lying about drug abuse. Others say that they feel bad about lying to the therapist and their family.

Usually, when such patients admit drug abuse after abstinence periods, they relate to themselves harshly with severe self-devaluation (*"I'm a failure"*, *"I'm worthless"*). Guilt is an anguished state of mind that arises out of internal conflict, particularly over self-worth (Hinshelwood, 1991). It is normal to feel guilt when one abuses drugs after abstinence periods, but sometimes the guilt can overwhelm, and Bronstein (2001) notes that being haunted by intense guilt may lead to a compulsive need for destruction. Blaming the patient may not help since it may lead to internalization of harsh superego and returning to active drug abuse.

Patients report that they fear admitting drug abuse in real time because of the fear that the therapist will end the therapy. In phantasy, they damaged therapy and the therapist himself, and there is fear from the therapist's aggression or retaliation (*"I decided to talk to you about the drug abuse knowing that it may well be the final session", "I wanted to talk with you about my relapse but I feared from your response"*). There are therapists and other professionals working with this population who report feeling offended, hurt and even betrayed in such situations. They wonder how a patient with whom they had close relations had hurt or damaged the therapeutic alliance. They do not understand how a patient who receives constant help, suddenly abuses drugs and conceals it.

First, the work with this population is indeed frustrating and may cause despair. Second, if therapist would contemplate about their attempts to struggle with unhealthy habits, such as cigarette smoking and emotional eating, they might acknowledge the difficulties in coping with addiction. Third, in therapy of patients who cope with addictions in private practice, the therapeutic alliance is recreated in every session, when the patient chooses to arrive and pay for therapy. In this action, despite the relapses, he chooses to cope with the challenges of the depressive position. Fourth, the therapist and the therapy, like other objects in this position, are objects toward whom the patient will feel anger, frustration and disappointment. Fifth, therapists should act professionally and learn in supervision how to distinguish between personal and professional issues. Finally, the scientific world defines drug addiction as a chronic, relapsing disorder characterized by compulsive drug seeking, continued use despite harmful consequences and long-lasting changes in the brain. Therefore, therapists should be aware that they are dealing with a phenomenon which is considered both a complex brain disorder and a mental illness (National Institute on Drug Abuse, 2020).

During therapy, the therapist will experience the patient's aggression, but will also feel his guilt and his fear to lose probably the only object who believes in his ability to rebuild his life. The therapist's reactions have influence on the patient's internalizations of his image and on the therapeutic relations. Therapists should be very direct and interpret the patient's destructiveness following relapses as well as his guilt and fear from the therapist's reaction. It is important to distinguish between persecutory guilt and depressive anxiety, since painful remorse is a good prognostic sign and an important stepping stone in the renewed commitment for drug abstinence, accepting responsibility and reparation. Gaining responsibility is possible through installation of a "valued and sustaining figure who gives him (the child) an inner strength. In Klein's words the child who was originally inside the mother now feels he has the mother within him" (Temperley, 2001, p. 49). These words describe well also the recovering patient, and the external figure can be a life partner, a family member, a friend or the therapist.

Internal reparations and external reparations

In the clinical material presented above, a major theme that is associated with the depressive position concerns the patient's reparations. The small home repairs are actually a way of repairing the object that was harmed in consequence of the patient's attacks, and there is concern for the mother, the good object that has survived the attacks. The reparation capacities constitute one of the strongest manifestations of the life instinct (Temperley, 2001), and any help to the mother and arrival to therapy consist a reparation attempt that stems from the life instinct. In this context, recovering drug abusers report that recovery, the term that denotes the rehabilitative process of drug addicts, means not only drug abstinence, but also recognition of problems, internal process, getting help and acceptance (Laudet, 2007).

These meanings reflect the equivalence between the depressive position and the recovery process because patients deal with internal reflection, an acknowledgment in the importance of external objects and readiness to participate in a therapeutic or rehabilitative process. Recovery is a process through which an individual tries to rehabilitate himself, and overcome the consequences of his destructiveness, when there is an anxiety which stems from the knowledge (K) that the power to either build or destroy lies in his hands. The following saying of a patient is an example for the anxiety that is associated with this responsibility: *"I know that if I will pass next to the old central bus station (a place which is associated with drug abuse), I might relapse. Therefore, I do not approach this area"*. Another recovering patient said: *"I have an annoying boss who tends to be very rude. Once if someone had dared to talk to me like that, I would beat the hell out of him. Now, I have learned that sometimes it is better to keep silent because I can get in trouble"*.

Such complex situations raise doubts among patients about their ability not to retaliate and harm their achievements. For patients in recovery, the depressive position is abundant with crossroads between the dreadful but familiar reality of active drug addiction and the goods, yet the uncertainty of the present and the future. In my opinion, these examples mostly emphasize the difficulties of keeping the equilibrium between the two positions (Steiner, 1992). Arguments and disagreements in interpersonal relations or working places raise also doubts among patients about their ability to live like people around them who do not use drugs. Such situations remind the Kleinian baby who is not assured that his attempts to repair and restore are associated with depression and despair, since the ego doubts its capacity to achieve these goals (Klein, 1935).

The creation of the phantasy of the good and beloved child of the good parent enables a renewed meeting with the family and symbolizes to the patient that he is welcomed into the family. Positive experiences with external objects in familial and occupational settings strengthen the belief in the reparation capacities and lead to internalization of good objects that influences on the internal matrix of object relations. Temperley (2001) notes that in the depressive position, positive experiences with external objects are introjected and modify bad internal objects and that more benevolent internal objects are then projected on to the external reality, which is perceived in a more favorable light. More complete perception of external objects is achieved through more complete perception of the self and acknowledgment of the internal goods that the infant possesses.

In the same manner as the baby learns that his ability to give love to external objects results in love and good experiencing, so do patients learn that caring for other people results in mutual caring. Such self-reinforcing cycles of trust help patients to be more assure of their own goodness. They learn that there is no need in using projective identification for receiving affection and tenderness, and so vicious circles of suspicion, aggression and internal dread are replaced by circles of closeness and trust.

During the recovery process, there are attempts to create such circles that enhance the confidence in external and internal objects. These attempts create positive experiences that reduce the annihilation anxiety and enable the patient to experience himself as a good person. If the patient is more assure that the addiction did not empty all the goodness from his insides, he is readier to continue in the mourning process. According to Kernberg (1980), mourning processes enhance the awareness for both reality and reality testing, and the availability of a good mother strengthens the baby's ability of loving and his confidence in his internal goodness.

There is high significance for the presence of supporting objects during the recovery process since they symbolize to the patient that his destructive phantasys did not destroy everything and that he contains also good parts. As one patient said: *"now that I returned from rehab and I don't abuse drugs, I help at home. I help in small reparations of electricity. I also helped a neighbor to repair his fence. My father was very proud of me"*. Another patient said:

> I clean the house, I go to the grocery store, buy food even cook sometimes. You know, its funny, I return with change. When I used drugs and had money, it vanished immediately. Now they trust me with the money. It's a good feeling.

According to Klein (1935), the reparation consists the major achievement of the depressive position. The patient who goes to the grocery store and does not vanish with the money and the one who helps in small reparations perform daily activities that we as therapists may wonder why they even mention it. But, it is important to understand that these patients are busy in making symbolic and concrete reparations toward their families and toward themselves. In my opinion, this is the reparation process which is described in Klein's writings and which is carried out of responsibility and concern to the object rather than only guilt (Dorban, 2002). The psychodynamic treatment, which relies on Klein work, leads to the discovery that the good breast is created from the patient's hard work, and every reparation enables the patient to be assured in the goodness inside of him and in the objects around him. The frustrations, the losses of life and the constant threat of internal destructiveness make the depressive position an achievement that is repeatedly lost and in need of re-establishing (Temperley, 2001).

Concluding remarks

The essence of the recovery process is keeping the balance between the two positions and developing ability to process the various anxieties every time anew until a more complex and integrative perception of the self and the world is achieved. Dorban (2002) writes that, since its early days, psychoanalysis, as a therapeutic system and as a thinking framework on the human condition, has dealt with the complex associations between life and death, construction and destruction, good and bad, and love and hate. I believe that these words describe precisely the internal world of recovering patients.

References

Britton, R. (1998). *Belief and imagination: Explorations in psychoanalysis*. Routledge.

Bronstein, C. (2001). What are internal objects? In C. Bronstein (Ed.), *Kleinian theory: A contemporary perspective* (pp. 108–124). Whurr Publishers.

Center for Substance Abuse Treatment. (1995). *Detoxification from alcohol and other drugs. Treatment Improvement Protocol (TIP) Series 19*. Center for Substance Abuse Treatment.

Dorban, Y. (2002). On love, hate and anxiety – An introduction to Kleinian thinking. In Y. Dorban (Ed.), *Melanie Klein – Selected writings* (pp. 7–38). Bookworm (in Hebrew).

Hinshelwood, R. D. (1991). *A dictionary of Kleinian thought*. Free Association Books.

Kernberg, O. F. (1980). *Internal world and external reality*. Jason Aronson.

Klein, M. (1935). A contribution to the psychogenesis of manic-depressive states. In *Love, guilt & reparation, 1921–1945* (pp. 262–289). Free Press, 1975.

Klein, M. (1936). Weaning. In *Love, guilt and reparation and other works 1921–1945* (pp. 290–305). The Free Press.

Klein, M. (1940). Mourning and its relation to manic-depressive states. *International Journal of Psychoanalysis, 21*, 125–153.

Klein, M. (1957). Envy and gratitude. In *Envy and gratitude and other works 1946–1963* (pp. 176–235). Vintage, 1997.

Klein, M. (1958). On the development of mental functioning. *International Journal of Psychoanalysis, 39*(2–4), 84–90.

Laudet, A. B. (2007). What does recovery mean to you? Lessons from the recovery experience for research and practice. *Journal of Substance Abuse Treatment, 33*(3), 245–256.

National Institute on Drug Abuse. (2020). The science of drug abuse and addiction: The basics. Retrieved from https://www.drugabuse.gov/publications/media-guide/science-drug-use-addiction-basics.

Ogden, T. (2004). This art of psychoanalysis: Dreaming undreamt dreams and interrupted cries. *International Journal of Psychoanalysis, 85*(4), 857–877.

Segal, H. (2001). Symbolization. In C. Bronstein (Ed.), *Kleinian theory: A contemporary perspective* (pp. 148–156). Whurr Publishers.

Steiner, J. (1992). The equilibrium between the paranoid-schizoid and the depressive positions. In R. Anderson (Ed.), *New library of psychoanalysis, 14. Clinical lectures on Klein and Bion* (pp. 46–58). Brunner-Routledge.

Temperley, J. (2001). The depressive position. In C. Bronstein (Ed.), *Kleinian theory: A contemporary perspective* (pp. 125–147). Whurr Publishers.

Chapter 5

Lapses and relapses

"Others remain stuck in the retreat despite the evident suffering it brings, which may be chronic and sustained or masochistic and addictive".
(Steiner, 1993, p. 3)

Lapse and relapse are two terms that are frequently used by clinicians and researchers in the addictions field. However, the different definitions of these terms harden on scientific measurement (McKay, Franklin, Patapis, & Lynch, 2006; Simonelli, 2005). Some suggest that they should be replaced with more morally neutral terms that aptly depict the experiences of those who cope with addiction and drug abuse problems since they are rooted in moral and religious conceptions of addiction (White & Ali, 2010). In the 12-step program, relapse is viewed as the first use of any drug after an abstinence period. In another common distinction in this field, lapse or slip is considered a one-time or a brief episode of drug abuse, whereas relapse relates to a resumption of more excessive drug abuse, which involves the return of the symptoms required for a substance use disorder (White & Ali, 2010).

However, many researchers consider relapses to be a more complex phenomenon and assume that lapses or slips have cognitive and behavioral processes that are quite different from relapses (Griffiths, 2005; Larimer, Palmer, & Marlatt, 1999). Additional definition of lapse is "any discrete violation of a self-imposed rule or a set of regulations governing the rate or a pattern of a selected behavior" (Wanigaratne, Wallace, Pullin, Keaney & Farmer, 1990, p. 11). In the basis of this model, it is assumed that patients can learn a new set of skills and behaviors that can assist them stop using drugs and identify risky situations (Marlatt & Gordon, 1985).

According to the medical model (Leshner, 1997), addiction is a chronic, relapsing disease that results from the prolonged effects of drugs on the brain. Drug addiction has many similarities to diseases, such as type 2 diabetes mellitus, asthma or hypertension, and genetic factors, environmental factors and personal choices have an essential role in the etiology and course of all these diseases (McLellan, Lewis, O'Brien, & Kleber, 2000). For example, a hypertonic patient who stops taking his medications or a diabetic patient who does not plan his meals probably will experience an intensification of the disease's symptoms. In the same manner, physiological and behavioral symptoms of drug addiction will appear following drug abuse (McLellan et al., 2000).

Relating to drug addiction, the most common relapse predictors include negative mood states, interpersonal conflicts and social pressure to engage in drug abuse (Festinger, Rubenstein, Marlowe, & Platt, 2001; Moos and Moos, 2006; Sanchez-Hervas et al., 2012). Other variables include low self-efficacy (Annis, 1990; Bandura, 1978), physical discomfort (Festinger et al., 2001; Marlatt & Gordon, 1985), pleasant feelings and experiences (Annis, Graham, & Davis, 1987), education level and employment status (Jin, Rourke, Patterson, Taylor, & Grant, 1998; Moos & Moos, 2006; Vaillant, 1988).

Relapses may lead to interpersonal conflicts, financial losses and job dismissal. There is also an influence on the therapeutic process, and patients might miss meetings or even dropout during relapses. Unfortunately, lapses and relapses do not receive much attention in the psychodynamic literature that deals with drug abuse and addiction. In the next lines, I will offer psychodynamic formulations of lapses and relapses, but first, I will present one of the prevailing approaches to drug abuse treatment, and I will explain how it relates to relapses.

A motivational interviewing perspective on lapses and relapses

Motivational interviewing is a client-centered, semi-directive method for enhancing intrinsic motivation to change by exploring and resolving ambivalence (Miller, & Rollnick, 2002). This approach relies on the transtheoretical model of change, which offers an integrative perspective on the structure of intentional change (Prochaska, DiClemente, & Norcross, 1992). In this model, behavior change is conceptualized as a process that unfolds over time and involves advancement through a series of distinct stages (Krebs,

Figure 5.1 The Wheel of Change.

Norcross, Nicholson, & Prochaska, 2018). The stages are usually illustrated by a figure of a wheel (the wheel of change) or of a circle. Figure 5.1 presents the wheel of change.

The first stage, precontemplation, denotes no intention of behavior change, and most people in this stage are unaware of their problems (Norcross, Krebs, & Prochaska, 2011). Relating specifically to drug addiction, family members and close friends are more aware of the suffering of the addicted individual and quite often suffer themselves. In contemplation, the second stage, there is awareness of the problem and serious thoughts about overcoming it but without any commitment to act (Norcross et al., 2011). People can stay stuck in this stage for extended periods (Prochaska et al., 1992). Relating to drug addiction, the addicted individual is aware of the consequences of his behavior but does not turn for help. In the preparation stage, people intend to act in the next month, and they have probably made some actions to change their behavior (Norcross et al., 2011). An addicted individual who contacts detoxification centers and asks about treatment is an example.

In the fourth stage, action, people make overt modifications in their behavior to overcome their problems. People are classified in this stage if they have successfully altered their behavior for a period of from one day to six months (Krebs et al., 2018). Relating to drug addiction, starting psychotherapy and entering a detoxification center are examples for actions. In maintenance, people work to consolidate their achievements and work to prevent relapse. This is not a static stage because people have to take various actions to preserve the changes, and for addictive behaviors, maintenance extends from six months to an indeterminate period past the initial action (Prochaska et al., 1992). For many years, the next stage of the model was termed relapse and represented the return of the unwanted behavior. Currently, relapse does not appear as a stage, although researchers note that relapse is the rule rather than the exception with addictions (Prochaska et al., 1992). However, relapse is not considered a failure of the person, and professionals understand that it is an integral part of the change process.

Motivational interviewing also relies on humanistic psychology principles of empathy and acceptance of the client (Rogers, 1961). Professionals who work within the motivational interviewing approach focus on the present, identify the stage in which the clients (not patients) are "stuck" and use different interventions in different stages to assist them (Miller, & Rollnick, 2002). They aim to increase the client's awareness of his problems and to their consequences by using reflective listening, asking open-ended questions, provision of affirmations and periodical provision of summary statements (Miller, & Rollnick, 2002). In a review that assessed the effectiveness of motivational interviewing for substance abuse on drug abuse, retention in treatment, readiness to change and the number of repeat convictions, the authors concluded that this approach could reduce the extent of substance abuse compared to no intervention (Smedslund et al., 2011). However, the evidence was mostly of low quality (Smedslund et al., 2011).

Relapse prevention interventions are mostly cognitive-behavioral and focus on skill learning for coping with stressful situations (Larimer et al., 1999), since stress is one of the most significant factors for cravings (Sinha, 2008). Stress elicits craving and drug-seeking behaviors in times of drug abstinence (Sinha, 2007). Taking even a small amount of a previously abused drug (de Wit, 1996) and environment-related cues (Blanco-Gandía, Aguilar, Miñarro, & Rodríguez-Arias, 2018; Lu et al., 2002) play critical roles in the incentive motivation underlying drug-seeking behaviors. Cognitive-behavioral models suggest that immediate determinants (e.g., high-risk situations, coping skills) and covert antecedents (e.g., lifestyle factors and urges and cravings) can contribute to relapse (Larimer et al., 1999). In the same manner, the 12-step program recommends its members to avoid people, places and things to avoid relapse (Narcotics Anonymous, 2008). Meaning, to avoid people (with whom the individual abused drugs with), avoid places (in which the individual abused or bought drugs) and finally to avoid and dispose of all objects related to drug abuse (rolling papers, bongs, needles and syringes).

Cognitive-behavioral therapy (CBT) focuses on mapping high-risk situations, monitoring craving, developing coping strategies and skills for emotional regulation. This approach emphasizes the covert route to relapse and the critical role of decision-making, but relapses may also stem from unconscious reasons (Cattano, 1996; Singleton & Gorelick, 1998). In the next lines, I will offer a psychoanalytic conceptualization of this phenomenon, which relies on the theoretical and technical contributions of neo-Kleinian analysts. The underlying assumption is that lapses and relapses are associated with difficulties in coping with processes that characterize the depressive position. More specifically, the transition to this position is so challenging because the good object representations are relatively few in comparison to the experiencing with bad objects and because of the difficulties to cope with threatening reality without any anesthetic substances that can expel the bad object.

Artificial manic defences ≈ relapses

Gideon, a 34-year-old male, abused cocaine intensively for a year. Following detoxification, he avoided cocaine for two months but experienced difficulty in coping with carving and maintaining a steady job. Due to pressure from his girlfriend, he turned to psychotherapy. She lived with him for four years and supported him, but, after suffering from the consequences of his addiction, she decided to pose an ultimatum. He appeared for two meetings and presented with different complaints, which included disputes in his workplace and craving for cocaine abuse. There was concern that his girlfriend would leave him if he abused drugs again. Gideon called me before the third meeting and canceled it, saying that he had been asked to stay in his work-place. He did not appear at the subsequent meeting and did not bother to contact or update me. When I tried to call him, he was not available.

A month after his sudden disappearance, he called me and asked for a meeting because of deterioration in his condition. When we met, he said, that during the past month, he had resigned from his work and spent much money on cocaine. He added that he had felt unpleasantness since he concealed the drug abuse from both his partner and me, and, for this reason, decided not to contact me. The event that led to the relapse was another dispute with his employer. During his work as a cook, his employer criticized him loudly, while Gideon thought it is the employer who was wrong. Gideon said that he was angry and considered pouring a hot cooking pot on his head:

> I've been angry with him for a few days. I saw how he was looking at me from day one. Who the hell he thinks he is?! Talking to me like that. Maybe I made a little mistake, maybe. But one little mistake and he shouts like a maniac? He should learn to talk properly to his employees. I am not the only one who hates him. All the employees do. If he talked to me in this way when I used cocaine, I would beat the crap out of him. I do not need him. I can find a job anytime.

As mentioned, this situation led to a relapse that lasted for a month, and the contents of the subsequent sessions dealt with coping with both the external and internal reality. Gideon had difficulties in containing negative emotions toward his employers, and often devalued them, although sometimes they praised him. Besides, he understood that his partner expects a marriage proposal but was afraid that he could not function as a husband and a father and concomitantly abuse cocaine. There was certain progress since the patient dealt with depressive anxieties, but on the other hand, there were difficulties in establishing this position.

According to Klein (1940), during the second position, unbearable feelings of guilt, mourning and despair arise, and the baby uses manic defences, such as idealization of the self, and triumph over the lost object (Klein, 1940). In my opinion, patients who relapse while coping with such issues are using artificial manic defence. According to Klein (1940), the child turns to manic omnipotence when he constantly feels his reparation attempts are failing and when he cannot rely enough on his constructing emotions. Drug abuse, and especially cocaine and amphetamines abuse, elicits euphoria and elation and enables the individual feelings of grandiosity and omnipotence. This drug abuse also enables denial of powerlessness and the inability to repair. In a study among cocaine abusers, the participants praised the drug for its stimulating properties and for conferring a strong sense of self-confidence and control (McCrystal, Mayock, & Hannaford, 2011).

The artificial manic defence (cocaine) allows the abuser aggrandization of the self, devaluation of the object and feelings of contempt and triumph over external objects and the painful reality of the depressive position. The cocaine abuse allowed Gideon to feel triumphant over the job difficulties, contempt toward his employer and even sadistic satisfaction of overcoming and humiliating, like the baby who uses such defences when he faces depressive anxieties (Klein, 1940). In this position, there are splitting and integrative processes between internal and external objects, and the ambivalence toward them allows the child to be more trustful toward internalized objects (Klein, 1940). At the same time, paranoid defences and anxieties are turned toward the bad objects.

In the external reality, Gideon experienced paranoid anxieties and could not accept that his employer provides constructive criticism. The complex external reality was characterized by financial dependence upon his employer and emotional dependence upon his partner. After two consecutive months of treatment, he revealed that he is afraid to stay alone. He could recognize the impact of his deeds on his partner and worried that she might leave him. Gideon revealed that he was afraid to find himself without a relationship and a job because not all employers were ready to put up with his temper. Those anxieties imply a fear of dependence in external objects that were screened continuously by cocaine abuse, a drug that enables a sense of control and even triumph upon the internal objects. This triumph is devastating because it is associated with distrust and persecution (Klein, 1940), which are embodied in Gideon's words about the hostile employer who wishes to harm him from his's first day at work.

Gideon reported that he started dreaming again but could not remember his dreams. He promised his girlfriend to stop using drugs and started again looking for a job. However, he did not like her threats to leave him if he will start abusing drugs again:

> who the hell she thinks she is?! In the last years, I hear it constantly. I had many girlfriends before her. If she leaves, another one will come. She does not understand what cocaine is. She wants me to go to therapy. I've been in therapy before. You only talk, and you do not do a thing.

These sayings are examples for states in which the ego cannot give up on his good internal objects, but on the other hand, tries to avoid any dependence upon them. It looks that Gideon tries to avoid any dependence upon his girlfriend, his employer and even the therapeutic setting and the therapist. The use of disregard, another manic defence, allows disengagement from the object without giving up on him. Gideon did not leave either his partner or therapy but relapsed again. Often during relapses, the relationships with external and internal objects are kept, but they are not integrative.

There are a few possible scenarios for relapses. In the first, the patient will abuse drugs several times, believing that he will succeed in maintaining the current interpersonal and occupational functioning. Based on colleagues' experience and my own, this phantasy shatters after a few weeks (if not days) and leads to drug addiction. For some patients, the first drug abuse is a slippery slope, which leads directly to addiction. In both scenarios, the movement toward the first position is quite quick. A third option involves regression to psychic retreats.

Relapses ≈ withdrawals to psychic retreats

In my opinion, Steiner's concept of withdrawal to psychic retreat applies to a dynamic that characterizes a patients' group who abuses drugs while coping with difficulties in processing the mental reality of the depressive position. These patients are drug abstinent for a few weeks or a few months, and they have a certain set of skills to cope with cravings and stressful situations. Their ego capacities are more mature, and their emotional regulation abilities are developed enough not to act impulsively. Their history shows that they have had several relationships in their life and significant employment periods. During therapy, they may show impressive progress, such as renewing family relations or getting a promotion at work.

Yet, the renewed encounter with the reality is associated with mental pain because with the new successes, appears the understanding that the patient will have to relinquish the possession of an object which enables elation and omnipotence. The patient copes with the ambivalence toward the drug and with mourning about lost opportunities and lost time. Meaning, recovery requires disengaging with any active drug abusers and creating new relationships without returning to drug abuse despite temptations or desires.

The patients' group that I refer to, has made significant progress and also has awareness of the consequences of drug abuse ("*using drugs isn't an option. I remember what I lost. I don't want that suffering again*"). However, despite the awareness, they have difficulties in accepting losses and dealing with negative emotions that arise during the encounter with frustrating reality. They may have sufficient skills to cope with drug craving, which is a derivative of the death instinct. But, when the anxiety intensifies, they withdraw to a hiding place or a refuge from both external reality and therapy. Phantasies about withdrawals to such places may appear in dreams and during wakefulness, but patients not always share it with the therapist.

According to Steiner (1993), withdrawals to psychic retreats occur during analysis when a significant contact with the analyst is conceived as threatening, painful and anxiety-provoking. Some patients will react to the anxiety while others will manifest schizoid superiority or mocking dismissal of the analyst's work, which implies that the analyst has touched upon a sensitive topic. In any case, those patients will retreat behind a robust system of defences which serve as a hiding place or protective armour (Steiner, 1993). Such behaviors also prevail among a subpopulation of drug abusing patients who display complacence and exaggerated self-confidence about the ability to avoid any drug abuse. I will demonstrate it in the following clinical material.

Michael was 28 years old when he had immigrated to Israel from western Europe. In the decade before his arrival in Israel, he abused cocaine and cannabis and sometimes had managed to work. Michael had a few relationships in the last years, and some of his girlfriends abused drugs with him. He reported that four years ago, he decided to stop abusing drugs and remained drug abstinent for two years. However, in subsequent years, he relapsed and decided to immigrate to Israel with the thought that a new beginning in a different country would be promising for him. In Israel, he did not find a job but started a new relationship and kept drug abstinent. His girlfriend knew about his addiction problem and supported him, although Michael used to flirt with other women. When his girlfriend had found out that he chats with other women on the internet, she started to suspect that he also conceals drug abuse. She was indeed right since he has started to abuse cocaine. With her encouragement, he turned to a detox center, and toward the end of his staying there, he contacted me with the request for psychotherapeutic treatment after his discharge.

In the first two months of therapy, Michael has improved his Hebrew and found a part-time job. The treatment focused on supporting his efforts to avoid any drug abuse and on the dishonest behavior in his current relationship. The intensity of the depressive anxieties about the annihilation of good internal objects (starting using drugs and ending the abstinence period) and good external objects (losing job), which appeared following detox, has lessened because of his successes. Michael was quite surprised because of his progress and began to talk about his lifelong phantasy of academic studies. However, the fear that he will start abusing drugs during the studies has accompanied the phantasy.

Four months after detox, he left his girlfriend and found an additional part-time job. He earned more money and was more self-confident than a few months ago. I asked him if he feels loneliness after the break up from his girlfriend and the distancing from his family, and he replied that he feels good. I asked him if he abuses drugs, and he denied. Michael added that this issue does not bother him. I experienced him quite haughty, but for some reason, despite knowing that this is a high-risk situation, I did not insist on asking him how he manages to keep drug abstinent in this sensitive period. I thought that maybe he manages to cope with his anxieties with the help of friends and coworkers.

In the subsequent session, he looked very anxious and confused. He said that a woman he dated, said to him that he is talented and asked what does he do with these talents. Michael experienced it like a wake-up call and started thinking thoughtfully about his life. He was fired during that time, because of manpower reduction and looked for a new job. Besides, he also checked the admission criteria for academic studies. When Michael reported that he still does not find a job, I suggested attending Narcotics Anonymous meetings, and he replied that he would think about it. He canceled the following meeting, and after about eight months in therapy, admitted that for the last two months, he has been occasionally using cocaine. I asked him why he reports it now, and Michael said that he feels he cannot lie any longer neither to his family that supports him financially nor to me because he feels that I care for him.

I wondered about therapy's efficacy when the patient abuses drugs and lies, and I thought about ending therapy. I asked him if he is afraid that I will end treatment because of his behavior. Michael replied that he thought about it, but then he knew that therapists who work with drug abusers know that relapses happen. I wondered if he takes advantage of this knowledge, but my passing thoughts were interrupted with his question: *"did I tell you about my last relationship in Europe before I came here?"* I said that he only mentioned it. Michael said that in this relationship, he abused drugs while his girlfriend did not. She went to college and did quite well, but after a few months, he persuaded her start abusing drugs. Consequently, she left college, and after two additional years, asked him for a serious answer concerning marriage. Michael had left her and immigrated. I said that it looks as if his drug abuse allows him to control his partner and to assure her staying. I said that professionals who work with drug abusers do understand that relapses may occur during recovery, but I think that he prepares me for prolonged drug abuse and wishes to put this treatment into stagnation as he did with his previous relationships.

In the subsequent session, he said that he is frustrated and thinks that he will never succeed in keeping drug abstinence even for a few months. He added that in the last week, he used cocaine only once. In contrast to the arrogance which I felt before, now I felt that Michael is afraid that his anxieties will be so overwhelming that he will have to stay in his psychic retreat to avoid reality. After a minute of silence, I asked him for a dream. He smiled and said that he had a dream which he even remembers (he used to say that he does not remember his dreams). In his dream, he flew over a crowded stadium with a helicopter, when unfamiliar people started shooting bullets at him. Michael returned fire and then woke up. I asked for associations about the helicopter.

MICHAEL: "The helicopter is a safe place for me. The bullets can't reach me there".

I: "It looks as is the helicopter is a hiding place that allows you avoiding mental pain. This place allows you hurting other people without getting hurt. When difficulties appear, you enter the helicopter and take off. In the last weeks, you started using drugs after a woman you dated asked you a question that has elicited anxiety. In the relationship prior to your immigration, you started using intensively when your girlfriend asked you to commit".

Michael just looked at me and seemed somehow curious.

I: "When you came emotionally closer, you felt that you might get hurt and you entered the helicopter and took off".

MICHAEL: "I feel guilty about the drug abuse of my former girlfriend in Europe. She was a good girl that started using because of me. When she asked me if I was going to marry her, I left. I was always selfish in relationships. I took money from them. I blamed them for not carrying enough about me. I did not have a healthy relationship".

I: "I think that now you understand that the bullets that you fired from your helicopter toward the people in your life, had hurt them".

Discussion

This example demonstrates how relapses among abstinent drug abusers may be related to withdrawals to psychic retreats. The woman's question during the date elicited annihilation anxiety in a period in which he felt evacuated from good internal objects and the withdrawal to psychic retreat allowed avoidance of emotional pain. Occasionally, Michael emerged from his retreat to look for a job or to take an interest in academic studies, but he withdrew again when he saw the admission criteria. He noted many times that after a few days of drug abstinence, something inside of him said that he can use drugs and that he deserves a gift in the form of one-time drug abuse for his progress. Drug abusers and therapists working in this field refer to this dynamic as a cunning ploy that aims to carry out a hidden intention of drug abuse.

This dynamic relates to the arousal of drug craving and the execution of a devious plan which is activated toward both the internal and the external realities. In my opinion, this devious planning is associated with a pathological organization which, according to Steiner (1993), is related to primitive destruction. Rosenfeld (1971) referred to this mental construct as a gang, and Meltzer (1968) described a narcissistic tyrannical regime that relies on terror and dread. This ploy, the pathological organization of drug abusers, is characterized by cunning inventiveness, wiliness, and destructiveness toward the overall good objects' matrix. The ploy is responsible for executing internal attacks on good internal objects (a healthy body, good self and good object representation) through drug abuse, and is accompanied with rationalizations, such as *"this use is temporary"*, *"it's only once"*, *"after so much time of abstinence, you can use drugs. No one will find out"*. The ploy is composed of destructive elements that take over the personality and offer a delusional world freed from pain and anxiety (Rosenfeld, 1971).

The pathological organization is related to narcissistic object relations which are based on idealization of destructive parts of the self (Rosenfeld, 1971). The pathology arises from internal sources of destructiveness manifested as primitive envy, which threatens to destroy the individual from within (Steiner, 1993). The part of the ego which contains such destructive impulses and phantasies is split off and evacuated through a process of projective identification. At the end of this process, the individual feels that he is attacked from without and uses various defences for coping (Rosenfeld, 1971).

In this context, in his writing on the destructive sides of narcissism, Rosenfeld miraculously describes a mental dynamic which may appear in transference relations. But, in the addictions field, this dynamic nourishes relationship of drug abusers with their life partners and other family members (Askian, Krauss, Baba, Kadir, & Sharghi, 2016; Johnson, 1988). Codependency is a term used by professionals in the addictions field to denote dysfunctional relationship patterns characterized by fusion, compulsive behaviors, and lack of awareness while focusing externally on another person (Prest & Protinsky, 1993). In this way, projective identification serves as a mechanism that helps to create enmeshed relationships in which drug abusers can strengthen their control of external objects and use them for their own needs. It should be noted that codependency is a concept which has attracted much criticism because of negative labeling and strong stereotyping (Calderwood & Rajesparam, 2014; Orford, 2005).

This dynamic describes well many of Michael's relationships. For example, he felt envious toward his girlfriend's achievements in college and her ability to live a drug-free life. After the projection of the destructive elements, he interpreted every criticism of his girlfriend as a persecutory attack. The girlfriend identified with the projected elements and actually became a member of a gang, which ensures avoidance from emotional pain.

According to Steiner (1993), the therapist may be recruited by the pathological organization to give rise to stuck periods of analysis, and I believe that Michael tried to turn me to a member of this gang, which represents the pathological organization. Six months into therapy, he negated any drug abuse, and perhaps the projection of haughty elements made me collaborate with the ploy. Therefore, I did not raise relevant questions about the instability in his life.

Several analysts described how the analyst's blindness contributes to the tendency to engage in collusive acting out (Langs, 1978; Rosenfeld, 1978), and perhaps the will to believe that the patient succeeds well after a relatively short time in therapy also contributed to this blindness. After a few weeks in the psychic retreat, Michael realized that staying there harms both his family and me and decided to emerge. The readiness to emerge from this place is one of the first steps in weakening the pathological organization's control over the patient's personality, and this action contributes to the patient's readiness to be seen.

Michel accepted my offer to attend Narcotics Anonymous meetings, checked out a few academic programs and even took a preparatory course. Nevertheless, once in two to three weeks, he abused cocaine. Michel described a phantasy in which he drives a car under drug influence wearing black sunglasses, when no one can see him. He added that in Europe, he did it and felt great. I said that the black sunglasses prevent any contact with reality and allow him to hurt others. Suddenly, he remembered how, as a teenager, he would sneak into the place where his mother stored medications and sought for medications with addictive potential. He said that as a teenager, he had smoked weed (cannabis) and used to lie to his parents. He described himself as a spoiled child who repeatedly deceived his parents and abused drugs. Yet, he felt regret following such events and did not understand why he lies to his parents. I said that I feel that the same situation had happened between us, and I asked him if he thinks that he is hurting me. Michael's eyes became red and he said that he is sorry and that he feels bad because he continues to hurt his parents by abusing their financial support to buy drugs.

I said that when he admits his drug abuse, he removes the sunglasses and allows me to see him exposed. He said that one of the things which bothered him since childhood is how other people think of him since he feels that he has no skills and that he is quite transparent. I replied that I believe that he achieved quite a lot since, during less than a year in a new country, he found work, learned a new language, gained friends and began to think about academic studies. I added that it shows that he has diverse skills and readiness for further progress, but the possibility of being seen by others, frightens him.

Emerges from psychic retreats

As part of the dynamic which characterizes this withdrawal (Steiner, 1993), Michael canceled a meeting. I think that he emerged from the psychic retreat because it became cruel and deadly (Steiner, 1993), and because a stable therapeutic connection has been created. I believe that the pathological organization wanted to see how I will react to the relapse, and whether the therapeutic process can be turned to as if therapy. Setting boundaries at the beginning of therapy helped Michael and (the pathological organization) to start and internalize that he may not be able to control the object. During such moments in therapy, the patient understands that the therapist is a complete object, that cannot always be manipulated. Consequently, the patient has to cope with the elements he tried to project onto the therapist, and a combination of firmness and sensitivity will allow the patient to start and internalize elements of responsibility, which he previously projected onto other objects. In other words, such experiences assist in the internalization and reconstruction of the superego.

During relapses and withdrawals to psychic retreats, therapists should ponder about the efficiency of therapy and on the patient's referral to detox.

Additional options include attending Narcotics Anonymous meetings, starting pharmacological treatment, or provision of urine tests in addition to therapy. The patient's readiness to continue in therapy and to accept one of these suggestions implies that he continues to emerge from the retreat and that he is more ready to be seen. As therapy proceeded, it looked as if Michael acknowledged the hurting in his former girlfriends and his family. He cried when he described how he let his parents believe he was working while, actually, he was spending their money on drugs. Michael mentioned that his life might have been entirely different if he would admit himself to detox back in Europe and stayed with a woman who loved him.

Mourning plays an essential role in the recovery of parts of the self which were expelled through projective identification, and if the analyst can contain, register and give meaning to the projected fragments, there is a movement toward integration as the patient feels less anxious and more understood (Steiner, 1993). Grief work is essential for any progress in therapy of drug abusers for a few reasons. First, grief means an understanding that old relationships and lost opportunities will not come back. Second, in a successful mourning process, drug abusers will give up on the phantasy of controlling the object and the expectation that individuals would act according to their will.

Third, Steiner (1993) describes mourning processes in which patients can regain personality parts of eroticism, desires and spontaneity. I believe that mourning processes among drug abusers involve the recovery of libidinal personality elements as well as recovery of aggressive personality elements. In other words, through projective identification, the therapist transforms the sadistic and persecutory aggression, which was used to hurt and control other objects into a more moderate form of aggression, which can be contained by the patient. At the end of the process, the need in projection of persecutory anxiety lessens since the patient does not feel haunted from the inside, and he is ready to take responsibility for previous hurts and avoid future hurts.

After fourteen months in therapy, Michael went for a few job interviews. He reported that he does not abuse drugs and began to attend Narcotics Anonymous meetings more frequently. He always saw those who attended these meetings as weak, called them 'junkies', and was ashamed to be identified with them. In the meetings he attended, he understood that they are not different from him. He described a few dreams which he had since he started attending the meetings. The first dream quite frightened him since he saw unfamiliar people being cut on large blades. I asked for associations about the blades, and he said: "*airplanes have blades...helicopters have blades*" and became silent. I felt his sadness. I said that the helicopter, his safe place has crushed, and now he feels unprotected in the face of the reality. In response, he described another dream where he is in a large paddock and then he ascends in an elevator to an upper floor of a high tower. There he meets unfamiliar people and feels not belonging.

These dreams describe the shame and the dread which patients feel during emergence from psychic retreats. Michael's constant attendance at Narcotics Anonymous meetings indicates that he started internalizing that he does not differ from objects he previously mocked. Simultaneously, attending job interviews and pre-academic courses involve encounters with individuals without addiction issues and sharpen questions about self-worth and be-longingness. The encounter with the external reality following emergence from psychic retreat raises intense anxiety about the ability to recreate goods and the fear that it will be destroyed again by the patient's aggression (drug abuse).

The emerges from psychic retreat involve exposure, and in this case, exposure of different personality elements in different settings. Meaning, Michael could talk about his lack of responsibility and deceit without any criticism at Narcotics Anonymous meetings, and he could present different facets of his personality at job interviews. The next sessions dealt with the fundamental insecurity and inadequacy feelings he had felt from a young age and the falsehood he adjusted for not letting anyone approach his inner world inside his psyche. After an additional month without any drug abuse, he began to look for a job as a waiter. Once he thought that such work is be-neath his dignity, and was afraid that one of his friends would see him. But, now he decided that starting any work is more important.

The readiness of the patient of being seen is bounded with repetitive ex-posures to shameful elements of the self and the surrounding's gaze. Such situations elicit shame and humiliation, but they contain a yearning for af-firmation and acceptance. In therapy, I said to Michael that I understand his fear of being humiliated, but I can see that once he decided to get out of the car and remove his sunglasses and walk in the street, the people he meets in job interviews or in his class only praise him. Steiner (1993) notes that when patients leave their psychic retreats, there is a danger of withdrawal. This is a very relevant issue in the treatment of drug abusers because the narcissistic organization or the ploy try their luck when the patient is ex-posed and assure him elation and pain-free reality if he withdraws to the psychic retreat (drug abuse).

In summary, the danger of withdrawal to psychic retreats always exists and especially when the inner world of the patient is characterized by dead-ness and emptiness. As mentioned earlier, the retreat is experienced as a safe hiding place, but sometimes it may have persecutory and cruel qualities. Steiner (1993) notes that patients may be stuck in the retreat with familiar and chronic masochistic suffering, which includes a relationship with par-tial objects. Relating specifically to drug addiction, this chronic suffering includes illness following the abuse of poisonous drugs, shame and guilt feelings, fear of any personal exposure, and especially feelings of stuckness. Interestingly, both Meltzer (1968) and Steiner (1993), analysts who did not treat patients who suffered from addictive disorders, use the word addictive for describing the pathological organization which is responsible for the withdrawal to psychic retreats.

The use of this word implies on the difficulty of patients to relinquish this place and therapists who treat such patients should be ready for relapses to psychic retreats during treatment. The therapeutic process requires much patience and hardiness since patients do not always tell the truth or might disappear when they withdraw to psychic retreats. The emergence from such places is so complicated for patients not only because of shame but mainly because of the difficulties in relinquishing the phantasy associated with the withdrawal to psychic retreats.

Concluding remarks

Individuals with addiction history who abuse occasionally cocaine and cannabis have a phantasy about simultaneously functioning well and continuing using drugs. When the therapist asks if they had managed to do both simultaneously, they unwillingly admit that either they quit their job or started abusing drugs intensively. Meaning, either they experienced loss, or the drug abuse became drug addiction. These patients regularly mention that once they have heard of a person who does succeed in working and occasionally abusing cocaine or cannabis. Interestingly, no one has managed to meet this mysterious person who represents the patients' phantasy. However, patients are not ready to give up on this phantasy so quick because they wish to be like other people who smoke cannabis at the end of the day or snort cocaine only in parties. Unfortunately, they tend to ignore the fact that the people they talk about, do not have an addiction history.

Usually, these patients turn to therapy following the environment's pressure. Actually, they try to avoid therapy because both the therapist and his interventions represent the reality which they try to avoid. In therapy, their wish of control shatters on the cliffs of the depressive position time after time. Unconsciously, they hate therapy and the therapist, who is experienced as a persecutory superego of the restricting reality. Like Oedipus, who did not want to face the truth, they retreat from truth to omnipotence (Steiner, 1993), or attempt to stay at -K preferring not to feel any of the pain involved in emotional growth (Bion, 1962; Potik, 2010).

These patients run away from knowing that they will not be able to smoke cannabis or use cocaine like other people because they have an addiction predisposition. These patients run away from K, not only when they abuse drugs but also when they lie, miss sessions or switch from one therapist to another. They flee from the restricting reality to psychic retreats only to discover that time does not stand still and that they cannot stay there forever.

Some patients report that the recovery attempts become harder after each relapse, and I believe that, in every emergence, they discover that the working through of the depressive position is never finished and has to be re-worked in each new life sitution (Britton, 1998).

References

Annis, H. M. (1990). Relapse to substance abuse: Empirical findings within a cognitive social learning approach. *Journal of Psychoactive Drugs, 22*(2), 117–124.

Annis, H. M., Graham, J. M., & Davis, C. S. (1987). *Inventory of Drinking Situations (IDS): User's guide.* Addiction Research Foundation.

Askian, P., Krauss, S. E., Baba, M., Kadir, R. A., & Sharghi, H. M. (2016). Characteristics of co-dependence among wives of persons with substance use disorder in Iran. *International Journal of Mental Health and Addiction, 14*, 268–283.

Bandura, A. (1978). Reflections on self-efficacy. *Advances in Behavioral Research and Therapy, 1*(4), 237–269.

Bion, W. R. (1962). *Learning from Experience.* Maresfield Library, 1984.

Blanco-Gandía, M. C., Aguilar, M. A., Miñarro, J., & Rodríguez-Arias, M. (2018). Reinstatement of drug-seeking in mice using the conditioned place preference paradigm. *Journal of Visualized Experience, 136*, e56983.

Britton, R. (1998). *Belief and imagination: Explorations in psychoanalysis.* Routledge.

Calderwood, K. A., & Rajesparam, A. (2014). Applying the codependency concept to concerned significant others of problem gamblers: Words of caution. *Journal of Gambling Issues, 29,* 1–16.

Cattano, J. (1996). The influence of unconscious fantasy process in addictions and relapse. *Journal of Clinical Social Work, 24*(4), 429–442.

de Wit, H. (1996). Priming effects with drugs and other reinforcers. *Experimental and Clinical Psychopharmacology, 4*(1), 5–10.

Festinger, D. S., Rubenstein, D. F., Marlowe, D. B., & Platt, J. J. (2001). Relapse: Contributing factors, causative models, and empirical considerations. In F. M. Tims, C. G. Leukefeld, & J. J. Platt (Eds.), *Relapse and recovery in addictions* (pp. 122–142). Yale University Press.

Griffiths, M. (2005). A "components" model of addiction within a biopsychosocial framework. *Journal of Substance Use, 10*(4), 191–197.

Jin, H., Rourke, S. B., Patterson, T. L., Taylor, M. J., & Grant, I. (1998). Predictors of relapse in long-term abstinent alcoholics. *Journal of Studies on Alcohol, 59*(6), 640–646.

Johnson, B. (1998). The mechanism of codependence in the prescription of benzodiazepines to patients with addiction. *Psychiatric Annals, 28*(3), 166–171.

Klein, M. (1940). Mourning and its relation to manic-depressive states. *International Journal of Psychoanalysis, 21*, 125–153.

Krebs, P., Norcross, J. C., Nicholson, J., M., & Prochaska, J. (2018). Stages of change and psychotherapy outcomes: A review and meta-analysis. *Journal of Clinical Psychology, 74*(11), 1964–1979.

Langs, R. (1978). Some communicative properties of the bipersonal field. *International Journal of Psychoanalytic Psychotherapy, 7*, 87–135.

Larimer, M. E., Palmer, R. S., & Marlatt, G. A. (1999). Relapse prevention: An overview of Marlatt's cognitive-behavioral model. *Alcohol Research Health, 23*(2), 151–160.

Leshner, A. I. (1997). Addiction is a brain disease, and it matters. *Science, 278*(5335), 45–47.

Lu, L., Xu, N. J., Ge, X., Yue, W., Su, W. J., Pei, G., & Ma, L. (2002). Reactivation of morphine conditioned place preference by drug priming: Role of environmental cues and sensitization. *Psychopharmacology, 159*(2), 125–132.

Marlatt, G. A., & Gordon, J. R. (1985). *Relapse prevention: Maintenance strategies in the treatment of addictive behaviors.* Guilford Press.

McCrystal, P., Mayock, P., & Hannaford, S. (2011). *A study of cocaine use in Northern Ireland 2009.* Department of Health, Social Services and Public Safety.

McKay, J., Franklin, T., Patapis, N., & Lynch, K. (2006). Conceptual, methodological and analytical issues in the study of relapse. *Clinical Psychology Review, 26*(2), 109–127.

McLellan, A.T., Lewis, D. C., O'Brien, C. P., & Kleber, H. D. (2000). Drug dependence, a chronic medical illness: Implications for treatment, insurance, and outcomes evaluation. *Journal of American Medical Association, 284*(13), 1689–1695.

Meltzer, D. (1968). Terror, persecution, dread: A dissection of paranoid anxieties. *The International Journal of Psychoanalysis, 49*(2-3), 396–401.

Miller, W. R., & Rollnick, S. (2002). *Motivational interviewing: Preparing people for change* (2nd Ed.). Guilford Press.

Moos, R. H., & Moos, B. S. (2006). Rates and predictors of relapse after natural and treated remission from alcohol use disorders. *Addiction, 101*(2), 212–222.

Narcotics Anonymous (2008). *Narcotics anonymous* (6th Ed.). Narcotics Anonymous World Services.

Norcross, J. C., Krebs, P. M., Prochaska, J. O. (2011). Stages of change. *Journal of Clinical Psychology, 67*(2), 143–154.

Orford, J. (2005). *Coping with alcohol and drug problems: The experiences of family members in three contrasting cultures.* Routledge.

Potik, D. (2010). Possessive objects and paralyzing moods. *Psychoanalytic Quarterly, 79*(3), 687–715.

Prest, L. A., & Protinsky, H. (1993). Family systems theory: A unifying framework for codependence. *The American Journal of Family Therapy, 21*(4), 352–360.

Prochaska, J. O., DiClemente, C. C., & Norcross, J. C. (1992). In search of how people change: Applications to addictive behaviors. *American Psychologist, 47*(9), 1102–1114.

Rogers, C. R. (1961). *On becoming a person.* Houghton Mifflin.

Rosenfeld, H. (1971). A clinical approach to the psychoanalytic theory of the life and death instincts: An investigation into the aggressive aspects of narcissism. *The International Journal of Psychoanalysis, 52*(2), 169–178.

Rosenfeld, H. (1978). Notes on the psychopathology and psychoanalytic treatment of some borderline patients. *The International Journal of Psychoanalysis, 59*(2–3), 215–221.

Sanchez-Hervas, E., Gomez, F. J., Villa, R. S., Garcia-Fernandez, Garcia-Rodriguez, O., & Romaguera, F. Z. (2012). Psychosocial predictors of relapse in cocaine dependent patients in treatment. *The Spanish Journal of Psychology, 15*(2), 748–755.

Simonelli, M. C. (2005). Relapse: A concept analysis. *Nursing Forum, 40*(1), 3–10.

Singleton, E. G., & Gorelick, D. A. (1998). Mechanisms of alcohol craving and their clinical implications. In M. Galanter (Ed.), *Recent developments in alcoholism: Volume 14. The consequences of alcoholism* (pp. 177–195). Plenum Press.

Sinha, R. (2007). The role of stress in addiction relapse. *Current Psychiatry Reports, 9*(5), 388–395.

Sinha R. (2008). Chronic stress, drug use, and vulnerability to addiction. *Annals of the New York Academy of Sciences, 1141,* 105–130.

Smedslund, G., Berg, R. C., Hammerstrøm, K. T., Steiro, A., Leiknes, K. A., Dahl, H. M., & Karlsen K. (2011). Motivational interviewing for substance abuse. *Cochrane Database of Systematic Reviews, 5,* CD008063.

Steiner, J. (1993). *Psychic retreats: Pathological organizations in psychotic, neurotic, and borderline patients.* Routledge.

Vaillant, G. E. (1988). What can long-term follow-up teach us about relapse and prevention of relapse in addiction? *British Journal of Addiction, 83*(10), 1147–1157.

Wanigaratne, S., Wallace, W., Pullin, J., Keaney, F., & Farmer, R. (1990). *Relapse prevention for addictive behaviours.* Blackwell Scientific.

White, W., & Ali, S. (2010). Lapse and relapse: Is it time for a new language. Retrieved from www.facesandvoices of recovery.org.

Chapter 6

Therapeutic issues

Internal destructiveness, countertransference and projective identification

> "The analyst seems to be the only person in the room who is actively concerned about change, about progress, about development".
>
> (Joseph, 1982, p. 137)

Professionals who work with drug abusers encounter many challenges and significant therapeutic issues which stem from the unique characteristics of this population. Some issues concern the therapist's difficulties containing the patient's internal destructiveness, which is expressed in prolonged drug abuse, despite the consequences, and in intensive projective identification. Actually, the encounter with such hard patients is an encounter with the death instinct that threatens to annihilate the patient, the therapist's ability to exist analytically, and the therapeutic process.

The dominance of the death instinct and drug addiction

Drug abuse and addiction have harmful consequences. First, the recurrent attacks on the body have physical and mental consequences. Second, the interpersonal relations of drug abusers with their families and friends, as well as their functioning, are damaged. Third, drug abusers eliminate their material resources and may turn for criminal activity to obtain money for financing the addiction. Drug addiction may lead to encounters with law enforcement agencies and even incarceration, which can negatively affect possible future career opportunities. Engagement in prostitution is another way to obtain drug money, and studies emphasize the negative and shocking consequences of prostitution (Sanders, Cunningham, Platt, Grenfell, & Macioti, 2017). In summary, drug addiction has many negative and traumatic facets.

Psychotherapy of drug abusers summons to therapists encounters with patients who not only hurt themselves in the past but also continue to harm themselves in the present. In my opinion, one of the therapists' enormous difficulties is to witness the harms that patients bring upon themselves, and especially on their bodies when they continue abusing drugs during therapy.

This issue is prominent in outpatient addiction treatment programs and opi-oid maintenance treatment programs in which therapists, counselors, phy-sicians, and nurses encounter patients who inject drugs into various body parts (legs, groins, neck). Consequently, wounds appear in those body parts, but not always patients will turn for medical assistance. Sometimes they might continue to inject drugs into those body parts.

Psychodynamic treatment of drug abusers also includes providing infor-mation about the hazardous consequences of drug abuse. Besides psychosis (Bramness & Rognli, 2016), amphetamines and cocaine abuse may cause heart and cardiovascular problems (Havakuk, Rezkalla, & Kloner, 2017; Indave et al., 2018; Sordo et al., 2014). Cannabis abuse may cause mental and cardio-vascular disorders (Goyal, Awad, & Ghali, 2017; Royal College of Psychiatrists, 2016). The opioid epidemic has many casualties in North America, although patients are informed about the harmful effects of abusing these medications (Chopra & Marasa, 2017). Next to psychological and physical suffering, drug abusers may suffer from drug abuse-related problems, such as homelessness, hunger, exposure to cold, diseases and violence. Some drug abusers report that a lifestyle which includes drug abuse and violence provided them thrills while others explain that they were merely in denial regarding the possible risks of their addiction. Sensation seeking and lack of awareness may explain why drug abusers abused drugs in the past. However, once those individuals have already begun treatment and continue abusing drugs, it is hard for therapists to under-stand why patients continue the hazardous lifestyle of drug addiction.

In these descriptions, I refer to a group of patients who continue abusing drugs intensively and risking their lives daily. In fact, sometimes the intensive addiction had brought them to the verge of death, when they overdosed or entered a coma. At some drug treatment centers, there is a possibility to imple-ment sanctions against such patients, but doubtfully if it will lead to the desired change. Psychoanalysts who wrote on drug abuse and addiction presented elaborated theoretical formulations and interesting case material, but they did not address to this group of patients. A legitimate question which arises in such situations is whether patients who abuse drugs intensively during the treatment despite the dreadful consequences are, actually, trying to nullify their lives.

In a review of empirical studies which dealt with the association between alcohol and drug abuse and suicidality, a significant association was found between alcohol abuse and suicidality (Wilcox, Conner, & Caine, 2004). A moderate association between opioid injection and suicidality was found, and the authors noted that there are not enough studies which examined the association between cannabis abuse and suicidality (Wilcox et al., 2004). The findings of this review provide a partial support for the association be-tween intensive opioid abuse and suicidal intents, and simultaneously it also supports Freud's ideas about the dominance of the death instinct.

The death instinct was initially described in *Beyond the Pleasure Prin-ciple* (Freud, 1920/1961), and provided a new epistemological framework of the operating forces in the human life. The death instinct (Thanatos), is expressed in aggressive actions and destructiveness, and it represents an unconscious wish "to lead organic life back into the inanimate state" (Freud 1923/1955, p. 41). Clues for the appearance of the death instinct had already appeared in an earlier essay in which Freud explained that the origin of cruelty and egoistical acts lies in archaic impulses searching for gratification (Freud, 1915/1957). This essay was written in a period in which for the first time Europe experienced mass and futile killing (an external expression of the death drive).

Self-inflicted pain and destruction of the body are derivatives of the death instinct which final goal is death (Freud, 1920/1961). In drug addiction, the death instinct operates through gradual destruction of body tissues and functions, when it promises to the addicted individual serenity and effort-lessness. While life constantly demands investment of inner resources and coping, drug addiction is a means for achieving the desired state of complete restfulness in which neither society nor the abuser have any demands towards himself.

The therapeutic interventions derived from this conceptualization of drug addiction include analysis of defences or examination of the repetitive compulsion of drug abuse, because repetition compulsion is one of the expressions of the death instinct (Freud, 1920/1961). However, such therapeutic interventions among drug abusers who incessantly abuse drugs may probably prove inefficient. Attempts of analyzing dream material or asking for free associations may encounter resistances. Soon the therapist will find out that the patients' defences level is quite immature and he might become the subject of projection of aggressive impulses. Most likely, patients who abuse drugs intensively will not be ready to address interpretations or to transference relations. In other words, the classical Freudian conceptualization of the death instinct provides an explanation for the dominance of the destructiveness in the psychic life of drug abusers, but adherence to traditional psychoanalytic technique may lead to impasse. In such cases, the ideas of a Kleinian analyst who treated hard-to-reach patients may prove useful and lead to breakthrough.

Drug addiction as addiction to near-death

In a very mind-provoking article, Joseph (1982) describes a particular group of patients whose mental life are controlled by a malignant type of destructiveness, which reminds addiction to near-death. She describes patients whose internal life is characterized with hopelessness and who overeat, overwork or rarely sleep. This group of patients is involved in activities that seem destined to destroy them mentally and physically (Joseph, 1982), and perhaps Joseph describes a group of patients with addictive or compulsive behaviors. These patients do not look for nirvana or relief from problems, and they are more interested in creating and spreading despair and hopelessness in themselves and in the analyst (Joseph, 1982).

She does mention that some of those patients drink alcohol excessively but does not relate to drug abuse or drug addiction. In my experience, Joseph's ideas are highly relevant for a group of drug abusing patients who intensively uses opioids, cocaine, synthetic cannabinoids and cannabis. The encounter with this group of patients implants despair, frustration and powerlessness because it seems that they do not respond to any therapeutic intervention. Common sayings of therapists who treat such patients are *"there is nothing more to do with these patients"*, *"nothing more could be done"*, *"only hitting rock bottom, will change them"*.

According to Joseph (1982), these patients try to cause the therapist to collude with the despair, and to be harsh, critical and even verbally sadistic towards them. If the therapist indeed reacts in such manner, these patients achieved the wished for triumph since the therapist has lost his analytic balance and his ability to help them. Such patients repeatedly describe their lack of successes and unhappiness with a masochistic excitement, as if they unconsciously attempt to make the analyst be critical towards them or accept their actual despair (Joseph, 1982). In my experience, such situations appear in therapeutic encounters with a group of patients who abuses drugs intensively and the next vignette demonstrates this point.

Danny is a 25-year-old homeless patient who is being treated in an opioid maintenance clinic. He has infectious diseases (HIV, HCV) and he continues to inject cocaine and heroin intensively for over two years. In the last month, he has started to inject drugs into the jugular vein because he can no longer inject drugs into the peripheral veins. His mother lives with his older brother in a remote area in Israel and experiences difficulties in coping with the brother's gambling addiction. In the past, Danny told his therapist that he is very sorry for his brother since the brother helped Danny a lot in difficult times in the past.

THERAPIST: "We received the result of your last urine test. Heroin and cocaine again".
DANNY: "I told you before that it is impossible to be homeless and not to use drugs".
THERAPIST: "You did. However, you started abusing drugs before you ended up on the street. Two years ago, you had your own apartment and you got help from the social services. You did not abuse any drugs. We already have seen that you can live differently".
DANNY: "Yes, but it is hard to live on the streets, my bag was stolen again yesterday, and I cannot find any apartments for rent".
THERAPIST: "In the past year, we searched together apartments for rent on the internet and we agreed that you will check those places, but you did

not do it. Yesterday, I heard a few therapists who asked you why you are homeless for such a long time, and you said that you and I could not find any apartments for rent on the internet".

Danny does not talk.

THERAPIST: "Besides, for more than two months I scheduled you several appointments at the social welfare department which assist homeless people, but you did not arrive once".

DANNY: "I was busy" (smiling).

The therapist is shocked to hear this answer and starts to feel anger.

THERAPIST: "You were so busy that you could not find time for a meeting which aim was to help you find accommodation?!"

DANNY: "I told you that I'm working. I collect metals, I sell it and then I have money".

THERAPIST: "Money for what?! For drugs?! you waste your entire social security disability pension for buying drugs. Do drugs make you feel so good?"

DANNY: "Finding drugs may be hard and the withdrawal can be like hell, but drugs also make people feel good".

THERAPIST: "You inject drugs in dumps, you hangout in crime areas when you were already robbed, you neither arrive to meetings in the social welfare department nor to the immunological clinic where you were supposed to start HIV treatment. You received referral for an emergency room because of necrotic wounds, yet you didn't do a thing".

silence

THERAPIST (RAISES HIS VOICE): "Two years of injecting heroin and cocaine, and recently into the neck. I think that you simply want to die, and you wait until the drugs will kill you. I had warned you that if you will not stop abusing drugs, you will be transferred to another opioid maintenance clinic and now we are going to carry it out. In the next two weeks you will receive your treatment in another clinic, and I hope that during this time you will think thoughtfully about your deeds and about stop abusing drugs".

I think that this example illustrates the vicissitudes of projective identification in this group of patients. The patient succeeds in projecting despair into the therapist, and the therapist acts out of this despair and provides critical interpretation. In this case, when the therapist answered with cynicism to the patient, he colluded with the patient's internal object that enslaved him to a devastating lifestyle. Joseph (1982, p. 136) describes intelligibly this interplay:

the analyst carefully, maybe tactfully, pushes, tries to get the patient's interest or to alert him. The patient briefly responds only quietly to withdraw again and leave the next move to the analyst, and a major piece of psychopathology is acted out in the transference. The patient constantly is pulling back towards the silent kind of deadly paralysis and near complete passivity. When these lively parts of the patient remain so constantly split off it means that his whole capacity for wanting and appreciating, missing, feeling disturbed at losing, etc., the very stuff that makes for real whole object relating is projected and the patient remains with his addiction and without the psychological means of combatting this.

In this kind of projective identification, the despair is so effectively loaded into the analyst until a feeling of internal crushing and paralysis (Joseph, 1982). It seems that in this case, the despair and the powerlessness were so unbearable and threatening that it led to acting out which was expressed with raising the voice at the patient. Joseph (1984) notes that when self-destructiveness is intensified, the patient pushes the therapist into acting out, and Bell (2001) notes that in every interaction which involves projective identification a new object-relation is perpetuated. In this case, perhaps the temporary transference of the patient to another clinic stemmed also from the punitive parts that were projected into the therapist.

In the next lines, there is another clinical vignette taken from a session which took place after Danny's return from the temporary transference.

PATIENT: "I know you for about four years and you never shouted at me".

THERAPIST: "I also thought about it a lot. I think that I felt your despair and your frustration from your addiction and your lifestyle. I understood that you wanted to make me give up on you in a certain sense – not to summon you to meetings, not to help you find accommodation and not to mention you again and again about going to the immunological clinic".

Danny keeps silent

THERAPIST: "And then I thought about your brother and I have remembered that you told me how significant he is for you. It was the only time I saw you cry. I told myself that the reasonable action is to stop abusing drugs and try to help him. But, afterwards I understood that maybe your brother is one of the reasons for the intensive drug abuse".

DANNY: "My brother was always the most stable person in the family. Dad left the family years ago when we were young, and my brother started working to support us. When I started to use drugs, he took me to many rehab centers. Two years ago, he was about to get married but then he had suddenly separated from his girlfriend and started to gamble. He does not stop. Every time we meet, we almost get into a fight. I talked to him a lot, but nothing helps. Our mother is despairing because he constantly asks for money and even steals from her".

THERAPIST: "In these two weeks that you were not in the clinic I understood that you do want to be with your family but at the same time you are very afraid from the consequences of the meeting with your brother. You are afraid from your own aggression".

DANNY: "I endlessly scream at him and I almost kicked him out of the house. I don't know what happened to him! He was always the responsible person in the family! He has debts and he has started to talk with our mother about selling her house in order to get more money. I already threatened him that if he will talk to her again about this issue, I will throw him out of the house. After every conversation with my mother, I see myself going home and hitting him. I called him a few times and I told him that mother is not a healthy woman, and if she will say to me even once that he nags her about giving him money, I will simply kill him. Those drugs are killing me, I hate to use it, it does give me a certain thrill, but after I return to reality, it is the same problems. I do not see any way out".

A week after this session, Danny asked to be transferred temporarily for a month to an opioid maintenance clinic which is in the same town where his family lives. After his return, he said that his brother still gambles, but he will try to stop abusing drugs and will try to help him. According to Joseph (1982), the pull towards life and sanity are also projected into the analyst, and I think that, besides the despair, hope and desire for change were projected into the therapist. However, the therapist understood this only after he colluded with the sadistic and punitive parts of the patient and sent him to receive treatment in a distant clinic. Only after identification with different aspects of the patient's experiences could the therapist see the patient's anxiety from his own aggression and his entrapment in a provocative sado-masochistic fantasy, in which he both hurts and is being hurt (Joseph, 1982).

In the patient's external world, a significant good object becomes a bad one, and simultaneously creates an unbearable internal reality in which he demolishes everything good which remains in his chaotic world. The patient is threatened by both an annihilation anxiety (withdrawal syndrome), by his own aggression and by his own bad objects (anger, despair, frustration and powerlessness). He turns to intensive drug abuse and the needle which penetrates the body in a mixture of excitement and pain transmits him to a phantasmatic territory which phantasy preserves entrapment.

Joseph (1982) found that patients with near-death addiction avoided feeling envious or frustrated nor have they been able to express anger towards the object. Danny's father disappeared when he was young, and the mother had to raise two children by her own. Consequently, he could not express anger toward the missing object nor towards his mother since it was associated with guilt. Additional significant experiences that contributed to his internal chaos occurred during his childhood, when the communist country in which he lived collapsed and all the values he was raised on, lost their significance. Accumulation of personal capital became an accepted norm as well as manifest expressions of bribe. Witnessing events such as buying grades for money by wealthy parents and bribery for avoiding military service led him to withdraw into his internal world.

His mother's attempts to persuade him that success in life demands persistence in school and in work failed. In such situations, there is a withdrawal into a secret world of sexual violence as parts of the self turn one against the other and parts of the body are identified with the offending object. Since childhood, Danny developed a habit of picking at scabs. Such behavior as well as nail-biting and head-banging are accompanied with repetitive mental activity which Joseph (1982) terms 'Chuntering'.

Another variation of 'chuntering' is complaining or grumbling about external objects. Sean, another patient in an opioid maintenance clinic, always complained about the workers he met at different bureaucratic offices and described how, in his next visit there, he would shout out against injustices, and will throw chairs so finally he will receive the proper attention. The workers will call the police, but he will feel victorious since he did not allow the workers to humiliate him. A similar mental activity appeared when he described interactions with patients who threatened him near the clinic. In his phantasy, he used to torture them until they asked him to stop the pain. When I noted his attention to these phantasies, the conversation led to feeling anger towards his mother because she did not protect him from his father's violence. Besides, Sean felt guilty for leaving his home and his little brothers to cope alone with the father's violence.

In my experience, the physical chuntering, which is expressed in masturbational and sexual violence towards the body, is the more prevalent form of chuntering among drug abusers. Investigation of their phantasy world reveals that many of these patients started smoking cannabis as teenagers and then have begun injecting methamphetamines and\or opioids intensively. This form of drug abuse perpetuates life in an internal world without the need of rageful tongue-lashing towards external objects. Cannabis addiction includes rolling cigarettes or preparing bongs, which remind obsessive masturbation. Heroin and cocaine addiction also include a ceremony of preparing the drug and the different tools before the abuse. This activity induces pleasure, but it is also a self-harming behavior because of the incorporation of toxic substances into the body.

Not every form of drug abuse is near-death addiction. Among the drug abusing population, this phenomenon relates to frequent and intensive drug abuse of patients who do not wait for the drug's influence to wear off or for the appearance of withdrawal symptoms, and abuse drugs again. In my opinion, this is near-death addiction, which constitutes an attack on thinking processes and allows avoidance of guilt feelings and ambivalence, which symbolize movement towards the depressive position. The therapeutic encounter with this population may be emotionally annihilating, and although Joseph did not treat drug abusers, she amazingly and accurately described their internal world, the therapist's experience, and the therapeutic dynamic with these patients:

> slowly the picture builds up. The analyst seems to be the only person in the room who is actively concerned about change, about progress, about development, as if all the active parts of the patient have been projected into the analyst.
>
> (Joseph, 1982, p. 137)

Pain, loneliness, despair, and hopelessness are projected into the therapist and cause passivity and paralysis, which preserve the transference relations in every meeting. There is enormous difficulty in holding alive these parts when the therapist feels attacked by the destructive material of the patient who has a speechless dialogue with death. The attack is carried out in two ways – projection of despair and frustration next to exposing the therapist to the physical consequences of the intense drug addiction in sadomasochistic enjoyment. Common examples of the latter kind of attack include skin picking, picking at scabs, showing marks of drug injections, or necrotic wounds, although the therapist asks patients not to do so in his room.

When the picture clears slowly, the therapist indeed comes to a point in which he says to himself that he is the only person in the room who is interested in the cessation of drug abuse and a significant change in the patient's life. Then, he stands before a crossroad – either to say to himself and his environment that nothing would help the patient, or to continue and act upon the living parts that were deposited onto him. I believe that the second option, meaning containing the living parts of the patient and providing appropriate interpretations, is possible only after the therapist has experienced the patient's paralysis and the psychic deadness.

Countertransference and projective identification in treatment of drug abuse and addiction

Countertransference toward drug abusers

In comparison to populations who do not abuse drugs, drug abusing patients are considered a hardcore population for treatment, and one that raises complex countertransferential reactions (Imhof, Hirsch & Terenzi, 1983; Najavits et al., 1995). Countertransference is a term that relates to all thoughts, feelings, and reactions the therapist has toward the patient (Goldstein & Goldberg, 2004). Countertransference includes not only internal reactions, such as feelings, emotions, and thoughts but also external reactions, such as verbal and non-verbal behavior toward the patient (Gelso & Hayes, 2007). In the literature which deals with countertransference towards substance abusing populations, this term receives an extensive interpretation and relates to the entire emotional reactions of therapists and counselors towards their patients (Najavits, Crits-Christoph, & Dierberger, 2000).

In various drug rehabilitation programs around the world, some of the professionals who treat drug abusers have a history of drug abuse. Drug abuse counselors consist of a diverse group with a range of education levels and backgrounds (Nielson, 2016), which could influence their perception of their patients and on the countertransferential reactions. In a study among counselors, recovering counselors tended to see drug abusers as qualitatively different from those who do not abuse drugs and hence themselves as like their patients. In contrast, non-recovering counselors tended to see drug abusers as experiencing a specific variety of a basic human struggle everyone experiences (Nielson, 2016).

Sometimes, counselors may find themselves in a dual relationship. Meaning, in the encounter with the patient, they may find themselves in two roles – in that of the counselor and that of an individual in a recovery process (Doyle, 1997). A counselor who meets his patient in a Narcotics Anonymous meeting is an example of this complexity because it raises anonymity and confidentiality issues. Therefore, counselors should be aware that emotions, thoughts and behaviors which are related to their addiction history may affect their behavior. In a few studies among drug abuse counselors, having addiction history was indeed related to strong feelings during encounters with drug abusers (Davis, 2013; Nakajima & Muto, 2006).

Countertransference reactions may also be related to the therapeutic or rehabilitative framework, which guides therapists, counselors and other professionals in this field. For example, the emergence of harsh confrontation techniques in the mid-20th century in the United States in alcohol treatment centers was laid upon Tiebout's ideas about the role of the helper (White & Miller, 2007). He believed that professionals should help the patient move from superficial verbal compliance towards a process of surrender and personality reconstruction (Tiebout, 1949, 1953, 1961).

Hence, the concept of "break 'em down to build 'em up" was a guiding principle in the encounters with patients despite possible harmful consequences. White and Miller (2007) note that without a theoretical foundation, such an approach can be conceived as unrestrained countertransference and as a violation of professional ethics. Countretransference reactions towards this population can be complex since the treatment and case management include addressing not only to psychic conflicts and interpersonal difficulties, but also to family problems, medical issues (Najavits et al., 2000), and difficulties in activities of daily living.

Patients arrive for treatment in times of crisis and experience withdrawal symptoms. Often, shouting and rude behavior that accompanies such situations are considered a violation of rules, while actually, these are expressions of mental pain. In this context, Forrest (2002) notes that therapists who end sessions or treatment because of such behaviors act out of countertransference. Blaming patients for inappropriate reactions to the expectations of the therapeutic setting is another example of behavior that could stem from countertransference and not from understanding the therapeutic situation and processing of the emotional experience of staff members (Forrest, 2002; Teyber & Holmes McClure, 2011).

In a quite extensive article on this topic, Weiss (1994) notes that the countertransference of substance abuse therapists stems mostly from the patient's behavior. Although Weiss focuses on countertransference toward individuals with alcohol use disorders, his ideas are highly relevant for therapists who treat drug abusers. These patients tend to project the instability of their interpersonal relations on the therapist, who usually reacts with anger. Often, such reactions stem from a lack of control on the patient's condition and expressed in hate and rejection. The interpersonal encounter with this unique population raises negative feelings and ambivalence among therapists because of the attitude and the behavior of the patients. Meaning, the denial of the addiction, under-reporting of drug abuse during the therapy, and disregard towards the rules of the treatment center – all raise negative emotions among therapists (Weiss, 1994). Training staff members for more awareness toward such issues is highly essential, and previous research has shown that knowledge of countertransference and ability to manage it increases patients' success in substance abuse treatment (Seiden, Chandler & Davis, 1994 in Yerks, 2002).

Projective identification in treatment of drug abusers

Concerning the intense emotional countertransference, one of the issues which did not receive much attention in the psychoanalytic literature which dealt with drug abuse and addiction is projective identification. Borderline personality disorder and borderline personality organization frequently co-occur with drug abuse (Hiebler-Ragger, Unterrainer, Rinner, & Kapfhammer, 2016; Trull et al., 2018). In my opinion, much of the complexity of treating drug abusing patients stems from the patient's projective identification and the difficulty in containing and processing the projected material. Persecutory anxiety, annihilation anxiety, envy and greed are projected onto the therapist who finds himself defending against recurrent attacks which are designated to control him, empty him of his goods or turn him to an ally of the narcissistic organization.

Other attacks are carried out through devaluations, unrealistic demandingness and dissatisfaction. Because of the patient's immature object relations, such attacks may suddenly appear and surprise the therapist, who thought that he had managed to straighten the therapeutic alliance. The transitions between such states are quick, and therapists may find themselves one moment thanked and feeling appreciated and on the next moment feeling hated and conceived as an object that wishes to harm the patient.

I will demonstrate this point in the next vignette, which is taken from psychotherapy in an opioid maintenance clinic. Therapists and counselors in such centers have the role of case managers who provide psychosocial treatment and refer their patients to various agencies and services (Hagman, 1994). The work does not focus solely on psychotherapy and involves the coordination of care with a team of professionals in the clinic and the community (Hagman, 1994). Besides, when patients violate the clinic's rules, they are summoned to their therapists and counselors for clarification of their behavior.

Maya is a 47-year-old patient who is involved in various behavioral transgressions in the clinic, such as violence and selling benzodiazepines to other patients. Her parents refuse to be in touch with her as well as her 20-year-old son. Her urine tests indicated cocaine abuse and the psychosocial treatment focused both on cessation of drug abuse and the alienation from her family. Another goal was helping the patient to make suitable payment arrangements of her debts with the municipality.

THERAPIST: "I called you since lately you behave inappropriately and shout on staff members".

MAYA: "I don't know what you're talking about. You all blame me for nothing".

THERAPIST: "A few staff members approached me about this issue. Recently, I have also noticed that you are more nervous. Can it be because of cocaine abuse?"

MAYA: "What cocaine? I didn't use anything. The staff members here do not do a damn thing for the patients".

THERAPIST: "I can see that you are angry, but where is your responsibility for your behavior?"

MAYA: "I'm already one year in treatment, but I'm not progressing. What do you do for me?"

THERAPIST: "In the last year, you mostly complained about your debts. We talked to the municipality and we arrived at an arrangement, but you don't pay the monthly pays, so what do you expect?!"

MAYA: "I got the electricity cut again".

THERAPIST: "We talked to them a week ago, and you were supposed to pay a payment. Did you pay?"

MAYA: "No, why do you think that I have any money?"

THERAPIST: "It seems that you have money for cocaine. Look, we try to solve the problems gradually. At the beginning of the treatment, you said that you want to settle your debts. I wrote you letters about your financial status, and you were supposed only to arrive at the customer service, but you didn't even arrive there. Look Maya, I see the difficulties you experience, and I do want to help you, but you are supposed to arrive to the municipality with my referrals. They called a few days ago and said that you did not arrive. Yet, you have time to sell here medications or to shout at staff members".

MAYA (SHOUTING): "You and all the others here receive money for doing nothing! You sit on your butts all day...you don't have a clue about what I'm going through!"

Maya continued to shout and emptied her entire bag on the floor while cursing the therapist and the entire clinic. The therapist was amazed by Maya's aggression when suddenly she tore her pearl necklace from her neck and threw it in the room as she continues blaming the therapist in all her problems. As the pearls scattered across the room, Maya made her way out and said to her therapist that he is worthless and does not help her, and only harms her. During Maya's acting out, the therapist felt how evil fragments spread in the room and aim to annihilate him. He was completely confused since only a week ago, Maya brought him a flower bouquet and thanked him for his help. Then, he felt that he could not stay in the room and went out, recalling how in his previous work with sex offenders, he felt emotionally flooded at the end of the day after encounters with evil.

In supervision, the therapist understood that his associations during the incident reflect Maya's internal reality and the quick transitions between his perception as a good and then a bad object. In the two months prior to this session, with the encouragement of the therapist, Maya tried to contact her father after a long disconnection. She felt much anger towards him and blamed him for not caring for her during most of her life. Besides, during that period, When Maya brought the therapist flowers and thanked him for his help, the therapist understood that there is an erotic transference but decided not to discuss with the patient this issue because he thought that such a complex issue should be addressed later in therapy.

Perhaps if the therapist had indeed chosen to relate to the erotic transference, he could have helped her in understanding her internal world and reduce some of the anxiety. Addressing her gesture could reduce some of her innate aggression, frustration, and help her see herself also as a good object in contrast to the negative comments she received throughout her life. In any case, this vignette demonstrates the therapist's difficulties in surviving the destructiveness and the persecutory anxiety projected onto him. The violent attacks on the therapist and his alpha function disturb his ability to process raw material and returning it to the patient in a digestible form. This vignette also demonstrates the intense transference relations and why it is so essential to address the latent contents which appear during the treatment.

Transference focused psychotherapy as a proper treatment for drug abusers

Such vignettes emphasize the intense transference relations and the patients' pathology of personality organization. Therefore, a treatment modality which directly addresses such issues might prove useful. Transference Focused Psychotherapy (TFP) is specific psychoanalytic psychotherapy for patients with severe personality disorders and borderline personality organization (Kernberg, Yeomans, Clarkin, & Levy, 2008). The theoretical premise which underlies this psychotherapy method centers on identity diffusion and predominance of aggressive internalized object relations over idealized ones. These patients suffer from a failure of psychological integration and ego fixation and hence the use of primitive defence mechanisms, such as projective identification, devaluation and splitting. Additional characteristics include inability to establish and maintain stable intimate relationships, incapacity to accurately assess the emotional state of the self and others in-depth, and significant difficulties to persist in work (Yeomans, Clarkin, & Kernberg, 2015).

TFP is a manualized, evidence-based treatment that focuses on helping patients to advance to an integrated internal world through the analysis of their ongoing experience of their relationship with the therapist (Clarkin, Levy, Lenzenweger, & Kernberg, 2007). Much like Dialectic-Behavioral Therapy (DBT, Linehan, 1993), TFP focuses on behavioral changes and cessation of self-destructive behaviors. However, unlike DBT it uses techniques of clarification, confrontation, and interpretation that are used within the evolving transference relationship between the patient and the therapist (Yeomans, Delany, & Levy, 2017).

TFP begins with establishing a treatment contract, which includes general guidelines and delineating the patient's and therapist's responsibilities and roles in the therapy (Kernberg et al., 2008). In the first step of therapy, the therapist helps the patient to clarify his experience and to put it into words. In the second step, confrontation, the therapist calls into the patient's attention the contradictory nature of his experiences. In the third step, the therapist interprets the defensive function of the split-off parts to increase awareness of the impact of unconscious material on the patient's life (Yeomans et al., 2015; Zerbo, Cohen, Bielska, & Caligor, 2013).

TFP may prove valuable and efficient for the treatment of drug abusing populations since many patients are characterized by borderline personality organization. Second, it focuses on managing self-destructive behaviors to facilitate better behavioral control and affect regulation (Levy, Meehan, & Yeomans, 2012). Third, this approach does not focus solely on intrapsychic material and relates to conflicts that appear during the treatment, even if they are not transference-dominant at that point (Kernberg et al., 2008). Since the disturbed object relations of the patients appear in almost any interpersonal, social or occupational settings, the therapist has much clinical material.

The next vignette is a common situation in OMT clinics and other drug abuse treatment centers where patients are required to provide urine tests. When these tests indicate positive results for various drugs, the therapist or the counselor summons the patient to clarify this point. Such situations have an explosive potential once the patient denies any drug abuse or does not ready to acknowledge his responsibility. Such situations relate directly to the trust between the patient, the therapist and the entire treatment setting, and they may bear unpleasant consequences for patients with take-home doses in opioid maintenance clinics.

THERAPIST: "I called you because your recent drug test indicates drug abuse".

PATIENT: "It's a mistake. I'm not using any drugs".

THERAPIST: "I did not say that you used. I said that a positive drug test had arrived and by your reaction, it looks like it annoyed you".

PATIENT: "Yes. What is this nonsense? I have already heard from other patients that you tend to confuse between the patients' urine tests".

THERAPIST: "I was also surprised when the result of this test had arrived and that's why I called the laboratory and asked them to examine it again. It was positive for drug abuse".

PATIENT: "So, what's now?"

THERAPIST: "I'm interested in hearing your explanation".

PATIENT: "There is nothing to explain".

THERAPIST: "Look, there is a drug test which indicated drug abuse and I'm interested in hearing you".

The patient keeps quiet.

THERAPIST: "This situation saddens me a lot, you know the clinic's rules. You know that the sanctions on positive drug tests include daily arrival for to the clinic and temporary cancellation of your privileges".

PATIENT: "Why do you cancel my privileges? I thought that you're in my favor, and you are interested in my progress".

THERAPIST: "I am very interested in your progression and I'm happy for your achievements. Nevertheless, your last drug test indicates drug abuse and we temporarily cancel privileges because of positive drug urine tests".

PATIENT: "I know that there are staff members who want to fail me, I didn't think that you're one of them".

THERAPIST: "You're actually telling me that before this incident, I was on your side and I was happy in your successes But, after this drug test, you are saying that I'm against you. The staff members, including me are all interested in your recovery. There are not any groups among the staff. Sometimes, patients think that a staff member who takes the urine tests or their therapist plot against them because they asked them to provide a urine test, but they are simply doing their job. This is our best indication for knowing if patients abuse drugs and to offer them help".

PATIENT: "So you're blaming me for using drugs?"

THERAPIST: "I do not blame you. I hear you say that I want you to fail or that I do not want you to succeed".

PATIENT: "Until now, you did not talk to me like this".

THERAPIST: "like what?"

PATIENT: "Disgustingly".

THERAPIST: "Until this moment, you had negative urine tests and we never had addressed this issue. When we referred to this issue today, you became angry. I think that there is a question of responsibility here and are you ready to take responsibility for this relapse. Cancellation of privileges is not a personal action against you, and the clinic's rules apply to all patients. I remind you that when you entered the clinic you received a delineated explanation about the rules. The fact that I sit and talk to you on non-pleasant issues and sanctions does not say that I'm against you. I feel that you're angry at me from the moment that I raised the issue of the positive drug test today and you think that I want to fail you. Yet, I feel that you know that you're important to me".

SILENCE OF A FEW SECONDS.

PATIENT: "I'm such a failure...".

THERAPIST: "What do you mean?"

PATIENT: "I thought that it would not come out in the urine test...I cleaned my house and I found some weed. I was upset because I had a fight with my boyfriend. I hesitated a lot if to throw it, but finally, I smoked. I'm such a failure. I cannot cope with stress. This is not the first time that I relapse. I'm tired of it. I cannot hold a steady job. My mother always told me that nothing good would come out of me".

TFP facilitates the (re)activation in the treatment of the patient's split-off internalized object relations that are then observed and interpreted in the transference (Kernberg et al., 2008). The conditions of treatment facilitate the reactivation of internalized object relations in the here and now, and TFP interventions may prove efficient because such enactments appear during therapeutic sessions in opioid maintenance clinics. The borderline personality organization is characterized by multiple split-off object relations, positive and negative, as each of them reflects a dyadic unit of a self-representation, an object-representation and a dominant affect linking them.

In this vignette appears a dyad of blaming mother and a defenceless child when anger is the affect which links them. The therapist tries to clarify the patient's emotional experience, while the patient uses primitive defence mechanisms during the entire dialogue. The conversation includes clarifications of the split-off representations of the therapist through confrontations and attempts to remain neutral and avoid blaming the patient directly and bluntly for the drug abuse. An empathic attitude is essential when inviting the patient's observing ego to relate to the interpretations of the conflict that arises during treatment. Following the empathic comment, the patient had identified with the object relation which was previously projected onto the therapist and provided important unconscious material. A significant aim of TFP is to change the patients' psychological structure through the analysis of transference relations. However, as therapists who work with drug abusers know, the road towards integration is paved with numerous devaluations, splittings, frustration and impasses.

References

Bell, D. (2001). Projective identification. In C. Bronstein (Ed.), *Kleinian theory: A contemporary perspective* (pp. 125–147). Whurr Publishers.

Bramness, J. G., & Rognli, E. B. (2016). Psychosis induced by amphetamines. *Current Opinions in Psychiatry, 29*(4), 236–241.

Chopra, N., & Marasa, L. H. (2017). The opioid epidemic. *International Journal of Psychiatry in Medicine, 52*(2), 196–201.

Clarkin, J. F., Levy, K. N., Lenzenweger, M. F., & Kernberg, O. F. (2007). Evaluating three treatments for borderline personality disorder: A multiwave study. *American Journal of Psychiatry, 164*(6), 922–928.

Davis, M. (2013). *Chemical dependency counselors' perceived countertransference and its relationship to personal experience with substance use (master's thesis).* The College at Brockport, State University of New York.

Doyle, K. (1997). Substance abuse counselors in recovery: Implications for the ethical issue of dual relationships. *Journal of Counseling and Development, 75*(6), 428–432.

Forrest, G. G. (2002). *Countertransference in chemical dependency counseling.* The Haworth Press.

Freud, S. (1915/1957). Instincts and their vicissitudes. In J. Strachey (Ed.), *The standard edition of the complete psychological works of Sigmund Freud* (vol. XIV, pp. 109–140). The Hogarth Press.

Freud, S. (1920/1961). *Beyond the pleasure principle.* (J. Strachey, Ed.). W. W. Norton & Co.

Freud, S. (1923/1955). The Ego and the Id. In J. Strachey (Ed.), *The standard edition of the complete psychological works of Sigmund Freud* (vol. XVIII, pp. 1–283). The Hogarth Press.

Gelso, J. C., & Hayes, J. A. (2007). *Counter transference and the therapist's inner experience: Perils and possibilities.* Lawrence Erlbaum Associates.

Goldstein, W. N., & Goldberg, S. T. (2004). *Using the transference in psychotherapy.* Jason Aronson.

Goyal, H., Awad, H., & Ghali, J. (2017). Role of Cannabis in cardiovascular disorders. *Journal of Thoracic Disease, 9*(7), 2079–2092.

Hagman, G. (1994). Methadone maintenance counseling: Definition, principles, components. *Journal of Substance Abuse Treatment, 11*(5), 405–413.

Havakuk, O., Rezkalla, S. H., & Kloner, R. A. (2017). The cardiovascular effects of cocaine. *Journal of American College of Cardiology, 70*(1), 101–113.

Hiebler-Ragger, M., Unterrainer, H. F., Rinner, A., & Kapfhammer, H. P. (2016). Insecure attachment styles and increased borderline personality organization in substance use disorders. *Psychopathology, 49*(5), 341–344.

Imhof, J., Hirsch, R., & Terenzi, R. (1983). Countertransferential and attitudinal considerations in the treatment of drug abuse and addiction. *International Journal of the Addictions, 18*(4), 491–510.

Indave, B. I., Sordo, L., Bravo, M. J., Sarasa-Renedo, A., Fernández-Balbuena, S., De la Fuente, L., Sonego, M., & Barrio, G. (2018). Risk of stroke in prescription and other amphetamine-type stimulants use: A systematic review. *Drug and Alcohol Review, 37*(1), 56–69.

Joseph, B. (1982). Addiction to near-death. In M. Feldman, & E. B. Spillius (Eds.), *Psychic equilibrium and psychic change: Selected papers of Betty Joseph* (pp. 127–138). Routledge, 1991.

Joseph, B. (1984). Projective identification: Some clinical aspects. In M. Feldman, & E. B. Spillius (Eds.), *Psychic equilibrium and psychic change: Selected papers of Betty Joseph* (pp. 168–180). Routledge, 1991.

Kernberg, O. F., Yeomans, F. E., Clarkin, J. F., & Levy, K. N. (2008). Transference focused psychotherapy: Overview and update. *International Journal of Psychoanalysis, 89*(3), 601–620.

Levy, K. N., Meehan, K. B., & Yeomans, F. E. (2012). An update and overview of the empirical evidence for transference-focused psychotherapy and other psychotherapies for borderline personality disorder. In R. A. Levy, J. S. Ablon, & H. Kächele (Eds.), *Psychodynamic psychotherapy research: Evidence-based practice and practice-based evidence* (pp. 139–167). Humana Press.

Linehan, M. M. (1993). *Cognitive-behavioral treatment of borderline personality disorder.* Guilford Press.

Najavits, L. M., Crits-Christoph, P., & Dierberger, A. (2000). Clinicians' impact on substance abuse treatment. *Substance Use and Misuse, 35*, 2161–2190.

Najavits, L. M., Griffin, M. L., Luborsky, L., Frank, A., Weiss, R. D., Liese, B. S., Thompson, H., Nakayama, E., Siqueland, L., Daley, D., & Onken, L. S. (1995). Therapists' emotional reactions to substance abusers: A new questionnaire and initial findings. *Psychotherapy: Theory, Research, Practice, Training, 32*(4), 669–677.

Nakajima, Y., & Muto, T. (2006). Impact of compensatory secondary control on the recollection of emotions and the self in respect to past adversity. *Japanese Psychological Research, 48*, 46–53.

Nielson, E. M. (2016). Substance abuse counselors' recovery status and self-schemas: Preliminary implications for empirically supported treatment implementation. *Journal of Drug and Alcohol Research, 5*, 235982.

Royal College of Psychiatrists. (2016). *Cannabis and mental health.* Retrieved from http://www.rcpsych.ac.uk/healthadvice/problemsdisorders/cannabis.aspx (accessed 14th January 2020).

Sanders, T., Cunningham, S., Platt, L., Grenfell, P., & Macioti, P. G. (2017). *Reviewing the occupational risks of sex workers in comparison to other 'risky' professions.* University of Leicester.

Sordo, L., Indave, B. I., Barrio, G., Degenhardt, L., de la Fuente, L., & Bravo, M. J. (2014). Cocaine use and risk of stroke: A systematic review. *Drug and Alcohol Dependence, 142*, 1–13.

Teyber, E., & Holmes McClure, F. (2011). *Interpersonal process in therapy: An integrative model* (6th Ed.). Brooks/Cole.

Tiebout, H. (1949). The act of surrender in the therapeutic process, with special reference to alcoholism. *Quarterly Journal of Studies on Alcohol, 10*(1), 48–58.

Tiebout, H. (1953). Surrender versus compliance in therapy, with special reference to alcoholism. *Quarterly Journal of Studies on Alcohol, 14*(1), 58–68.

Tiebout, H. (1961). Alcoholics Anonymous: An experiment of nature. *Quarterly Journal of Studies on Alcohol, 22*, 52–68.

Trull, T. J., Freeman, L. K., Vebares, T. J., Choate, A. M., Helle, A. C., & Wycoff, A. M. (2018). Borderline personality disorder and substance use disorders: An updated review. *Borderline Personality Disorder and Emotion Dysregulation, 5*, 15.

Weiss, R. (1994). Countertransference issues in treating the alcoholic patient: Institutional and clinician reactions. In E. Levin, & R. Weiss (Eds.), *The dynamics and treatment of alcoholism* (pp. 407–420). Jason Aronson.

White, W., & Miller, W. (2007). The use of confrontation in addiction treatment: History, science and time for change. *Counselor, 8*(4), 12–30.

Wilcox, H. C., Conner, K. R., & Caine, E. D. (2004). Association of alcohol and drug use disorders and completed suicide: An empirical review of cohort studies. *Drug and Alcohol Dependence, 76*(Suppl7), S11–S19.

Yeomans, F. E., Clarkin, J. F., & Kernberg, O. F. (2015). *Transference-focused psychotherapy for borderline personality disorder: A clinical guide.* American Psychiatric Publishing.

Yeomans, F. E., Delaney, J. C., & Levy, K. N. (2017). Behavioral activation in TFP: The role of the treatment contract in transference-focused psychotherapy. *Psychotherapy, 54*(3), 260–266.

Yerks, S. (2002). *Countertransference knowledge and substance abuse treatment* (Master's thesis, St. Catherine University and University of St. Thomas, St. Paul, Minnesota). Retrieved from https://sophia.stkate.edu.

Zerbo, E., Cohen, S., Bielska, W., & Caligor, E. (2013). Transference-focused psychotherapy in the general psychiatry residency: A useful and applicable model for residents in acute clinical settings. *Psychodynamic Psychiatry, 41*(1), 163–181.

Chapter 7

Methadone maintenance treatment (MMT) as transitional phenomena*

David Potik, Miriam Adelson and Shaul Schreiber

"However, there are many patients who need us to be able to give them a capacity to use us. This for them is the analytic task. In meeting the needs of such patients, we shall need to know what I am saying here about our survival of their destructiveness. A backcloth of unconscious destruction of the analyst is set up and we survive it, or alternatively, here is yet another analysis interminable".

(Winnicott, 1971, p. 94)

Methadone maintenance treatment (MMT) is a very effective treatment for opioid dependence (Kaplan & Sadock, 1998; Marsch, 1998; Sees et al., 2000). The object of MMT is to bring about a cessation of the use of opioids and other street-drugs with addictive potential (sedative-hypnotic drugs and minor tranquillizers). MMT is useful in both reducing the risk of HIV and hepatitis infections resulting from the drug addiction as well as the criminal activity which accompanies drug addicts' lifestyles (Carroll, 1997; Kaplan & Sadock, 1998; Marsch, 1998). Psychosocial counseling is an integral component of MMT, and it deals with personal, family and employment problems to achieve improvement in functioning and a return to a productive lifestyle (Ball & Ross, 1991). Psychosocial counseling is an important ingredient of MMT (Ball & Ross, 1991; Hubbard et al., 1989; McLellan, Woody, Luborsky, & Gohel, 1988; Preston, Umbricht, & Epstein, 2000), and evidence shows that MMT with psychosocial counseling is more effective than methadone maintenance alone (McLellan, Arndt, Metzger, Woody, & Obrien, 1993).

Studies in methadone programs indicate that patients who receive psychotherapy in addition to counseling show major advancement in their lives, enter the job market and stop using drugs (Luborsky, McLellan, Woody, Obrien, & Auerbach, 1985; Woody et al., 1983). Many studies point to the

* This chapter was previously published as a journal article: Potik, D., Adelson, M., & Schreiber, S. (2007). Drug addiction from a psychodynamic perspective: Methadone maintenance treatment (MMT) as transitional phenomena. *Psychology and Psychotherapy: Theory, Research and Practice*, *80*, 311–325. © 2010 John Wiley and Sons, reprinted by permission.

efficiency and necessity of psychotherapy in methadone programs but do not elaborate on the contents and the dynamic processes, which occur in patients' lives during therapy. This chapter analyzes how psychotherapeutic interventions may be implemented among drug addicts in methadone centers and programs. The major premise of this work is that patients undergo certain changes in their lifestyles and behavior, which are parallel to transitional phenomena, when the setting is being used as an intermediate area of experience (potential space) while both methadone and the therapist serve as transitional objects.

Psychodynamic approach to drug addiction

The psychoanalytic literature offers many theories regarding the etiology and treatment of drug addiction (Glover, 1932a, 1932b; Goodman, 1993; Hagman, 1995; Kohut, 1977; Limentani, 1968; Rado, 1928; Wieder & Kaplan, 1969). Hagman (1995) and Jerry (1997) have tried to integrate psychoanalytic and psychodynamic thought in counseling and psychotherapy of drug addicts. Hagman (1995) offers a psychodynamic psychology of MMT using the self psychology perspective. He (Hagman, 1995) explains the selfobject function of methadone in the repair of self-deficits, specifically in the area of affects regulation, and he expands the dynamics of self-repair to the relational and pragmatic 'context of care' of methadone maintenance.

Jerry (1997) offers an object relations approach based on Malan's (1979) and Winnicott's (1965a, 1965b, 1968, 1986, 1988) work and demonstrates its relevance in a case study of a young woman using cocaine (not in an MMT program). Although Jerry uses many of Winnicott's important concepts, he does not mention one of Winnicott's most important contributions to psychoanalytic theory and psychotherapy – the idea of the transitional object. We believe that this idea and Winnicott's theory of child development may suggest one more possible explanation (to the so many existing ones) to the addiction phenomena and may be very helpful in the treatment of some drug addicts.

Drug addiction as absolute dependence

Winnicott (1953, 1971) sees addictions to drugs, alcohol and food and to sexual promiscuity as attempts to re-find the lost object through direct physical gratification. In that sense, addictions are similar to transitional phenomena because they represent the mother and yet are recognized as not being the mother (Summers, 1994; Winnicott, 1971). Unlike the child's transitional possessions, addictions are not given up naturally because they are regressive response to deprivation and an effort to regain an earlier relationship with the mother before deprivation. Consequently, rather than moving the developmental process forward, addictions tend to remain fixated (Summers, 1994; Winnicott, 1971).

Winnicott (1953) describes addiction to transitional objects in a seven-years-old child who obsessively dealt with strings to deny separation from his depressive mother. Following Winnicott's advice, the mother talked about the subject with her child and found him to be eager to talk about his relations with her and his fear of a lack of contact with her. She went over all the separations she could think of and soon the string play ceased. The mother's most significant comment was that it was not just her leaving but her lack of contact with him because of her complete preoccupation with other matters (Winnicott, 1971).

Four years after this incident, the father reported a new phase of string preoccupation, associated with a new depressive episode of the mother. The child played with a number of teddy bears, which represented children to him and to which he gave a lot of affection. Any attempt to treat the child away from home was impractical because he kept running back to his home. During adolescence, the boy developed new addictions, especially to drugs, and could not leave home to receive an education (Winnicott, 1971).

There is an evident similarity between drug addicts and infants in the absolute dependence phase. In Winnicott's view (1960), absolute dependence is the first phase during development, in which the infant is not aware of an external mother that satisfies his needs and is not aware of his dependence on the environment. The infant lives in a magical world (detached from reality) in which needs are self satisfied. His experience lacks any sense of continuity in himself or others and the time factor is missing. The pleasure principle is a central characteristic in the infant's magical and omnipotent world and all his actions are aimed toward getting satisfaction (Winnicott, 1960).

Among drug addicts, the equivalence of an absolute dependence on 'an external mother' is the dependency upon various illicit and legal drugs. Many drug addicts deny their addiction and do not admit that their life had become uncontrollable. Common phrases among drug addicts like "*I can stop it whenever I want*" or "*I am not addicted, and can manage without drugs*" are parallel to the infants' denial and lack of awareness. Constant pursuit after drugs is a pursuit after constant pleasure and a will to create a perfect world without suffering and pain, similar to the primary world of the infant. In both cases, there is a lack of awareness regarding the environment, self-directedness and centering on personal needs when the reality is out of the experience (Fassino, Daga, Delsedime, Rogna, & Boggio, 2004; Le Bon et al., 2004).

The withdrawal syndrome is a reaction of the body to the cessation or reduction of drugs after a prolonged abuse and contains physical and psychological symptoms like tremor, stress, pain, diarrhea, agitation and restlessness (Kaplan & Sadock, 1998). The psychological component of withdrawal is actually an exposure to reality, which threatens the pleasure experience of the abuser and is similar to annihilation anxiety and external threat on the omnipotent world of the infant. In the same manner as withdrawal is accompanied by physical symptoms of psychomotor agitation and strong mental dependence, absence of the mother brings restlessness among infants (Winnicott, 1960).

In this situation, fantasies appear, which protect against the implosion of the reality into the personal world, and every experience in the external reality is interpreted and adapted according to them and brought to the omnipotent range. Omnipotent defences in this phase result in the development of borderline and narcissistic personality disorders (Summers, 1994). These defences help substance abusers to survive, but more than anything, they protect the loss of a world with perfect satisfaction.

Cessation of addiction to drugs is a process, which is parallel to transition from absolute dependence to relative dependence. Relative dependence includes developmental processes comprised of breaking of the omnipotence of the absolute dependence, the acceptance of reality and the ambivalence toward objects (Summers, 1994). The first mission in this phase is the management of a separation anxiety (from the mother) and awareness that the infant cannot provide his/her own needs. Primary coping with craving phenomena after admission to a methadone program and some degree of recognition that the current lifestyle cannot continue can (and should) be the first objectives in MMT counseling. Ambivalence is a later objective, since the outlook of drug addicts is characterized by a huge split between good and bad, and there is a long way to go until the patients recognize the therapists and counselors as both assisting entities and as punishing ones.

Relapses are frequent at the beginning of entering an MMT program, although patients are repeatedly informed that they will not feel any euphoria if they take heroin with methadone. Some patients may switch from heroin use to sedative-hypnotics abuse, possibly as a means of self-medication of the negative feelings that flood them after heroin cessation, or because of unwillingness to relinquish the pleasure experience. Minor tranquilizers' (or sedative-hypnotics') abuse for MMT patients is parallel to addiction to a new transitional object and unwillingness to totally depart from absolute dependence.

Methadone as transitional object

Various medications (most sedative-hypnotics, some antidepressants and even some antipsychotics) can serve as transitional objects (Adelman, 1985; Gutheil, 1982; Hausner, 1985; Schlierf, 1983; Shred, 1963) since they are readily available, reduce anxiety, provide relaxation and can be used before sleep, like children's usage of transitional objects (Winnicott, 1953, 1971). Methadone itself can serve as a transitional object since it reduces pain and stops withdrawal syndrome. Methadone is an opioid agonist drug that interacts with the same receptors as heroin, and its action lasts 24–36 hours (Kaplan & Sadock, 1998). Unlike heroin, methadone does not induce acute physical or emotional reactions, and oral daily dosage allows physiological stability without tolerance (Kaplan & Sadock, 1998).

Methadone can serve as a transitional object since it acts on two major fields and saves many worries for patients in MMT programs and for drug addicts who consume methadone unofficially. On the physical level, withdrawal symptoms and agitation cease, and on the mental level, many anxieties that exist during addiction dissipate. Drug addicts constantly worry about finance of the next dose of drug, and frequently need to engage in criminal activity in order to obtain the money, leading to constant fear of entanglement with the law enforcement agencies.

MMT provides release from a world of drug addiction and sedative-hypnotics trade and abuse, selling of personal and family objects for financing of drugs and entanglement with law enforcement agencies. Transitional phenomena can occur in MMT programs especially because of the object consistency it provides for patients with an extremely chaotic lifestyle. The MMT clinic is actually a special setting, with physicians who constantly follow-up the patients' condition, their blood tests and methadone dosages, and counselors who accept each one of them whenever not feeling well. This creates a perception of a special place, focused only on patients' health and well-being. These characteristics distinguish between MMT clinics and other harm-reduction or abstinence programs.

The pouring of methadone right under the patients' eyes and not behind a counter is an important component in treatment, since patients can see that no one tries to manipulate their treatment. Patients approach the pouring desk, receive the methadone dose, drink it and receive take-home doses in small bottles. Many patients report that they find themselves touching these bottles (in the purse or pocket) times and again when passing by places associated with drug abuse and relax. Patients report that this happens whenever they happen to see drug addicts looking for drugs or in a poor medical condition. These reports remind the child's interaction with the transitional object especially in times of anxiety and depression (Winnicott, 1971).

MMT creates the predisposition for counseling and for mental and behavioral changes among patients. Methadone does not induce euphoria, and one of the main objects of counseling is to cope with the mental dependency (craving). The absence of drugs and lack of euphoria arouse high intensity of negative emotions during counseling since, for the first time without artificial means, patients have to cope with disturbing contents and painful feelings, which were repressed for a long time.

The setting as the intermediate area of experience

Patients with borderline personality disorder live in an intermediate area of infancy in which the child goes back and forth between merger and separation. This intermediate area may be seen as parallel to a transitional period between substance use (absolute dependence) and a world without substance use (relative dependence). The intermediate area of experience exists between oral eroticism and true object relations, and includes transitional objects and transitional phenomena (Winnicott, 1971). The counseling room and the setting can be seen as a potential space in which there is an interplay that allows maturation.

The intermediate area of experience is a part which cannot be ignored and to which both inner reality and external life contribute (Winnicott, 1971).

> It is an area that is not challenged, because no claim is made on its behalf because except it shall exist as a resting- place for the individual engaged in the perpetual human task of keeping inner and outer reality separate yet interrelated.
>
> (Winnicott, 1971, p. 3)

The counseling is affected by both an inner and an external reality, but it has to stay neutral and objective resting-place and as a haven against dangers in the external and internal world (Greenson, 1978). For example, Allen, a 26-year-old patient, homeless, used to come to the clinic neglected and dirty. On the first meeting, when asked about his appearance, he said that he is homeless and sleeps in some friends' house. Allen repeatedly said that he does not feel comfortable talking to the therapist because of his looks. When first introduced to the setting, it was emphasized that he was welcomed no matter how he looked but, he did not come to sessions regularly and frequently avoided his therapist in the clinic.

During the brief sessions he did attend, Allen did not talk much. One day, while the therapist was sitting alone in his office, Allen opened the door and looked inside. When he saw that there was nobody else inside, he sat down quickly in the chair and cried for a few minutes. He then wiped his tears and left the room without uttering a word. In an analytic setting, holding provides space and time and allows for the patient's 'being' (Khan, 1969; we believe that space comes before time). We do not know if Allen felt a sense of being, but we do believe that his action resulted from conceiving the function of counseling or the setting as a resting-place from external reality and as a place in which his inner reality will not be judged or ridiculed.

The time factor in counseling and therapy is not entirely in the counselor's hands, and it is composed of many components, such as the patient's will to participate in counseling and/or his emotional maturation. The therapist can provide a space in which holding can be the starting point of counseling, and we believe that a non-verbal message is transmitted in this setting. This message is, that patients can express their genuine feelings during counseling and that there is a place to which they can come without disguises, as they frequently do while in prison or in their regular interpersonal relationships.

When planning the setting of drug addicts and patients with borderline personality organization, it is important to introduce the counseling as a non-judgmental place that emphasizes confidentiality. Many addicts spent many years in courts, and in prison and in evasion from law enforcement agencies, so they really lack some feeling of constancy. Heroin does not provide constancy because its influence dissipates after four-to-five hours, and drug addicts have to face another day of struggle to obtain "the next dose". Their struggles represent an attempt to return to the absolute dependence phase.

'Object consistency' is not a familiar concept to these patients because usually their lives are scattered with long histories of neglect, abuse, lack of parental figures during childhood or constant transition between dormitories or adoptive families. It is very important that the counselor present himself as the person responsible for treating the patient's problems, including those of emotional distress and security in social situations. The non-verbal message is that there is a place in which the counselor will be available for the patient and where the patient can address the counselor on any matter.

The therapist as a transitional object

A few studies (Gunderson, 1996; Last, 1988; Rosenthal, 1981) point to the importance of transitional phenomena in the treatment of clinical populations such as children with behavioral disorders, girls with eating disorders and patients with borderline personality disorder. However, we found no study mentioning transitional phenomena among drug addicts. Many addicts have cluster B personality traits or personality disorders (American Psychiatric Association, 2000), or they have a borderline personality organization (Kernberg, 1975). Many cases of borderline personality disorders fit Winnicott's (1960) concept of trauma in the phase of relative dependence (Summers, 1994). Overwhelming dependence ties and acting out that are so characteristic of such patients can be seen as efforts to 'lay claim' to something in the world and to use people or things as transitional objects in an effort to regain a lost maternal bond (Summers, 1994, p. 171).

The relation of the infant to the transitional object is parallel to pathological narcissism, which characterizes borderline and narcissistic personality disorders (Kernberg, 1975). Drug addicts also display pathological narcissism since they tend to see people around them either as 'objects with supply', which can be extracted, or as 'empty and worthless objects'. Drug addicts experience objects in their control course and as such they can be used freely. They often sell personal and family objects without permission of the parents or ask them for money but do not admit that the money is for financing drugs. Drug addicts have developed behavior patterns of exploitation, lying, deceit and manipulability toward the environment in order to obtain drugs.

Many addicts promise their parents that the current drug abuse is the last time and that they would stop, and many parents cannot bear to see their children suffer (withdrawal symptoms) and give them money.

Many addicts have borderline personality organization, which manifests in split ego states that alter frequently and lack integration capacity, which allows them to see people as 'whole'. These patients cannot conceive the counselor both as an assisting person and as a punishing one (difficulty to conceive the counselor as a 'feeding breast' and as a 'frustrating one'). There is only a small capacity for empathy, and their primitive defence mechanisms such as denial, splitting (which represents ego weakness), projective identification and idealization and devaluation characterize borderline personality organization (Kernberg, 1975).

Many transferences during counseling and therapy are characterized by fluent projections of either 'all bad' or 'all good' object images, which preserve dangerous world and threatening images. These object images protect against this dangerous world and there are lying and megalomaniac self-images, whereas underneath lie inferiority feelings. An avenging tendency to destroy frustrating objects is another common characteristic of patients with borderline personality disorder (Kernberg, 1975) and drug addicts. This avenging tendency is manifested through verbal or physical violence toward counselors after ruling of rights. Transferences and behavior patterns of patients may be seen as attempts to control the counselor as transitional object in attempt to regain a lost maternal bond.

Drug addicts and people with borderline personality disorder look for a transitional object, and the counselor's therapeutic role is to adapt as much as possible to the patient's longing for a gratifying object (Summers, 1994). In this way, the therapist places himself in the position of a transitional object and represents a symbol of maternal gratification to be discarded when no longer needed. This type of adaptation unblocks the arrested maturational process (Summers, 1994).

The following is a description of a few meetings of psychodynamic psychotherapy of a 27-year-old client who presented to the first author with a history of a prolonged heroin addiction, accompanied by snorting and intravenous use of cocaine and benzodiazepines. Although permission was obtained from the client to use her material, certain details, including names and locations, are disguised to ensure confidentiality. This case study demonstrates how counseling and the counselor may serve as transitional objects.

Patient background

Betty, a 27-year-old woman, was already two years in treatment in the MMT clinic when D.P. was appointed as her counselor. She had already had a prolonged history of addiction to various drugs, including opioids, cannabis, benzodiazepines and methamphetamines, and was currently using cocaine. She was accepted to the MMT program after many unsuccessful attempts of detoxification and rehabilitation in various therapeutic communities and many entanglements with the law, which resulted in a long criminal record.

Betty came from a family that included her father and her stepmother. Her biological mother died when Betty was two years old. Her family was not very attentive to her needs: her father was addicted to opioids and did not take care of the family and her childhood was characterized by constant transitions between dormitories and abuse. Betty got married at a young age and abused substances with her husband. They were married for four years and had two children who lived with Betty for three years, following the couple's divorce. After three years, her husband had succeeded to rehabilitate and remarry, and then claimed custody of the children. Betty struggled with him in the Family Court but lost custody rights since she was still using drugs. She had gone through a hard period of time that included drugs trade, sexual promiscuity and admission to a mental health center for a few months.

Betty was discharged from the mental health center with a diagnosis of borderline personality disorder and entered the MMT clinic to stop her opioid abuse. She has made progress since her admission to the MMT: she took up a cosmetics course and began to train in a gym. She had had a good therapeutic alliance with her counselor and gradually stopped using street-drugs. She also appealed to the Family Court again, in order to regain custody of her children. Betty's counselor supported her efforts to act in a legal way and helped her when she entangled with the law. Betty's ways of coping, however, were maladaptive: she used to appear at her ex-husband's house or in the children's school yard, shouting and demanding to see her children and sometimes even taking them away from school.

The Family Court did not approve of her behavior and ruled that she would see her children only in a neutral place and with professional supervision. Betty could not accept this ruling, repeatedly violated the court's order and the police were occasionally involved in these incidents. In light of her behavior, the court decided to deprive her of the right to see the children at all for the time being and recommended that she should reestablish contact with her children only gradually, first through letters and only later through assisted meetings.

At this point, Betty relapsed to using increasing quantities of cocaine and behaved violently in the clinic and outside. She threatened to physically harm her supportive counselor, and the clinic's staff held an emergency meeting with Betty to discuss her treatment and the need to stop her unacceptable behavior. During this meeting, Betty blamed the clinic for all the failures in her life and said that her present condition was caused by the clinics' staff. She did not miss the opportunity to directly accuse her counselor by saying: *"Maybe I do not have any problem? Maybe you have a problem. Maybe you did not treat me well? Did you think about it?".* In order to be allowed to remain in treatment in the clinic, Betty was asked to sign a 'therapeutic contract', in which she had to re-accept certain rules, including 'behaving properly'. She accepted, but while signing, she said that this was a humiliating agreement.

After this meeting, D.P. was appointed as her counselor. Betty did not talk much during the first session, but repeated that no one can help her and that the only way to help her is to let her talk to her children 'here and now'. The therapist said that they can renew the contact with the children gradually (through letters), and she immediately answered that she is a free human being and would sent letters only when she will be in prison. During the first sessions, Betty expressed considerable anger toward her environment: her ex-husband would not allow her to see her children, the social workers in the family center hate her (and took her children away from her) and the clinic's staff humiliates her.

In these sessions, she used to cry a great deal and to talk about her difficulties in the sessions. She would exclaim: *"you sit, listen and only occasionally say anything"*. She repeatedly said that, her life developed and she did many things during her previous counseling, but now, with her present counselor, her life 'has hit bottom'.

> When I was with my former counselor, I just started to talk and she already knew what to say and everything was good. Now, I am at the bottom, I am in counseling with you. With my former counselor, we were one person, we completed each other…I did my counselor so good…I don't have strength for another counseling… I cannot start all over again and talk about painful things. But with the former counseling, all the mess in the clinic started and I was hurt.

During this period, Betty used cocaine continuously, and it was decided that if she could not stop it (as demonstrated by two consecutive urine tests being negative for cocaine), she would be transferred to another clinic for a month.

During the fourth meeting, Betty said: *"I know that it is not common to ask therapists this question, but how do you see me and how do you see this counseling going on?"*. The therapist said that she tends to compare between the overall good situations that happened before she came to this counseling (which manifested in personal development and the relationship she had with her children while she had custody of them) in contrast to the present deterioration accompanied by despair and depressive feelings. The therapist tried to mirror her conflict and said that she felt she was hurt in a place she thought was safe for her (the clinic), so *"isn't it obvious that she would be hurt in a new place?"* Betty did not talk, and just asked: *"what will happen with me now?"*

The therapist said that it depended on her expectations and on her appearing for sessions (Betty did not attend to the last two meetings). The therapist said that it is a difficult decision to talk or to share unpleasant feelings, but that he is here for her, ready to listen and help. Betty, who used to present herself as a perfect mother when the children were with her, said that her children suffer in her ex-husband's house. She added that she did not understand why they do not leave the father's house and come to stay with her. She used to cry a lot when she talked about her loneliness and the lack of support that appears often in her life (Betty's family did not want any contact with her and she spent the weekend and holidays on her own. Her father had recently managed to rehabilitate, but did not want any contact with Betty since she was still using drugs).

Following this meeting, Betty appeared regularly to counseling during that month and talked a great deal about yearning for her children, depression and despair. She cried during the first sessions and said: "*I do not know what happens when I enter the room, I automatically burst into tears*". Betty's urine tests demonstrated constant decrease in cocaine use and she had one negative urine test about one month later. The therapist appealed to the clinic's manager, asking to postpone her impending 'transference' for a few more days beyond the program in order to enable her to give a second negative urine test. This was granted, and finally, 36 days after starting treatment with the present therapist, Betty's second urine test returned negative and she was cocaine free. Betty did not come to counseling in the next two weeks despite repeated invitations, and the therapist was surprised to be summoned to the manager's office and find her there, complaining about him and the whole counseling.

Special qualities in the relationship to the transitional object

Betty told the manager that during her counseling sessions, other patients use to enter the room constantly and talk with the therapist. She wanted the door to be locked so that no one would enter and interrupt. She was told that a patient may knock on the door but nobody enters when they see her inside and that we do not lock the doors during sessions. Betty was quiet for a few moments and then said that she has difficulties talking to the therapist, since she is a woman and he is a man, and added that she "does *not get anything in counseling and has to leave the room dissatisfied*". The therapist mentioned the latest laboratory findings and noted that her complaints about lack of progress are contrary to her negative urine tests. He added that people do not always feel happy and satisfied after counseling, and sometimes, they leave the room feeling anxious due to painful contents, and coping with these feelings and contents is part of the counseling process.

The manager informed her that it was the therapist who had asked him to postpone the planned 'transference' for a few more days in order to provide her a second negative urine test. Betty's belligerent attitude changed instantly, she kept silent for a few minutes and then left the room. The conversation in the manager's office can be interpreted as an attempt to break the setting's boundaries and as an attempt to create a split in the clinic's staff, but, above all, this situation demonstrates the special qualities of the relationship with the transitional object. The transitional object is the first possession, which is "not-me", and the infant assumes rights over the object (Winnicott, 1971).

Betty assumed rights over her therapist when she said that she is responsible for her former counselor's abilities. The therapist's refusal to lock the door represents the abrogation, which represents the state of the transitional object from the start (Winnicott, 1971). Betty's devaluations during counseling and in the manager's office are parallel to the pure aggression of the infant toward the transitional object. Perhaps Betty was surprised to find that the transitional object gives warmth (his request to postpone her transfer), but maybe her silence symbolizes some understanding that the transitional object has vitality or reality of its own (Winnicott, 1971).

Betty did not use any street-drugs for a few months after this incident. She said that she feels some elation regarding the cessation of cocaine use and added that she has started to accept certain things in her life and does not try to fight against the whole world. For the first time, she pondered about the possibility to leave her children with her ex-husband *because they live well there"* and wanted to get in touch with them gradually. The therapist mirrored her past sayings that her children suffer when they are not with her, and she answered that she tends to project her feelings on her children. He said that maybe she hopes that they would act like she had acted in her youth. Betty agreed and added that she has difficulties to understand that her children do not feel like she does and that they are independent individuals with individual wills.

The therapist was rather surprised by the transition that occurred during the last few months. He tried to mirror this transition from a position of power, omnipotence and ultimate fighting to a position of acceptance, serenity and relaxation in order to emphasize her progress. She said that during the first meetings, she had noticed only one of the pictures on the wall, that of two dogs playing and pulling a rope from both sides, and that she now sees another picture on the other wall *'the picture of the touching hands'* (Michelangelo's 'The Creation of Man'). When asked what comes to her mind when she sees the picture, she said: *"It gives you a feeling that there is someone, like if you would make a little effort to reach, there will be someone to catch you".*

The term 'transitional object' describes "the infant's journey from the purely subjective to objectivity and is what we see of this journey of progress towards experience" (Winnicott, 1971, p. 6). Perhaps the ability to look on her own life with objective eyes grew out of her cessation of drug abuse and her readiness to participate in a therapeutic process that survived several attempts of mutilation. We believe, however, that this change was also possible due to counseling and the setting, which created a potential space between her internal reality and the environment.

From the very beginning, the baby has maximally intense experiences in the potential space between the subjective object and the object objectively perceived, between "me- extensions" and the "not-me" (Winnicott, 1971, p. 100). The counseling served, in this case, as a potential space in which Betty could play and have intense experiences toward objects. In this potential space, "appears creative playing that arises naturally out of the relaxed state; it is here that there develops a use of symbols that stand at one and the same time for external world phenomena and for phenomena of the individual person who is being looked at" (Winnicott, 1971, pp. 146–147).

Absence of the transitional object

Two months later, Betty suddenly announced that she must serve a few days in prison because of an old criminal record. Her attorney did not succeed in canceling this record, and Betty considered the possibility of running away and not serving any time at all. She knew that if she decided to avoid this imprisonment, she would have to serve an extra six months in prison. She feared that she might use again substances in jail. Feelings of loneliness and sorrow related to possible future loss of her present drug-free condition became stronger toward her imminent arrest. She said time and again that no one will be with her in jail, and that again, like every other time in her life, she is powerless and lonely. Every attempt of empowerment or reinforcement of recent achievements encountered resistance and sayings such as: "*I always used drugs in jail, this is the only way to survive*".

Betty was released after five days and said that she used various drugs in jail. She said that she feels weak, and emphasized that no one was in prison with her. She did feel, however, that the clinic was concerned about her condition (a letter was faxed to prison authorities asking that a social worker helped Betty), but she was alone in prison. The therapist said that the fact that she served only five days and not one year is an achievement, and a brief relapse does not mean total failure. She said: "*I am tired of ups and downs… maybe it's better for me in jail…I talked with prisoners who said that they feel good there…the prison decides everything for you and you do not have to do a thing*".

During the next meetings, feelings of helplessness and worthlessness were prominent, and they were accompanied with suicidal ideation. Betty demanded to see her children immediately and said that she understands her children more than anyone. The therapist was on vacation during the next few days and Betty was heard cursing him loudly and exclaiming: "*where is he when you need him?*" Betty left a letter in his box, describing strong depressive feelings, worthlessness and despair, and another letter, which said: *"After many thoughts, I decided to admit myself to a psychiatric institute...I am not capable any more...I cannot talk to you when I need, so figure it out".*

During the next meeting, she looked calm and smiled. The therapist asked her about the letters and she said that she was angry, but now she is calm. When asked how she was coping with the craving in the last days, she cried and said: *"I am alone...all my life alone in dormitories...in prison...and there is no one for me...I am used to it".* The therapist asked if this anger is similar to anger toward other people in different situations in her life and added that from a young age she was alone in dormitories, courts and imprisonments, and always appears the question who is with her and who cares for her? The therapist told her that if he is not available, it does not mean that he does not care for her. Betty kept crying and said: *"now I sit here and talk and everything is fine, but then I go out and feel empty again. Why when I leave this place, I do not feel well? Why outside is not like here inside?"*

The regression to drug abuse and to available transitional object was evident since the time of her imprisonment. Betty's expressed wish to either be imprisoned or admitted to a psychiatric hospital reflects her wishes to return to absolute dependency and to a state in which she does not have to worry about her needs since they are determined by external objects. Her letters to the therapist demonstrate that at times, counseling and the counselor do have functions of transitional object. In Betty's letters, the clear need for a transitional object appears when there are difficulties in the external reality and when anxieties flood the internal reality. At this difficult time, a question is turned to the counselor: 'where are you when I need you?'

Aggression appears in the absence of the transitional object and there is a will to carry it everywhere, especially when there are feelings of sadness, emptiness and depression. Betty says in no uncertain terms that she feels well in counseling but that she feels alone and cannot cope with these feelings outside the room. Perhaps her words come from a constant wish or a phantasy that the counselor (or the transitional object) will always be with her, at home or in jail, and that she would like to carry them everywhere and use them when unpleasant feelings appear.

Greenbaum (1978) and Greenson (1978) describe similar sessions in which they served as transitional objects for patients who wanted to hold them, hit them and carry them everywhere they went. These patients hit pillows or other objects when they talked about these wishes and added that they wanted to hit the walls, to tear the pillows to small pieces or to throw them at the therapist during treatment (Greenbaum, 1978; Greenson, 1978). Winnicott (1971) believes that transitional phenomena occur at times of loneliness or when a depressed mood threatens. The transitional object becomes vitally important to the infant for use at the time of going to sleep and is a defence against anxiety, especially of the depressive type (Winnicott, 1971).

The craving for the transitional object intensifies when the coping with the negative feelings and the craving for substances is harder, and there is a clear question directed toward the transitional object: 'where are you when I need you?' When the option of counseling and the counselor are absent, the distressed individual turns to a transitional object that is always available and which never fails – illicit drugs.

Concluding remarks

The objective of this chapter was to present drug addiction from a psychodynamic perspective and to show how psychodynamic interventions can be implemented in counseling MMT patients in particular and drug and alcohol abusers in general. The added value and importance of psychotherapy in treatment and rehabilitation of drug addicts were impressively demonstrated by Woody, McLellan, Luborsky, & O'Brien (1995). In their study, 84 patients were randomly assigned to receive drug counseling, whereas the other group received drug counseling and individual psychotherapy (Woody et al., 1995). During the study, both groups had similar proportions of opiate-positive urine samples, but the patients receiving individual psychotherapy had fewer cocaine-positive urine samples and required lower doses of methadone.

One month after the extra therapy ended, both groups had made significant achievements, with no significant differences between them. At follow-up six months later, many of the achievements made by the drug-counseled patients had diminished, whereas most of those made by the patients who received psychotherapy persisted or were still evident. Many significant differences emerged, all favoring the addition of individual psychotherapy (Woody et al., 1995).

Methadone (or other chemical substance) counseling does not have to rely solely on a psychodynamic orientation, since substance abuse is a widespread phenomenon with both biological and social aspects. Drug counseling and psychotherapy are effective when they are accompanied by mental processes that manifest in behavioral changes. These processes can have psychodynamic conceptualization (as they may have other conceptualizations, e.g., cognitive-behavioral (CBT), interpersonal approach, etc.), and an analytic viewpoint may be helpful in clinical interventions and policy decisions (Hagman, 1995; Wiedner, 1977).

The complex nature of these phenomena requires a few considerations from counselors and therapists who work in this field. First, the nature of this phenomenon requires a certain change in the patients' environment, and so there is a need to provide information to the close circle of relatives and friends. Second, a variegated approach or some degree of eclecticism is vital on the part of counselors and therapists in the field of addictions. The complex nature of addiction requires seeing the person as a whole, thus focusing only on one aspect of the phenomena would bring about a total failure to see treatment objectives. For example, adoption of only a biological point of view of the abuse of opiates or cocaine phenomena, and focusing solely on the role of a few neurotransmitters and receptors in the brain without paying attention to the patients' experiences, may result in the cessation of drug abuse but only for a short period of time (O'Connor et al., 1998).

Interventions based on other therapeutic approaches and especially CBT are useful since drugs are a positive reinforcement that provides pleasure and euphoria, and a negative reinforcement which reduces such unwanted feelings as tension, anger, boredom, self-hatred, depression, disappointment and emptiness (Weinberg, 1982). Perhaps the most effective index for measuring the efficacy of counseling and change is the nature of the individual's behavior during the transition period and after it. However, since drug addiction is considered a chronic-relapsing disease (Leshner, 1997), as it is an "addictive disease" and a chronic-relapsing disorder, it is difficult to rely upon successful rehabilitation as the only measure of treatment success. Individual and group counseling in addictions require an overview of the person, the addiction and the interaction between them. Therefore, some reference to certain characteristics of the abuser's personality is mandatory.

References

Adelman, S. A. (1985). Pills as transitional objects: A dynamic understanding of the use of medication in psychotherapy. *Psychiatry, 48*(3), 246–253.

American Psychiatric Association. (2000). *Diagnostic and statistical manual of mental disorders, 4th edition, text revisited.* American Psychiatric Association.

Ball, J., & Ross, A. (1991). *The effectiveness of methadone maintenance treatment.* Springer-Verlag.

Carroll, K. M. (1997). Integrating psychotherapy and pharmacotherapy to improve drug abuse outcomes. *Addictive Behaviors, 22*(2), 233–245.

Fassino, S., Daga, G. A., Delsedime, N., Rogna, L., & Boggio, S. (2004). Quality of life and personality disorders in heroin abusers. *Drug and Alcohol Dependence, 76*(1), 73–80.

Glover, E. (1932a). Common problems in psychoanalysis and anthropology: Drug ritual and addiction. *British Journal of Medical Psychology, 12*(2), 109–131.

Glover, E. (1932b). On the aetiology of drug addiction. *International Journal of Psychoanalysis, 53*, 63–73.

Goodman, A. (1993). The addictive process: A psychoanalytic understanding. *Journal of the American Academy of Psychoanalysis, 21*(1), 89–105.

Greenbaum, T. (1978). The "analyzing instrument" and the "transitional object". In S. Grolnick & L. Barkin (Eds.), *Between reality and fantasy* (pp. 193–202). Jason Aronson.

Greenson, R. R. (1978). On transitional objects and transference. In S. A. Grolnick & L. Barkin (Eds.), *Between reality and fantasy* (pp. 205–209). Jason Aronson.

Gunderson, J. G. (1996). The borderline patient's intolerance of aloneness: Insecure attachments and therapist availability. *American Journal of Psychiatry, 153*(6), 752–758.

Gutheil, T. (1982). The psychology of psychopharmacology. *Bulletin of the Menninger Clinic, 46*(4), 321–330.

Hagman, G. (1995). A psychoanalyst in methadonia. *Journal of Substance Abuse Treatment, 12*(3), 167–179.

Hausner, R. S. (1985). Medication and transitional phenomena. *International Journal of Psychoanalytic Psychotherapy, 11*, 375–398.

Hubbard, R., Marsden, M., Rachall, J., Harwood, H., Cavanugh, E., & Ginzburg, H. (1989). *Drug abuse treatment: A national survey of effectiveness.* The University of North Carolina Press.

Jerry, P. A. (1997). Psychodynamic psychotherapy of the intravenous cocaine abuser. *Journal of Substance Abuse Treatment, 14*(4), 319–332.

Kaplan, H. I., & Sadock, B. J. (1998). *Synopsis of psychiatry* (8th Ed.). Lippincott Williams & Wilkins.

Kernberg, O. F. (1975). *Borderline conditions and pathological narcissism.* Jason Aronson.

Khan, M. M. R. (1969). Vicissitudes of being, knowing and experiencing in the therapeutic situation. *British Journal of Medical Psychology, 42*(4), 383–393.

Kohut, H. (1977). Preface. In J. D. Blaine & A. Julius (Eds.), *Psychodynamics of drug dependence* (pp. vii–ix). (NIDA Treatment Research Monograph # 12). National Institute on Drug Abuse.

Last, J. M. (1988). Transitional relatedness and psychotherapeutic growth. *Psychotherapy, 25*(2), 185–190.

Le Bon, O., Basiaux, P., Streel, E., Tecco, J., Hanak, C., Hansenne, M., Ansseau, M., Pelc, I., Verbanck, P., & Dupont, S. (2004). Personality profile and drug of choice; a multivariate analysis using Cloninger's TCI on heroin addicts, alcoholics, and a random population group. *Drug and Alcohol Dependence, 73*(2), 175–182.

Leshner A. I. (1997). Addiction is a brain disease, and it matters. *Science (New York, N.Y.), 278*(5335), 45–47.

Limentani, A. (1968). On drug dependence: Clinical appraisals of the predicaments of habituation and addiction to drugs. *International Journal of Psychoanalysis, 49*(4), 578–590.

Luborsky, L., McLellan, A. T., Woody, G. E., Obrien, C. P., & Auerbach, A. (1985). Therapist success and its determinates. *Archives of General Psychiatry, 42*(6), 602–611.

Malan, D. H. (1979). *Individual psychotherapy and the science of psychodynamics.* Butterworths-Heinemann.

Marsch, L. A. (1998). The efficacy of methadone maintenance interventions in reducing illicit opiate use, HIV risk behavior and criminality: A meta-analysis. *Addiction, 93*(4), 515–532.

McLellan, A. T., Arndt, I. O., Metzger, D. S., Woody, G. E., & Obrien, C. P. (1993). The effects of psychosocial services in substance abuse treatment. *Journal of the American Medical Association, 269*(15), 1953–1959.

McLellan, A. T., Woody, G. E., Luborsky, L., & Gohel, L. (1988). Is the counselor an 'active ingredient' in substance abuse rehabilitation? *Journal of Nervous and Mental Diseases, 176*(7), 423–430.

O'Connor, P. G., Oliveto, A. H., Shi, J. M., Triffleman, E. G., Carroll, K. M., Kosten, T. R., Rounsaville, B. J., Pakes, J. A., & Schottenfeld, R. S. (1998). A randomized trial of buprenorphine maintenance for heroin dependence in a primary care clinic for substance users versus a methadone clinic. *The American Journal of Medicine, 105*(2), 100–105.

Preston, K. L., Umbricht, A., & Epstein, D. H. (2000). Methadone dose increase and abstinence reinforcement for treatment of continued heroin use during methadone maintenance. *Archives of General Psychiatry, 57*(4), 395–404.

Rado, S. (1928). The physical effects of intoxication: Attempt at a psychoanalytical theory of drug addiction. *International Journal of Psychoanalysis, 9*, 301–317.

Rosenthal, P. A. (1981). Changes in transitional objects: Girls in midadolescence. *Adolescent Psychiatry, 9*, 214–226.

Schlierf, C. (1983). Transitional objects and object relationship in a case of anxiety neurosis. *International Review of Psychoanalysis, 10*, 319–332.

Sees, K. L., Delucchi, K. L., Masson, C., Rosen, A., Clark, H. W., Robillard, H., Banys, P., & Hall, S. M. (2000). Methadone maintenance vs 180-day psychosocially enriched detoxification for treatment of opioid dependence: A randomized controlled trial. *Journal of the American Medical Association, 283*(10), 1303–1310.

Shred, M. (1963). The influence of the doctor's attitude on the patient's response to antidepressant medication. *Journal of Nervous and Mental Diseases, 136*(6), 555–560.

Summers, F. (1994). The work of D. W. Winnicott. In F. Summers (Ed.), *Object relations theories and psychopathology* (pp. 137–190). The Analytic Press.

Weinberg, J. R. (1982). Counseling the person with alcohol problems. In N. G. Estes, & M. E. Heinemann (Eds.), *Alcoholism – development, consequences, and interventions* (pp. 294–303). Mosby.

Wieder, H. (1977). Needed: A theory (an historical perspective). In J. D. Blaine & A. Julius (Eds.), *Psychodynamics of drug dependence* (pp. 26–35). NIDA Treatment Research Monograph # 12. National Institute on Drug Abuse.

Wieder, H., & Kaplan, E. (1969). Drug use in adolescence: Psychodynamic meaning and pharmacogenic effect. *The Psychoanalytic Study of the Child, 24*(1), 399–431.

Winnicott, D. W. (1953). Transitional objects and transitional phenomena. *International Journal of Psychoanalysis, 34*(2), 89–97.

Winnicott, D. W. (1960). The theory of parent-infant relationship. *International Journal of Psychoanalysis, 41*, 585–595.

Winnicott, D. W. (1965a). The concept of trauma in relation to the development of the individual within the family. In C. Winnicott, R. Shepherd & M. Davis (Eds.), *Psycho-analytic explorations* (pp. 130–148). Harvard University Press, 1994.

Winnicott, D. W. (1965b). The value of the therapeutic consultation. In C. Winnicott, R. Shepherd, & M. Davis (Eds.), *Psycho-analytic explorations* (pp. 318–324). Harvard University Press, 1994.

Winnicott, D. W. (1968). On "the use of an object". In C. Winnicott, R. Shepherd, & M. Davis (Eds.), *Psycho-analytic explorations* (pp. 217–239). Harvard University Press, 1994.

Winnicott, D. W. (1971). *Playing and reality.* Tavistock Publications.

Winnicott, D. W. (1986). *Home is where we start from – essays by a psychoanalyst.* Norton.

Winnicott, D. W. (1988). *Human nature*. Schocken Books.

Woody, G. E., Luborsky, L., McLellan, A. T., O'Brien, C. P., Beck, A. T., Blaine, J., Herman, I., & Hole, A. (1983). Psychotherapy for opiate addicts. Does it help? *Archives of general psychiatry*, *40*(6), 639–645.

Woody, G. E., McLellan, A. T., Luborsky, L., & O'Brien, C. P. (1995). Psychotherapy in community methadone programs: A validation study. *American Journal of Psychiatry*, *152*(9), 1302–1308.

Chapter 8

Towards independence

Detoxification during opioid maintenance treatment

> "Once these things are established, as they are in health, the child is able gradually to meet the world and all its complexities, because of seeing there more and more of what is already present in his or her own self".
> (Winnicott, 1963, p. 91)

Dependence in general and dependence upon an object in particular are central terms in Winnicott's developmental theory (Winnicott, 1960a, 1987). Dependence upon a drug or a rewarding behavior consists significant issue in drug addicts' lives; therefore, this theory is highly relevant for understanding the mental processes that patients undergo during opioid maintenance treatment (OMT). In the previous chapter, I described transitional phenomena that occur during the transition from active drug addiction and entrance to methadone maintenance treatment (MMT), meaning movement from the absolute dependence stage toward the relative dependence stage. In the following, I will relate to the third stage in Winnicott's developmental theory – towards independence in the context of detoxification from OMT.

In comparison to the other developmental stages, the third developmental stage, towards independence, receives less attention in Winnicott's writings. His formulations of this stage are synonymous with the main themes of the oedipal phase (Summers, 1994), but also include references to latency and adulthood. In this stage, the child has a more integrated sense of self and growing intellectual understanding, and he is less dependent on physical needs than in previous stages (Winnicott, 1960a, 1963c). The mental development continues into latency and includes socialization when the parents have an important role in setting and maintaining boundaries for the exploration attempts of adolescents.

The name towards independence suggests that Winnicott believed that no one ever reaches absolute independence, and there is always interdependence between the individual and the environment. Relating to detoxification and coming off OMT, in my opinion, drug treatment and rehabilitation facilities offer drug abusers two main paths towards independence, meaning toward drug abstinence. The first includes an intermediate stage of relative dependence, whereas the second consists of a quite direct transition from absolute dependence towards independence.

Opioid detoxification in professional literature

Drug detoxification, which is also known as medically managed withdrawal, is a medical intervention for withdrawal symptoms associated with the reduction or the stop of drug use (Substance Abuse and Mental Health Services Administration, 2006). This process may or may not involve the administration of medication as the dose is calculated to relieve the withdrawal syndrome and is gradually tapered off as the patient recovers (World Health Organization, 2008). There are detoxification centers and rehabilitation facilities in which the treatment lasts between two weeks to a month, when the patients are treated by medical staff, counselors and instructors. Drug abstinence following such detoxification process enables release from physical dependence and some release from psychological dependence. But doubtfully, if such a short period enables learning necessary skills for coping with craving and stressful life situations.

Low success rates were found in a longitudinal study that followed heroin addicts after detoxification (Hser, Hoffman, Grella, & Anglin, 2001). The sample was composed of male heroin-dependent criminal offenders who had been referred to compulsory drug treatment program for heroin. At the end of the study, half of the participants died. Among those who lived, 20% had positive drug urine tests for heroin, whereas 40% reported on heroin use in the past year. Besides, almost 10% of the participants refused to provide urine tests, whereas 14% could not provide it since they had been incarcerated (Hser et al., 2001). In another study that examined differences in onset of prescription opioids and heroin abuse and dependence among adults, the average time to remit from opioid abuse was 7–10 years (Wu, Woody, Yang, Mannelli, & Blazer, 2011).

One of the conclusions that arises from a recent review of national trends and characteristics of inpatient detoxification for drug use disorders in the United States is that many efforts are needed to improve engagement for receiving detoxification follow-up treatment to prevent relapse (Zhu & Wu, 2018). Another important finding is that treatment of comorbid medical and mental disorders is essential to facilitate recovery (Zhu & Wu, 2018). Therefore, a prolonged therapeutic–rehabilitative work that relates to significant life aspects, such as processing intrapsychic issues, creating and maintaining interpersonal relations, developing social support networks, helping patients in finding employment and managing leisure time, is vital. In certain countries, those who complete a short detoxification program can continue their treatment in drug treatment units that belong to the social services departments. Usually, such units provide individual counseling, group counseling and weekly urine drug testing.

Another treatment method is the therapeutic community (TC). The TC is a drug-free residential setting that focuses on long-term (from half a year to a year) psychosocial rehabilitation (De Leon, 2000; Sella, 2002). The TC is a structured environment that is characterized by clear boundaries and presents the members with requirements and moral criteria (Sella, 2002). The TC consists a drug-free environment in which individuals with addictive problems live together in an organized way to promote change toward recovery and reinsertion in society (Vanderplasschen et al., 2013). The staff and the more veteran members serve as role models and help new members to understand that any attempts for integration in the community will yield only failures if they continue in their deceiving behavior.

The TC facilitates a process of resocialization through feedbacks and confrontations, and in this way, individuals learn new values and norms that prevail both in the TC and in society. Positive reinforcements will help new members to learn and adapt values, norms and alternative behaviors. In the group interactions, the new member will develop self-care skills, personal responsibility, working relations and mutual help (De Leon, 2000; Sella, 2002). The treatments ensemble in the TC varies and may include individual and group counseling or psychotherapy, pharmacotherapy, 12-step groups, family interventions, creative art therapy, yoga and complementary medicine.

Actually, the TC provides a holding environment in which the member is expected to move from a stage of absolute dependence towards independence. In comparison to detoxification programs, the treatment in TCs is more complex and more intense. The TC helps the member to give up his hallucinatory omnipotence, by constant encounters with the reality and with other objects who have experienced similar processes and recovered. The meeting with similar objects who gave up on the attempts to possess the magical object (the drug) implants hope about the ability to recover. Successful treatment in TC can be expressed in personality changes and acquisition of a new set of (interpersonal, social, relapse prevention) skills, which would help them in their attempt of reintegration. Upon returning home, these individuals can attend Narcotics Anonymous meetings or turn to drug treatment units, which provide counseling that will assist them in continuing working on their recovery.

In a systematic review about the effectiveness of TCs, half of the participants stayed in treatment a third of the planned time, and the completion rate ranged from 9%–56%. Drug abuse decreased during the treatment, but the relapse rates were quite high and frequent after the treatment in TC had ended (Malivert, Fatseas, Denis, Langlois, & Auriacombe, 2012). These findings suggest that in the lack of the holding community, regressions to absolute dependence (relapses) in reaction to impingements may occur. Studies indicate that reintegration into the community indeed appears to be a critical point after treatment completion in a TC not only because of possible relapses but also due to employment and social difficulties (Brunette, Mueser, & Drake, 2004; Vanderplasschen et al., 2013). In another review that aimed to determine the effectiveness of TCs versus other treatments for drug abusers, little evidence was found concerning TCs' significant benefits in comparison with other residential treatments (Smith, Gates, & Foxcroft, 2006).

To provide appropriate solutions, some TC s opened hostels in cities that would enable the members more effective adaption after treatment completion in the TC. This action is the result of recurrent failures to continue moving towards independence after treatment completion in the TC and an understanding that without continuous holding, the regression toward absolute dependence is almost inevitable. The staff members in the hostels continue in provision of the holding environment of the TC, and this method allows members to learn different skills, practice them in the real world and return at the end of the day to the hostel. This method enables a constant learning process and frequent support on the members' path towards independence.

Despite the long-standing and relatively high availability of this treatment and rehabilitation method, TC s were criticized during the years for high drop-out and relapse rates, lack of rigorous empirical support for effectiveness and high costs of long-term residential treatment (Vanderplasschen et al., 2013; Vanderplasschen, Vandevelde, & Broekaert, 2014). Michael (2007) raises additional criticism toward this approach and notes that the TC's staff may prefer to act on his own instead of advising members who hold different roles in the community. Second, since the TC's members vary in their personality structure, some members may act out from obedience and fear. Goldfarv (1996) notes that the entire processes in the TC are directed toward fragmentation of the previous ego of the new members and building an institutional ego that fits the organization's ideology.

Sella (2002) completely disagrees with this argument and notes that many drug addicts behave in a way that indicates the existence of a false self. The TC's norms do not enable the new member adhering to a false identity that characterized their relation to themselves, their family and society (Sella, 2002). Issues of personal identity and authenticity concerning true and false self also appear during psychodynamic psychotherapy of OMT patients. Especially, in the relative dependence phase, after drug abstinence of a few years, patients deal with questions of falsehood and authenticity. Often, these are also the patients who are interested in detoxification from OMT.

Fantasy and reality in detoxification during opioid maintenance treatment

Many patients who enter OMT have the fantasy of leaving treatment one day and living without any drug dependence. In a study among MMT patients, 62% reported on high interest in treatment completion in the next six months (Winstock, Lintzeris, & Lea, 2011). Seventy-one percent reported previous withdrawal attempts, and 23% had achieved opioid abstinence for three months or even more following a previous withdrawal attempt. The most common attempts were jumping off independently (59%), physician-controlled detoxification (52%) or self-controlled (48%) gradual reduction (Winstock et al., 2011).

Among many older patients (mostly over 60), there is a certain acceptance about remaining in OMT until the end of their lives, whereas among younger patients prevails the fantasy of staying in treatment for a few years before coming off OMT. Common sayings of these patients are: *"I came here for treatment of a year or two"*, or *"for me, methadone is a final station before drug-free life"*. This fantasy enabled patients to survive years of suffering and to look for treatment. However, unfortunately, these patients do not understand that coming off opioids during OMT is complicated and may last years.

Based on my experience, most of the patients who leave OMT independently do not succeed in remaining drug abstinent for an extended period, entering the job market or building support circles. On the contrary, patients who stay in MMT succeed more than patients who drop-off treatment, when the relapses number is higher among the latter (Kleber, 2007). During MMT, patients receive medical and psychosocial treatment. They are referred to medical screening tests, such as hepatitis C, human immunodeficiency virus (HIV) and tuberculosis, and receive psychosocial counseling that concerns many life areas. Patients' health and functioning improve during MMT, but it may decrease with its discontinuation (Kleber, 2007).

Buprenorphine, sold under the brand name Subutex, is a long-acting, safe and effective medication for detoxification or maintenance of opioid dependence (Kleber, 2007; Wirfs, 2019). Buprenorphine is mostly taken by the sublingual route or orally. In order to prevent its misuse by intravenous injection, Suboxone, a medication that contains a combination of buprenorphine and naloxone was developed. Recently, there have been more advancements in the field of OMT as Sublocade, a once-a-month injectable form of buprenorphine, and Cassipa (buprenorphine and naloxone) sublingual film have received Food and Drug Administration (FDA) approval for adults with moderate to severe opioid use disorder (Wirfs, 2019).

In a few large meta-analyses (Amato et al., 2005; Mattick, Breen, Kimber, & Davoli, 2009, 2014), both buprenorphine and methadone were found as an effective medication for maintenance treatment of heroin dependence, but methadone was superior to buprenorphine in retaining people in treatment.

From my experience, a significant number of patients who leave OMT independently return to treatment following failure in the subsequent weeks or months. Another patients' group feels shame about returning to the same clinic and turns for OMT in another clinic. A third group of patients that leaves treatment returns to abuse drugs and does not return to treatment. The lack of success to remain drug abstinent after leaving OMT not only implies on lack of the necessary ego strength to deal with the recovery process and life's challenges, but also on the difficulties in creating a new lifestyle mostly without social and economic support.

The OMT population is diverse and includes people from diverse age groups and different social and ethnic backgrounds. One population segment is characterized with early onset of heroin abuse, diverse criminal offending, low socioeconomic background and lack of familial or social support. It is quite understandable that this group of patients will have significant difficulties finding their place in society after leaving OMT without a controlled and gradual detoxification process. Additional patients' group that reports on the fantasy of ending treatment includes patients with more mental resources and skills than the previous group. Some of them had worked before they began abusing drugs, and sometimes, they had managed to use drugs while working. These patients are stabilized on methadone or buprenorphine and receive take-home doses. During the treatment, they start working or even studying and strengthen their familial and social ties. A careful anamnesis reveals that their drug addiction has begun mostly because of economic or personal crises after their 20s.

In this population segment, one can find patients who were prescribed with opioids following car accident injuries or following army or work injuries. The combination of physical pain, depression, post-traumatic stress disorder (PTSD) or other mental malaises and the availability of opioids led to an addiction to those medications before turning to heroin. During OMT, a substantial part of this patients' group makes significant changes in their lifestyle and develops a routine that includes family life and work. These patients stay away from any involvement in criminal activity and see themselves as completely different from other patients due to their high functioning level. However, their personality organization is not necessarily high, and during the clinical encounter, the therapist discovers the contrast between high functioning and immature object relations.

Because of the high functioning and the frequent interactions with people without drug abuse and addiction history, these patients often wonder whether they will be able to stay drug abstinent following OMT discontinuation. In my opinion, the question about detoxification should appear during treatment in an intermediate space in which fantasy and reality meet. In such space, the patient presents his fantasy about a drug-free lifestyle, and the clinic's staff can hold both fantasy and reality. Sayings such as *"forget it"*, *"you don't have any chance"*, or *"many others had tried, failed and returned to treatment"* are problematic since they damage (or crush) the patients' fantasy. Some patients might react furiously to such blows to their omnipotence and try to leave treatment impulsively. In summary, the fantasy of coming off OMT independently or gradually exists among many patients, but it is not always discussed during the treatment.

In a study that focused on coming off OMT (Winstock et al., 2011), the authors noted that some patients may require lifetime maintenance and that the issue of coming off treatment is essential to numerous patients and should be continuously discussed throughout treatment. They add that the staff should provide clinical options for patients interested in leaving treatment (Winstock et al., 2011), and other researchers note that the ultimate goal of motivated MMT patients with good progress should be methadone detoxification (Hiltunen, Eklund, & Borg, 2011).

In cohort studies among patients who came off MMT, it was found that in comparison to patients with failed coming off methadone attempts, those who succeeded had higher quality of life and a more stable actual life situation (Eklund, Melin, Hiltunen, & Borg, 1994). However, another interesting finding was that patients who were satisfied with their situation were less inclined to make a withdrawal attempt. These well-functioning MMT patients did not try to quit treatment because they believed they needed the treatment and because they were familiar with other patients who experienced failures in such attempts. Another reason for not quitting MMT was low confidence in their ability coming off methadone (Hiltunen & Eklund, 2002).

A stable lifestyle should be an important consideration in the decision to discontinue treatment, and the OMT clinic staff should emphasize that this stability was achieved during the treatment. Therefore, the patient should consider whether he will be able to maintain those achievements without the clinic's support. Discussion about OMT detoxification should relate to the patient's skills, past detoxification attempts, current treatment, emotional maturity, social support sources and rehabilitative parameters (employment, leisure). The discussions about OMT detoxification should also relate to the following issues:

1   Opioid addiction as a disease – MMT is identified by many professionals with harm reduction because of its proven efficacy in reducing heroin abuse rates, drug-related criminal behaviors and drug-related infectious diseases (Sun et al., 2015; Wakeman, 2016). However, OMT relies on the medical model and on the premise that drug addiction in general and opioid addiction in particular is a brain disease (Bleich & Adelson, 2000; Volkow, Koob, & McLellan, 2016). Studies that show changes in human brain following chronic opioids use support this premise (Evans & Cahill, 2016; Younger et al., 2011), and patients should receive this important information when considering ending treatment. A common analogy that some physicians, therapists and counselors use in their conversation with OMT patients who want to come off treatment is that opioid addiction is a disease quite like diabetes or epilepsy that requires lifelong pharmacological treatment.

2   Providing information about success rates of OMT detoxification – A systematic review about the discontinuation of buprenorphine maintenance therapy shows that relapse rates to illicit opioid use exceeded 50% (Bentzley, Barth, Back, & Book, 2015). Concerning methadone, 15-year follow-up after the first 38 MMT patients in Stockholm raises some optimism, but usually most of the patients who come off treatment relapse (Brewer, Catalano, Haggerty, Gainey, & Fleming, 1998; Kleber, 2007; Magura & Rosenblum, 2001; Unnithan, Gossop, & Strang, 1992).

When patients are informed about these findings, some of the common reactions are: *"even though the majority relapses, there are those who do not relapse"* and *"maybe I can be one of the few who doesn't relapse"*. Such comments imply on the powerful fantasy to leave OMT and to move from relative dependence towards independence.

3   Providing information about the detoxification process – Voluntary tapering off from methadone should begin after a substantial period of drug abstinence during treatment, and as mentioned, a stable lifestyle should be an essential consideration in the decision to discontinue treatment (Henry-Edwards et al., 2003). Withdrawal from MMT should be gradual, and the staff should provide the relevant information and with a menu of clinical options (Henry-Edwards et al., 2003; Hiltunen et al., 2011; Winstock et al., 2011). Some OMT clinics present with the option of giving drug urine tests and psychotherapy or counseling for a year after detoxification from OMT. Other treatment options include drug treatment units that are located at the social services departments or attending Narcotics Anonymous meetings.

Many OMT patients who consider ending their treatment report on high anxiety level. This anxiety appears more often and more intensively with any further movement towards independence. Patients wonder if they will be able to remain drug abstinent without the protective setting of the clinic, which includes constant drug urine tests and psychosocial treatment. The psychotherapeutic treatment is the appropriate space for discussing such issues and understanding the patient's considerations and anxieties. For a considerable number of patients, the privilege of take-home doses consists a status symbol that distinguishes them from drug-abusing patients. Sometimes, patients who just entered OMT and those who do not receive take-home doses look up to them with some admiration and jealousy. Therefore, ending treatment means giving up a status symbol. In therapy, such patients deal with the issue of *"being a big fish in a small pond, or a small fish in a big pond"*. They understand that they function better than many other OMT patients, but they are not sure if they will be able to fully integrate into the society like their colleagues and neighbors who do not have any addiction problems. Sometimes, these patients start gradual detoxification and stop on low doses as their anxiety level intensifies.

Much of the anxiety concerns separation from significant objects such as the clinic and the holding environment that it offers. Besides, there is difficulty in separation from a chemical transitional object and a human one – the therapist. The detoxification process is characterized by many complexities because of the physiological and psychological processes that the patient experiences, and sometimes, it is suddenly abrupted by angry patients who leave treatment because they disagree with the detoxification program or due to another minor reason. In such situations, patients suddenly report distrusting the clinic's staff, or begin to argue about the clinic's rules.

This sudden change may surprise the staff that begins to wonder why a patient who receives take-home doses for years starts to argue or even violate the clinic's rules. In my opinion, such dramatic events produced by the patient's unconscious theater constitute repetition of past object relations, and indicate the difficulty of performing an organized and well-planned separation from significant objects. A sudden separation, while devaluing the therapist or other staff members either for not understanding or not providing with required needs, allows the patient to steadfastly in his righteousness and omnipotence.

My main argument in this chapter is that movement towards independence in OMT is associated with mental maturation that takes place during the psychotherapeutic treatment. In this long process, there are regressions toward relative dependence or absolute dependence for fulfilling developmental missions, which the patient could not achieve earlier because of the environment's impingements. Second, during this process, the therapist continues to serve as a transitional object. Third, during this process, the patient makes different object usages of the therapist and learns different object relating. In the next lines, I will demonstrate these arguments.

Case illustration

Lily (false name), a 32-year-old woman, turned to OMT at the age of 26 after a few unsuccessful detoxification attempts from heroin. She was the younger daughter of a father who was an artist and a mother who worked as a caregiver of disabled people. Lily had two older brothers with whom she was not in touch. She described a warm relationship with her father and, on the other hand, a horrible relationship with her mother that turned to mental and physical abuse at the age of eight when her father died. The mother sunk into a depression that lasted two years and included admission to a psychiatric department.

Lily reported that the death of the father was a terrible loss since he was the closest person to her. Following his death, she did not go to school, and her teachers called her mother, saying she has enormous potential and that she should care well for her. The mother responded to the school's staff that nothing good would come out of her. Lily deteriorated in her studies and began to miss school. The mother moved her away to boarding school, where she became an outstanding student. However, for an unknown reason, her mother brought her back home, and after a while, the behavioral problems started again. At the age of 16, Lily met a guy who was four years older, who introduced her to the world of drug abuse. She began to abuse cannabis, MDMA, and the two started stealing to finance the addiction. When he was imprisoned, she kept abusing drugs and used to call her boyfriend to prison. They broke up when he was released from prison, and in the next years, she found herself in the same relationship of joint heroin abuse and crime.

At the age of 24, she decided to end a relationship because she felt that she was exploited ("*I suddenly understood that I constantly has stolen to gain money while he had lame excuses. He was smarter than most of the addicts I knew, but I took all the risks and sponsored him*"). She was not in touch with her family and lived a lifestyle of addiction and crime. Lily turned to detoxification centers but could not remain drug abstinent after the treatment. As happens with most of the drug abusers, she was caught stealing and was incarcerated for almost a year. Subsequently, she decided to turn for OMT.

Lily received a woman therapist and had made impressive progress. She stopped any drug abuse and began to work at a clothes shop. After a year and a half in treatment, her therapist went to maternity leave for half a year and then decided to leave her work in the OMT clinic. In a staff meeting, a male therapist was appointed as her therapist. In the first meetings, Lily spoke of her disappointment from the former therapist's leaving, especially because she felt that she was her favorite patient. Lily said that the therapist supported her and for the first time in her life, she felt that somebody is proud of her. However, Lily also felt jealous of the therapist and felt that the future child took her place. In this period, she considered leaving treatment, and the therapist offered to see her a few times a week to help her to process the separation and the associated grief.

In the following year, Lily reported elaborately the horrible emotional and physical abuse of her mother, which included curses, devaluations and violence during her childhood. During these sessions, the therapist said that it is incredible that she could rise from such bottoms. He added that he thinks she is very talented, and therefore, he decided to send her to career counseling. In this counseling, she was found very skillful and the counseling center offered to finance her a professional course and even academic studies. She began to learn in a preparatory program in a local college and did quite well. She made friends with other students and received good grades. However, the success experience was strange for her because she used to think of herself as a failure. In this period, she started a controlled process of reducing her subutex dosage.

Winnicott, more than any other psychoanalyst, emphasized the importance of the environment to the growth and the development of the child (Summers, 1994). The patient's achievements and her reaction to the leaving of her first therapist imply on the solid therapeutic alliance she had with the therapist and on the facilitating environment that enabled progress. Prolonged drug abstinence, constant occupation and constant arrival for therapy imply on the transition from absolute dependence toward relative dependence. When her second therapist met her, he felt her pain and understood that the experience of going-on-being was abrupted. During the treatment, the therapist has attempted to put himself in the patient's place, like the mother fits herself into her infant's needs (Winnicott, 1956a). In this way, he could provide a setting in which Lily's constitution began to make itself evident, and the developmental tendencies have started to unfold (Winnicott, 1956a).

In her early years, the environmental provision was sufficient, but the father's death constituted a hold-up of the developmental process. Winnicott (1963a) notes that such states allow the development of ego-organization of a considerable degree, but there is failure in establishing internal development and becoming independent. This process, meaning deprivation, leads to the development of an antisocial tendency, which in turn forces the child to develop personality disorder and to become a recidivist offender (Winnicott, 1963a). In my opinion, this conceptualization describes well the personality development of drug abusing patients.

Good-enough holding allows the infant to feel undifferentiated from the mother and provides the basis for object usage and object relating (Winnicott, 1960a). The environmental holding is a necessary condition for maturational processes and the emotional growth of the child. The therapist's actions and sayings had the function of mirror role that validated Lily's emotional experiences (Winnicott, 1971), and it allowed the 'inherited potential' to become itself a 'continuity of being' (Winnicott, 1960a). Until this point in treatment, the therapist had many opportunities to interpret Lily's transference toward the former therapist or relate to the difficulty of seeing the former therapist as an independent person, who also thinks about her personal life. In this respect, Winnicott (1971) notes that psychotherapy is not about making clever interpretations, but a long-term process of giving the patient back what he brings.

In the year of her preparatory studies, Lily received high praise from many teachers who were ready to write her recommendation letters for graduate studies. She studied for exams with other students and was courted. In this period, the therapist met her once a week, and Lily used to call him between the sessions and described in detail her new and exciting academic experiences. Winnicott (1945) presents an example of a patient who reports every detail of his weekend and feels contented at the end that everything had been said. The analyst feels that no analytic work has been done, but at such moments, the patient is feeling integrated in the analyst (Winnicott, 1945).

Every therapist who met his recovering patient after he had begun any academic studies, or any professional course, will be amazed at how Winnicott had conceived so accurately a unique moment in therapy when theory meets reality. The flickering glimpse in the patient's eyes, when he talks fast and does not want to miss any detail, appears as Winnicott (1960a) noted when there is silent but vitally important ego support. In my opinion, such experiences occur only after the patients feel both physical aliveness and emotional aliveness, and the link between these two forms of aliveness gives birth to playfulness, spontaneity and vitality (Potik, 2010; Winnicott, 1954). At this stage of the recovery process, a new form of knowledge that has not been available, even though it exists within the patient, is now redeemed. This form of knowledge is the unthought known (Bollas, 1987), and it is expressed in Lily's discoveries of her academic skills.

False self and true self

Lily successfully finished the preparatory studies and was accepted to a fine arts graduate program. At that time, she was in a relationship that was characterized by financial exploitation. The therapist tried to reflect this point and to imply the repetitive choices of abusive partners during her life, but it seemed that Lily preferred to stay in an unhealthy relationship than to stay alone. After about six months, her partner left, and Lily was heartbroken. In therapy, she wondered what she had done wrong and why the relationship suddenly ended. Lily had difficulties in her daily functioning because of depressive symptoms and even mentioned suicide without a concrete plan. At the same time, she asked the clinic's physician to raise her subutex dosage. The concerned therapist offered to see her two and even three times a week when she stopped attending the classes and rarely left her house.

The holding that the therapist provided enabled experiencing the breakdown that has occurred in the past but was not experienced (Winnicott, 1974). In contrast to the withdrawal that took place after the leaving of Lily's former therapist, this regression to dependence revealed powerlessness, emotional pain and anger related to the early environmental failures (Winnicott, 1955b). Much of it because of the traumatic death of the loving father and the abuse by her mother, which included continuous projection of guilt and jealousy ("*the father died because of you*", "*you are horrible and should be punished*", "*he loved you more than anyone else*"). It turned out also that her partner left her because she started to set boundaries to his exploitation attempts, and Lily discovered that she was ready to pay enormous emotional prices for the presence of an object in her life.

The intense therapeutic work at this stage strengthened the therapeutic alliance, and Lily said a few times that for the first time in her life, she has someone close who cares for her in hard times. She said that she sees the therapist like the father she never had, and she wants him to be proud of her. Quietly, she added that she is jealous of other woman patients who are the therapist's patients in the OMT clinic. After about three years in treatment, occurred the next dialogue in one of the sessions.

LILY: "I wanted to thank you for all your support in this tough period. Shall we hug?"

THE THERAPIST FELT EMBARRASSED AND SAID: "Do you mean that you want us to hug?"

LILY: "Yes. I really appreciate what you have been doing for me, and I want to hug you".

THERAPIST: "I understand your will to thank me, and you indeed express it in your words. However, a hug can be problematic because it has different meanings. In therapy, there is a meaningful and intimate relationship between patients and therapists, and the therapist's caring can be interpreted as an invitation for intimate closeness. In this therapy, there is indeed intimate closeness, and I am delighted to see your progress".

LILY SEEMED CONFUSED AND, IN THE SUBSEQUENT SESSION, SAID: "It is strange that you don't want a thing from me".

THERAPIST: "What do you mean?"

LILY: "Every man I met in life tried to exploit me this way or the other. When I was an addict, I did not have where to live because my mother did not let me stay at her place. Many drug abusers offered me drugs for free, but I found out that they have a hidden interest. They all wanted to have sex with me or that I'll be a prostitute, and they will be the pimps. Men see a single woman and automatically think of how they can have sex with her. The world is cruel, and if you'll show any weakness or naiveness, people will exploit it. I made very clear to all those who wanted sex in return to drugs or accommodation that I'm not that kind of girl, and I survived on the streets alone. If you hear me raising my voice in the clinic or talking aggressively with other patients, don't think badly of me. The patients here are not boy scouts".

THERAPIST: "I understand that you have different aspects like we all do, but it seems that you do not want me to see you shouting or setting boundaries to other patients".

LILY: "I'm ashamed that you'll see me that way, you will think of me badly because of such behavior or because I stopped the detoxification after the separation. You know that lately I noticed that before almost any action, I think what you would expect me to do".

THERAPIST: "You are going through many changes, and one of them is learning how to set boundaries to other people in order to protect yourself. We are not born with this skill; we learn it. I also hear you saying that I am valuable to you. Thank you, you are also very valuable to me and I am excited to see your amazing progress throughout the years. You are the first patient in this clinic who studies in college, and I really think that this is the beginning of your success. You study in college, you have new friends, you receive compliments from your lecturers, and you even were invited to present one of your works in an exhibition. I feel that maybe for the first time in your life, you believe in yourself".

There are a few significant points in the clinical material, which has been presented until now. First, the psychosocial treatment in OMT includes both psychotherapy and rehabilitation. The therapist's involvement in the rehabilitative process affords him a better understanding of his patient and assists in strengthening the therapeutic alliance. Second, during psychotherapy in OMT, the therapist's room becomes an intermediate area of experience (Potik, Adelson, & Schreiber, 2007; Winnicott, 1971), in which the true self begins to emerge.

In these stages of treatment, patients feel safe to talk about events from their active addiction period, which include violence, exploitation, involvement in crime and prostitution, and the therapist can look at the falsehood cloak, which has helped the patients to survive the cruel world of addiction that is characterized with annihilation anxiety and objectification. Reflecting this point in this stage of therapy when patients are occupied in questions of authenticity and adaptation to the world is vital, and it allows them to develop the ego organization that is adapted to the environment (Winnicott, 1960b). In fact, frequent questions about authenticity and falsehood in daily situations imply on the movement towards independence.

The false self appears at the front of the stage to guarantee the mental and physical survival of the patients, while at the same time deep inside, there is a yearning for an enabling environment in which aspects of the true self can emerge safely. The false self often appears at the beginning of treatment to impress the therapist or to protect against any impingement from an object (the therapist), which represents the hated establishment. In this context, Winnicott (1960b) notes that at the beginning of the therapy, the therapist talks to the false self about the true self. My experience shows that the physical and verbal expressions of the false self appear in the patients' body language (posture, glance) and gestures just as the true self is expressed through spontaneous movement. The false self appears in treatment facilities not only in the therapist's rooms but mostly during interactions with other patients and staff members. It is quite amazing to see the expressions of the true and the false self when one moment patients talk about highly emotional experiences in the therapist's room, and after a few minutes, they talk bluntly with other patients outside the room.

In my opinion, the therapeutic work should not focus on the obliteration of the false self because patients during recovery still have certain interactions with drug-abusing individuals and because they need the protection of some aspects of the false self in order to cope with external reality's threats. Instead, it should focus on the development of mental flexibility from which the ability to compromise arises. According to Winnicott (1960b), the equivalent of the false self is the adaptation to social manner, and in treatment of patients in recovery, it is the ability to respond to the other's needs without feeling betrayal in the true self. For example, it is the ability of a patient in recovery to adhere to his employer's demands, although not always agreeing with him.

Towards independence

The appearance of transitional phenomenon and the finding of the therapist as a transitional object constitute the main psychotherapeutic achievements of OMT patients during their journey toward relative dependence.
However, many OMT patients, like those with borderline personality disorder, never had the opportunity to create the first possession because they
did not grow up in an enabling environment with a good enough mother.
The therapist is the patient's first possession, and the therapeutic relationship shares a few of the special qualities that the child shows toward the
transitional object. In healthy development, the transitional object must
survive instinctual loving, hating and pure aggression, and it is gradually decathected (Winnicott, 1971). However, in OMT, some patients are
not ready to let the transitional object be forgotten and cope more independently with emptiness, loneliness, separation, loss and with the challenges that the external reality poses.

The personal lives of the patients are characterized by emotional whirl-
pools and instability, and once they find an object that gives warmth and
survives their aggression, they are not ready to let it relegate to limbo. Progress in the recovery process, such as long periods of drug abstinence or
prolonged work experience, does not necessarily indicate the achievement
of integrated object relations. For some patients, the therapist constitutes a
transitional object also throughout the journey towards independence, and
when they discover that the therapist has vitality or reality of its own, they
will devalue him or find another minor reason to leave treatment. Such patients cannot tolerate the abrogation of their omnipotence and the separation and, therefore, the aggressive or the impulsive reaction.

In Lily's case, the therapist's refusal for a hug has begun the acknowledgment of his independence and selfhood but simultaneously begun a shat-
tering of the omnipotent fantasy of controlling the object. Such situations
are therapeutic crossroads, and if the patient continues arriving for therapy,
then he continues in his way towards independence.

Object usage

Lily continued in the gradual detoxification program, and after an additional year in which she studied at college and did well, she said to the therapist that she thinks about him and wants to be with him beyond treatment
hours. The erotic transference became the focus of the sessions and especially
Lily's fantasy of the therapist as a potential life partner. She said that he is
a good-looking and educated individual and added that usually, she "*gets
the men she likes*". The embarrassed therapist followed Freud's (1915/1959)
dictum of talking about but not acting upon the intensity of transference
neurosis. He talked about the oedipal nature of this transference, and in

response, she reported a dream about two snakes and was reluctant to share her associations. The therapist thought that the dream represents the dual relation toward him. Meaning the dream deals with oedipal desire toward the abstinent father but also relates to her perception of the therapist as an attractive man.

During this period, Lily said in one of the sessions that she talked to one of the staff members who speaks freely about her colleagues and found out interesting things about him.

> I talked with her about you. You know what they think about you in the clinic?! I asked her about your life and where do you live. She told me where you live and added that she does not know how you can effort yourself to live there with a salary of a public servant?!

The therapist became upset and said that it is an invasion of his privacy, and added that Lily has crossed the line. He became angry and said that patients do feel curious about their therapists, but this is exaggerated, and he will talk to his colleague about her inappropriate behavior. Lily said that she wants quick detoxification of a few days and left the room. In the next weeks, she arrived at the clinic only to take her take-home doses. The therapist contacted her on the phone and sent emails asking her to meet him. Lily declined and wrote an email saying she wants quick detoxification because her current goal is living without any dependence. After two months in which the therapist tried unsuccessfully to reach her, she appeared and seemed insulted. She said that she is happy that this incident had happened since now she can see his true colors, and she is sure now more than ever that she wants to end treatment.

Lily left the room, and the therapist tried to contact her again in the next days. She wrote to him that she is done with the treatment, and she is thinking about coming off subutex independently without the necessity of arriving for treatment. The therapist tried to mirror her impulsive actions in relation to her anger, and Lily replied that for quite a time she has been feeling that he does not show any interest in her life as before. He tried to talk on the extreme fluctuations in the therapeutic relations, but Lily was not ready to hear him. After about two exhausting months of reaching out attempts that were responded with verbal aggression and devaluations, Lily reappeared.

She said that she became curious about him and therefore talked to a few staff members. The therapist said that patients are curious about their therapists and usually try to find out various details about them on social networks. Lily said that she indeed did it at the beginning of treatment because she wanted to see how his life looks. The therapist said that he thinks that there is a difference between searching the internet and between interrogating staff members for receiving information. He added that he did not mean to offend her and that he reacted this way because he felt his privacy was damaged. Lily said that considering his reaction, she understands that he is not as perfect as she thought before and that she does not want him as a life partner because of his many flaws.

In supervision, the therapist reported that he indeed knew that Lily talked about him with other staff members, and he has assumed that she searched for information about him on the internet. However, the action of manipulating staff members for receiving personal information was experienced as a severe privacy invasion. In this context, Ofer and Durban (1999) note that curiosity may be motivated by attempts to annihilate the differences between the self and the other, and it has a persecutory and invasive meaning.

The therapist experienced Lily's deed not only as an act of curiosity but as an act of aggression and even destruction. Winnicottian conceptualization of this action will not necessarily refer to such behavior or perhaps transgression as an expression of destruction. Meaning, in healthy development, the infant looks at the mother, touches her face, her fingers, pinches her and even bites her. Winnicott (1950–1955) considered aggression as a primitive expression of love and noted that when a baby chews the nipple with his gums, it does not mean that he aims to destroy or to hurt. Aggression is associated with the basic life force, motility, and it is related to the enjoyment of pushing against the environment (Winnicott, 1950–1955). Excess of opposition from the environment hardens on the fusion between the aggressive potential and the erotic one.

Perhaps, in this case, the therapist's response was too harsh and led to difficulties in navigating between sexual attraction toward the therapist and between feelings of frustration and aggression following the therapist's refusal for physical intimacy. Consequently, Lily reacted furiously and left therapy. After a while, she returned to the weekly sessions and continued in the original detoxification program. She successfully finished three years of her graduate studies, but had difficulties in her relationships with some lecturers whom she felt did not like her. The sessions focused on the will to receive love and attention from lecturers who were perceived as being *"hard to get"*. In this period, Lily appeared to therapy and said that she heard from one of the staff members that her therapist is married. The therapist said that he is quite sure that she had already known it, but he feels that when she heard it today, something has happened. Lily replied that she indeed knew that he was married and added that lately, she feels that he is not responsive as he once was, and it takes him too much time to answer her calls when she calls the clinic or when she sends emails. Without a further word, she left the room. The therapist tried to reach her on the phone and in email, but Lily answered shortly that he *"had his chances"*, and he *"blew it"*. She added that she wants a quick detoxification program to leave the clinic as soon as possible.

During the next weeks, Lily avoided entering the therapist's room when she was in the clinic and only took her take-home doses. In one of the times they met in the clinic, he said that one of the therapeutic aims was to work on her extreme and impulsive responses during emotional conflicts. Lily said that the therapist could continue to treat his other clinic patients who are *"not talented and successful as she is"*, and she made her mind to end treatment. In the next months, the therapist tried reflecting her fantastic progress and relentlessly asked her not to throw the baby out with the bathwater. Lily either did not respond to his attempts or had responded with anger and devaluations. When she finally appeared to therapy, she said that she knew well that the therapist is married, but the saying of the staff member about his familial status ruined her fantasy.

THERAPIST: "I understand that you expected that I will leave everything behind and be with you".

LILY: "Yes, I thought that I would come off subutex, and we will leave this country and start a new life abroad. I know that you like me, and I see that you care for me. You do not want to be with me? Don't you think that I'm an attractive woman?"

THERAPIST: "I do find you attractive, and at the same time, I feel that this fantasy prevented you from meeting other men. I do care for you, and I said to you on previous sessions that some patients confuse the caring of their therapist with a will to closeness beyond therapy hours".

LILY: "This is the first time in my life that I have an emotional relationship that does not include any hidden interests or sex. It is strange".

THERAPIST: "This relationship, which includes emotional intimacy and not sexual intimacy, is one of the main things that enabled you to discover how talented you are and that you can succeed in the world of the people who do not abuse drugs".

LILY: "Now I know exactly how a relationship should be. Life partners should care and support each other at times of need. I know that I made progress and that you are proud of me. I heard from one of the staff members that you tend to mention my achievements in staff meetings. Don't be angry, it's not my fault that the staff here is very talkative".

The therapist smiled and there was a minute of silence.

LILY: "I indeed declined many offers to date other men, and I was angry that you are not loyal to me as I was loyal to you".

THERAPIST: "You and other patients see other therapists and me for an hour or two a week when I am attentive to you and think of your best. Therefore, patients think of their therapists as flawless and wish to be with them or even marry them. If this relationship turns to an intimate relationship, then this special place will be lost, and in fact, it would be an abuse of these close relations".

LILY: "After I saw your reaction to my conversation with your colleague about your address, I do not think any longer you're perfect. I have noticed that you can lose your temper quite as I do sometimes".

The therapist smiled without words and hesitated if to relate to this comment, which reminded him Winnicott's (1971) words about the mirror-role of the mother when Lily said:

> I didn't tell you, but in the last months, I've been reading about psychotherapy. I looked for cases when patients and their therapists were engaged in intimate relationships, but all those times ended with abuse and separation. I was very disappointed because I didn't find even one successful case. I have read accounts of women who had been hurt after having sex with their therapists. In fact, it made me appreciate you more because you could have exploited me so many times. I also understood that if you will be with me, you can lose your license and your work, and I don't want it to happen to you.

The main psychotherapeutic achievements of OMT patients during their journey toward independence are transition from object relatedness toward object usage and development of the capacity for concern. These processes are characterized by emergences of the true self, and they occur if the therapist is ready to place himself in the role of an object and be used. From a developmental perspective, a baby who can perceive the world objectively is a baby who had the experience of an object that withstood his destructiveness and survived (Abram, 2007). Lily's words in the last vignette illustrate the difference between pathological destruction and healthy destruction that appears in fantasy and its relation to the capacity for concern.

After an additional year in treatment, one of the staff members reproached Lily for being late. She said to her therapist that because of her achievements, she should not receive any negative comments from the staff. She added that she wants to leave treatment and she had enough of the clinic and the rude staff members. Any attempt to explain that the rules apply for every patient ended unsuccessfully. Lily did not appear for the next session, but after two weeks, she reappeared and said:

> in the last time that I felt offended and did not appear to the sessions, we said that the next time that it would happen, I would not act impulsively, and we will talk about it. So, here I am.

She added that during the last week, she felt sad because they could not be a couple, but she also felt worried about his health because he treats severe cases. Lily said that in the past, she did not like his leavings for vacations, but now she understands that he should take care of himself and encouraged him to do it more often. Additional sayings that appeared in this period were:

> I thought about the treatment a few days ago. How you tolerated my dramas all these years?! I would have given up long ago. I learned to appreciate you. If patients offend you, don't take it to heart what they say about you. They don't understand you're doing the best for them.

Winnicott (1955a) suggested the term the stage of concern as a substitute for Klein's concept of the depressive position. The capacity for concern develops following a repeated sequential dynamic, which is termed benign circle and includes instinctual experiences, acceptance of responsibility (guilt), working through and true restitutive gesture (Winnicott, 1956b). In her words, Lily accepts responsibility for her aggression toward the therapist and shows concern about his possible destruction by other patients. I believe that her words echo Winnicott's (1969) much-quoted passage that illustrates the journey from object relating to object usage, which is achieved through unconscious destruction (Abram, 2007).

Concern for an object implies further integration and emotional growth, and it is associated positively with the individual's sense of responsibility, especially in relationships into which instinctual drives have entered (Winnicott, 1963b). Concern is the result of the emergence of benign circles, which is a major indication that the patient is moving towards independence. Benign circles are characterized with a dim perception of the therapeutic experience, an inner working-through and reparation (Winnicott, 1956b), and they are created when therapists leave their chairs and sit with the patients on the floor in an intermediate position. Only there, on the floor, appear the significant processes that help the patient move from object relatedness toward object usage.

In the last stage of Winnicott's developmental theory, there is capability of meeting the world and all its complexities because of seeing there more and more of what is already present in his or her own self (Winnicott, 1963c). As therapy continued, it seemed that such process occurs in Lily's life as she created new social circles and was invited to present her works in galleries. Currently, she is on a low subutex dosage and still dealing with the question of when to complete the detoxification program. A major concern is that ending the pharmacological treatment means also ending psychotherapy.

During therapy, OMT patients realize that the detoxification process is quite long. As one patient who came off methadone after ten years in treatment said: *"when I entered treatment, I thought that I will come off methadone after a year or two. There are many patients who think like me. They don't understand that therapy is as important as methadone"*.

Concluding remarks

The vicissitudes that appear during gradual detoxification may vary between patients. Some patients who receive low methadone dosages report that low dosages are associated with more ability to feel various emotions, whereas high dosages are associated with emotional numbness. Other patients report increasing mental distress and especially anxiety symptoms, such as panic attacks, which are associated with low doses. Based on my experience, these symptoms appear mostly among patients who did not undergo significant psychotherapeutic processes during OMT and imply on threatening mental contents as well as on reality anxiety, which is related to the approaching treatment discontinuation. It is of value to remember that dependence is a keyword in Winnicott's developmental theory, and perhaps at such stages, physical withdrawal symptoms are entwined with mental contents.

As mentioned earlier, Winnicott (1963c) saw dependence as a critical element of human life and did not support the idea of complete independence. In my opinion, this saying corresponds with the awareness of the detoxified patient that, in certain situations, he may relapse and start abusing drugs again or even regress toward drug dependence. This awareness may lead some patients to continue psychotherapy or counseling after OMT detoxification or to attend Narcotics Anonymous groups. This realization is embodied in the following patient's words:

> I have to remember that I will never be like other people who have never been addicted. Others can smoke a joint at the end of the day or sniff a line of cocaine in a party. I know that I must be careful because I can become addicted again.

References

Abram, J. (2007). *The language of Winnicott*. Routledge.

Amato, L., Davoli, M., Perucci, C. A., Ferri, M., Faggiano, F., & Mattick, R. P. (2005). An overview of systematic reviews of the effectiveness of opiate maintenance therapies: Available evidence to inform clinical practice and research. *Journal of Substance Abuse Treatment*, *28*(4), 321–329.

Bentzley, B. S., Barth, K. S., Back, S. E., & Book, S. W. (2015). Discontinuation of buprenorphine maintenance therapy: Perspectives and outcomes. *Journal of Substance Abuse Treatment*, *52*, 48–57.

Bleich, A., & Adelson, M. (2000). Opiate addiction as a chronic brain disease: New concept of an old problem, and re-evaluation of methadone treatment. *Harefuah*, *138*(6), 454–457.

Bollas, C. (1987). *The shadow of the object: Psychoanalysis of the unthought known*. Free Association Books.

Brewer, D. D., Catalano, R. F., Haggerty, K., Gainey, R. R., & Fleming, C. B. (1998). A meta-analysis of predictors of continued drug use during and after treatment for opiate addiction. *Addiction*, *93*(1), 73–92.

Brunette, M. F., Mueser, K. T., & Drake, R. E. (2004). A review of research on residential programs for people with severe mental illness and co-occurring substance use disorders. *Drug Alcohol Review, 23*(4), 471–481.

De Leon, G. (2000). *The therapeutic community: Theory, model, and method.* Springer.

Eklund, C., Melin, L., Hiltunen, A., & Borg, S. (1994). Detoxification from methadone maintenance treatment in Sweden: Long-term outcome and effects on quality of life situation. *International Journal of Addictions, 29*(5), 627–645.

Evans, C. J., & Cahill, C. M. (2016). Neurobiology of opioid dependence in creating addiction vulnerability. *F1000 Research, 5,* F1000 Faculty Rev-1748.

Freud, S. (1915/1959). Observations on transference love. In J. Strachey (Ed. & Trans.), *The standard edition of the complete psychological works of Sigmund Freud* (vol. 12, pp. 157–171). Hogarth Press.

Goldfarv, A. (1996). *The myth of the therapeutic community therapy for drug addiction as a mechanism for social control among therapists and patients.* (Doctoral dissertation). Hebrew university of Jerusalem: Jerusalem, Israel. (in Hebrew).

Henry-Edwards, S., Gowing, L., White J. M., Ali, R., Bell, J., Brough, R., Lintzeris, N., Ritter, A., & Quigley, A. (2003). *Clinical guidelines and procedures for the use of methadone in the maintenance treatment of opioid dependence.* National Expert Advisory Committee on Illicit Drugs.

Hiltunen, A. J., & Eklund, C. (2002). Withdrawal from methadone maintenance treatment. Reasons for not trying to quit methadone. *European Addiction Research, 8*(1), 38–44.

Hiltunen, A. J., Eklund, C., & Borg, S. (2011). The first 38 methadone maintenance treatment patients in Stockholm: 15-year follow-up with a main focus on detoxification from methadone. *Nordic Journal of Psychiatry, 65*(2), 106–111.

Hser, Y., Hoffman, V., Grella, C. E., & Anglin, M. D. (2001). A 33-year follow-up of narcotics addicts. *Archives of General Psychiatry, 58*(5), 503–508.

Kleber, H. (2007). Pharmacologic treatments for opioid dependence: Detoxification and maintenance options. *Dialogues in Clinical Neuroscience, 9*(4), 455–470.

Magura, S., & Rosenblum, A. (2001). Leaving methadone treatment: Lessons learned, lessons forgotten, lessons ignored. *Mount Sinai Journal of Medicine, 68*(1), 62–74.

Malivert, M., Fatseas, M., Denis, C., Langlois, E., & Auriacombe, M. (2012). Effectiveness of therapeutic communities: A systematic review. *European Addiction Research, 18*(1), 1–11.

Mattick, R. P., Breen, C., Kimber, J., & Davoli, M. (2009). Buprenorphine maintenance versus placebo or methadone maintenance for opioid dependence. *The Cochrane Database of Systematic Reviews, 3,* CD002209.

Mattick, R.P., Breen, C., Kimber, J., & Davoli, M. (2014). Buprenorphine maintenance versus placebo or methadone maintenance for opioid dependence. *The Cochrane Database of Systematic Reviews, 2,* CD002207.

Michael, A. (2007). Addiction and recovery. Ach Publishers LTD. (in Hebrew).

Ofer, G., & Durban, G. (1999). Curiosity: Reflections on its nature and functions. *American Journal of Psychotherapy, 53*(1), 35–51.

Potik, D. (2010). Possessive objects and paralyzing moods. *Psychoanalytic Quarterly, 79*(3), 687–715.

Potik, D., Adelson, M., & Schreiber, S. (2007). Drug addiction from a psychodynamic perspective: Methadone maintenance treatment (MMT) as transitional phenomena. *Psychology and Psychotherapy: Theory, Research and Practice, 80*(2), 311–325.

Sella, E. (2002). Therapeutic communities in Israel. In D. Elisha & S. Marchevski (Eds.), *Alcohol and drug abuse and addiction* (pp. 185–216). Dyonon. (in Hebrew).

Smith, L. A., Gates, S., & Foxcroft, D. (2006). Therapeutic communities for substance related disorder. *The Cochrane Database of Systematic Reviews, 1,* CD005338.

Substance Abuse and Mental Health Services Administration. (2006). *Detoxification and substance abuse treatment. Treatment Improvement Protocol (TIP) Series, Protocol (TIP) Series, No. 45.* HHS Publication No. (SMA) 134131. Substance Abuse and Mental Health Services Administration.

Summers, F. (1994). The work of D. W. Winnicott. In *Object relations theories and psychopathology* (pp. 137–190). The Analytic Press.

Sun, H. M., Li, X. Y., Chow, E. P., Li, T., Xian, Y., Lu, Y. H., Tian, T., Zhuang, X., & Zhang, L. (2015). Methadone maintenance treatment programme reduces criminal activity and improves social well-being of drug users in China: A systematic review and meta-analysis. *BMJ Open, 5*(1), e005997.

Unnithan, S., Gossop, M., & Strang, J. (1992). Factors associated with relapse among opiate addicts in an outpatient detoxification programme. *British Journal of Psychiatry, 161,* 654–657.

Vanderplasschen, W., Colpaert, K., Autrique, M., Rapp, R. C., Pearce, S., Broekaert, E., & Vandevelde, S. (2013). Therapeutic communities for addictions: A review of their effectiveness from a recovery-oriented perspective. *Scientific World Journal, 2013,* 427817.

Vanderplasschen, W., Vandevelde, S., & Broekaert, E. (2014). *Therapeutic communities for treating addictions in Europe: Evidence, current practices and future challenges.* European Monitoring Centre for Drugs and Drug Addiction.

Volkow, N. D., Koob, G. F., & McLellan, A. T. (2016). Neurobiologic advances from the brain disease model of addiction. *The New England Journal of Medicine, 374*(4), 363–371.

Wakeman, S. E. (2016). Using Science to battle stigma in addressing the opioid epidemic: Opioid agonist therapy saves lives. *American Journal of Medicine, 129*(5), 455–456.

Winnicott, D. W. (1945). Primitive emotional development. *International Journal of Psychoanalysis, 26,* 137–143.

Winnicott, D. W. (1950–1955). Aggression in relation to emotional development. In *Through paediatrics to psycho - analysis* (pp. 204–218). Tavistock Publications, 1958.

Winnicott, D. W. (1954). Mind and its relation to the psyche-soma. *British Journal of Medical Psychology, 27*(4), 201–209.

Winnicott, D. W. (1955a). The depressive position in normal emotional development. *British Journal of Medical Psychology, 28*(2–3), 89–100.

Winnicott, D. W. (1955b). Metapsychological and clinical aspects of regression. *International Journal of Psychoanalysis, 36,* 16–26.

Winnicott, D. W. (1956a). Primary maternal preoccupation. In *Collected papers, through paediatrics to psychoanalysis* (pp. 300–305). Tavistock Publications, 1958.

Winnicott, D. W. (1956b). Psychoanalysis and the sense of guilt. In J. D. Sutherland (Ed.), *Psychoanalysis and contemporary thought* (pp. 15–32). Grove Press.

Winnicott, D. W. (1960a). The theory of the parent-infant relationship. *International Journal of Psychoanalysis, 41*, 585–595.

Winnicott, D. W. (1960b). *Ego distortion in terms of true and false self.* In *The maturational process and the facilitating environment* (pp. 140–152). The Hogarth Press and the Institute of Psycho-Analysis, 1965.

Winnicott, D. W. (1963a). Dependence in infant care, in child care, and in the psycho-analytic setting. *The International Journal of Psychoanalysis, 44*, 339–344.

Winnicott, D. W. (1963b). The development of the *capacity for concern. Bulletin of the Menninger Clinic, 27*, 167–176.

Winnicott, D. W. (1963c). From dependence towards independence in the development of the individual. In *The maturational process and the facilitating environment* (pp. 83–92). The Hogarth Press and the Institute of Psycho-Analysis, 1965.

Winnicott, D. W. (1969). The use of an object and relating through identifications. *The International Journal of Psychoanalysis, 50*, 711–716.

Winnicott, D. W. (1971). *Playing and reality.* Tavistock Publications.

Winnicott, D. W. (1974). Fear of psychoanalysis. *International Review of Psychoanalysis, 1*(1–2), 103–107.

Winnicott, D. W. (1987). *Babies and their mothers.* Free Association Books.

Winstock, A. R., Lintzeris, N., & Lea, T. (2011). "Should I stay or should I go?" Coming off methadone and buprenorphine treatment. *International Journal of Drug Policy, 22*(1), 77–81.

Wirfs, M. J. (2019). *The APRN and PA's complete guide to prescribing drug therapy 2020.* Springer.

World Health Organization. (2008). *Lexicon of alcohol and drug terms.* World Health Organization.

Wu, L. T., Woody, G. E., Yang, C., Mannelli, P., & Blazer, D. G. (2011). Differences in onset and abuse/dependence episodes between prescription opioids and heroin: Results from the national epidemiologic survey on alcohol and related conditions. *Substance Abuse and Rehabilitation, 2011*(2), 77–88.

Younger, J. W., Chu, L. F., D'Arcy, N. T., Trott, K. E., Jastrzab, L. E., & Mackey, S. C. (2011). Prescription opioid analgesics rapidly change the human brain. *Pain, 152*(8), *1803–1810.*

Zhu, H., & Wu, L. T. (2018). National trends and characteristics of inpatient detoxification for drug use disorders in the United States. *BMC Public Health, 18*(1), 1073.

Chapter 9

Drug abuse and addiction in the view of self psychology

> "Man can no more survive psychologically in a psychological milieu that does not respond empathetically to him than he can survive physically in an atmosphere that contains no oxygen".
>
> (Kohut, 1977, p. 253)

Over the years, analysts who work within the self psychology school of thought have provided interesting contributions regarding the treatment of drug abuse and addiction (Hagman, 1995; Levin, 1987; Ulman, & Paul, 2006). In the following lines, I will review central ideas about drug abuse and addiction, which rely on Kohutian thought. Then I will present a case illustration of a patient who turned to therapy while he was abusing cannabis, MDMA and cocaine. Since cannabis is the most prevalent abused drug in the world, and because many patients who seek therapy in both the public and the private sectors report on either past or current abuse of this drug, I found it appropriate to start with a short review on the prevalence and the harmful consequences of cannabis abuse.

Cannabis abuse and addiction

Cannabis is globally the most commonly used psychoactive substance under international control (World Health Organization, 2016). In 2013, an estimated 181.8 million people between the ages of 15–64 years used cannabis for nonmedical purposes globally (uncertainty estimates 128.5–232.1 million) (United Nations Office on Drugs and Crime, 2015). In other words, cannabis is probably either cultivated, trafficked and abused in almost every country on earth. About 147 million people, 2.5% of the world population, use cannabis (annual prevalence) compared with 0.2% consuming cocaine and 0.2% consuming opioids (World Health Organization, 2019).

The high increase in cannabis use rates has begun in the 1960s with the emergence of the hippie counterculture when cannabis became one of its most prominent characteristics (Davis & Munoz, 1968; Wesson, 2011). Ever since studies show that cannabis use is highly prevalent among the adult population in many countries around the world (World Health Organization, 2016), and the public discourse over the decriminalization of this drug is only growing. Much of the growing interest is probably because of the discovery of the cannabinoid system in the brain (Iversen, 2003; Pertwee, 2008) and the medical use of cannabis for treatment of various diseases and disorders (NASEM, 2017).

Drug abuse in general and cannabis abuse in particular has become a significant leisure activity of many adolescents and adults. Many individuals who abuse this drug have positive attitude toward cannabis abuse, such as *"cannabis is not dangerous"* and *"you cannot compare the hazards of cannabis use and heroin use"*. In a certain sense, the last saying is true because the harmful consequences of each drug class vary. The first saying is highly problematic because people either do not know or do not want to acknowledge the negative consequences of cannabis abuse. Cannabis abuse may impair the ability to process information efficiently (Solowij, Michie, & Fox, 1991), and it also impairs memory and attention (Solowij et al., 2002). Cannabis abuse also increases the risk for accidents, and it is associated with mental disorders (Barrigón et al., 2010; Hall, 2015; Moore et al., 2007).

Cannabis is the second most widely used intoxicant in adolescence, and massive cannabis abuse is associated with disadvantages in neurocognitive performance and alterations in brain functioning at this age (Jacobus & Tapert, 2014). Adolescent cannabis abuse is associated with an increased risk of psychosis (Mustonen et al., 2018), and adolescent initiation of cannabis abuse is associated with the emergence and severity of psychotic symptomatology and functional impairment (Bagot, Milin, & Kaminer, 2015). It should be noted that cannabis is a generic name for a plant from which hashish, hashish oil and marijuana can be extracted, and these substances vary in their potency. Epidemiological studies demonstrate that cannabis abuse is associated with an increased risk of psychosis and confirms a dose-response relationship between the level of abuse and the risk of later psychosis (Murray, Quigley, Quattrone, Englund, & Di Forti, 2016).

A common question concerns the addictive potential of cannabis. Individuals who abuse cannabis frequently often report cravings, decreased appetite, irritability, mood dysregulation and sleep difficulties within the two weeks after quitting (Budney & Hughes, 2006; Gorelick et al., 2012). This description suggests cannabis withdrawal syndrome, and this syndrome is actually a criterion of cannabis use disorders (American Psychiatric Association, 2013; World Health Organization, 2018). Findings of animal and human studies indicate that cessation of regular and long-term cannabis abuse precipitates a withdrawal syndrome with mainly behavioral and mood symptoms of light to moderate intensity, which can usually be treated in an outpatient setting.

Around 2004, appeared various substances named "Spice" or "K2" as legal alternatives for cannabis abusers, curious individuals or those who wished to avoid detection in routine drug tests (Vandrey, Dunn, Fry, & Girling, 2012; Winstock & Barratt, 2013). Soon, the harmful effects of these synthetic cannabinoids were discovered when the number of emergency department visits related to these substances increased sharply (Bush & Woodwell, 2014). During the last years, the accumulative evidence suggests that acute synthetic cannabinoids intoxication is associated with poisoning and deaths (Adamowicz, 2016; Law et al., 2015; Shevyrin et al., 2015) and with serious physical complications and psychopathology (Mensen et al., 2019; Tait, Caldicott, Mountain, Hill, & Lenton, 2016).

The growing evidence from clinicians and pharmacological studies led to illegalization of such substances in many countries, but synthetic cannabinoids are constantly changing in attempts by manufacturers to evade legislation (Hudson & Ramsey, 2011). The ensemble of such events - marketing of designer drugs or illegal synthetic, laboratory-made chemicals, the detection of their harmful consequences and finally illegalization, reminds a "cat-and-mouse game", when the legislators constantly lag behind.

Self psychology conceptualization of drug abuse and addiction

Kohut did not treat patients who abused drugs, but he related to this subject a few times in his writings. In one of his early papers, he noted that the addicted individual does not has the capacity for self-soothing nor can he make the transition to a sleeping state. He added that the origin of addiction is in a failure to transform early childhood experiences of going to sleep into solid psychic structures (Kohut, 1959). Consequently, drugs turn to substitutes for missing tension-regulatory capacities. The abuser's dependence will appear in therapy not as a transference, but rather as a need for soothing. Hence, the primary therapeutic task involves acknowledgment of the dependence on other selfobjects as the patient will see the therapist as the carrier of his projected fantasies (Kohut, 1959).

Although some of these ideas bear a certain resemblance to those presented by a British psychoanalyst a few years earlier (Winnicott, 1953), Kohut's intuition about the treatment of people with addictive disorders is quite impressive. First, he emphasizes the lack of self-regulation capacities that characterize this population. Second, he notes that individuals with addictive disorders hold a set of grandiose fantasies that provide temporary support, and later studies confirmed the link between narcissistic pathology and addictions (Bruno et al., 2014; Carter, Johnson, Exline, Post, & Pagano, 2012). Third, Kohut (1959) related also to the psychoanalytic technique by hinting that the classical method of eliciting insight and understanding of unconscious conflicts will not prove beneficial for treatment of drug abuse.

Kohut's most significant contribution to the addictions field appeared at a later stage of his career in a preface to a National Institute on Drug Abuse (NIDA) monograph, which had focused on psychoanalytic treatment of drug abuse and addiction. He noted that narcissistic disorders, perversions, delinquent behaviors and addictions are different conditions that vary in their symptomatology but share the same etiology (Kohut, 1977a). A personality defect lies in the basis of all these pathologies and motivates a repetitive search after a merger with a selfobject that will provide a desired state of mind. This defect was created during the child's development when he was supposed to feel omnipotence over his capacities, but his selfobjects could not provide him this experience. Consequently, addictions constitute unsuccessful reparation attempts to cure the major defects in the structure of the self, and the addicted individual craves for the drug because he believes in its ability to repair the defects in his selfhood (Kohut, 1977a).

Meaning that the drug has become the selfobject that failed the addicted individual during a specific life period, and it provides the required selfobject needs for development. The aim of addiction, whether it is drug addiction or behavioral addiction, such as compulsive buying or compulsive gambling, is to fill structural voids in the structure of the self. Kohut (1977a) compares the addiction to an abnormal opening in the digestive tract, which prevents digestion of the food and causes a constant feeling of hunger, although the individual eats. In other words, addiction is much the same as a bottomless pit or a black hole.

Gradually, the recurrent drug abuse becomes a complex aspect of a defence system aimed to strengthen the grandiose self, and the drugs become a substitute for healthy selfobjects (Ulman & Paul, 2006). Drug addicts are characterized by low self-image (Kohut, 1977a), and drugs provide them a false grandiosity and arrogance, which assists in simultaneously increasing self-esteem and avoiding intense feelings of shame (Ulman & Paul, 2006). Individuals with an incohesive self may turn to drug abuse also because the ingestion of the drug provides a symbolic mirroring and an acceptance by the selfobject, or because it allows a merger with his magical power (Kohut, 1977a). When the drug becomes a symbolically sustaining and accepting selfobject, a tendency to addiction is created (Tolpin, 1996). Flanagan (2002, p. 189) emphasizes the importance of feeling twinship for human development and notes that: *"too much time without a feeling of twinship can make people feel like they are unraveling and losing touch with themselves"*. Difficulties in achieving a feeling of twinship during childhood can lead to loneliness, alienation feelings and to a search for external means, which will assist in dissipating such feelings (Jenkins & Zunguze, 1998; Mora, 2011).

Drug abuse allows avoiding an encounter with the inner world and assists in adopting an identity while socializing with other drug abusers. Drugs constitute a sort of bridge to the companion of drug abusers and elicit feelings of twinship during the joint drug abuse. In my opinion, Becker's (1963) seminal study on social deviance demonstrates how marijuana serves as not only as a means of entrance to a specific community but also as means of establishing a distinct identity. Authentic selfobjects allow development, transformation and provide the essential support and nourishment for the personality's consolidation, whereas false selfobjects (drugs) do not enable any development and damage the consolidation of the personality construct (Ulman & Paul, 2006). Individuals who abuse drugs try to fix the self's defects, but this abuse sentences them to an eternal and elusive search for an authentic selfobject, when the self-structure is constantly harmed (Tolpin & Kohut, 1980).

Addiction constitutes a curtain that hides significant defects in the self-structure, and it stems from an absence of internal mental structures that are responsible for significant functions (Kohut, 1971, 1977a). Hence, when examining the structure of the self, addicted individuals differ from non-addicted individuals in the lack of mental structures that allow emotional regulation. The recurrent drug abuse constitutes a compensation attempt for the absent mental structures (Van Schoor, 1992), and it is also a reaction to the fragmentation of the self (Kohut, 1977a).

I will relate to these ideas and present new ones about the relations between specific drugs and the self-structure in the following clinical material.

Case illustration

Peter, a 22-year-old single male, turned to a therapist who works in the addictions field but made it clear that drug abuse issues are not the main reason for which he came for treatment. Peter worked many hours in a family coffee house with a few of his brothers, but felt frustrated because his wills varied from his family's plans for him. During most of Peter's childhood, the father was addicted to drugs, and the mother struggled to support the family. Peter described how, as a child, he noticed that the father tends to enter the bathroom quite often alone for long minutes and how he found many tools used for smoking cocaine in the house. The family suffered from hunger since the father had spent the family's savings on buying drugs. He had also taken many loans, which he could not return. Peter added that the father was not very concerned about the growing debts, and the authorities came several times to confiscate the family's property. His older brothers did not attend school and had begun to work in order to pay for the father's debts.

Peter described himself as a mischievous child who had difficulties in sitting in class and listening to teachers. In his home, no one talked to him about the importance of receiving a proper education, and he became bored in school. Peter has never undergone any evaluation for diagnosing attention deficit and hyperactivity disorders or learning difficulties. Soon, he became involved in violent acts in school, and his parents had been continuously invited to the principal's office when they also heard about school tardiness and frequent absences. However, the parents did not always arrive at those meetings or to parent–child conferences. Peter did not attend high school regularly and spent his days with friends outside school. He noted that from an early age, he was flirtatious with girls.

Professional basketball was an anchor in his chaotic life. He had begun playing at a young age and advanced to play in different professional teams. Two years before he turned to therapy, he argued with his coach about his role in the team, and subsequently, he quit playing professional basketball. The therapist, who also played professional basketball in his adolescence until his injury, asked Peter if he will return to play professional basketball in the future, and Peter answered negatively. The therapist said that he feels sad for Peter to give up his childhood dream. Peter answered that he is not in shape, and that professional sport requires constant practicing. He considered himself a good player, but returning to professional basketball requires full time practicing, and currently, he is committed to the family business. Peter added that famous coaches predicted him a promising future. However, he had understood that his professional career is over. The therapist listened carefully and asked Peter not to give up his dream. Deep down inside, he knew that he was not talking only to the patient.

Peter's family supported him over the years, and he heard his father saying numerous times that he would have a better life because of his talent. Upon retirement, he felt obliged to recompense his family for their prolonged investment and support and went to work in the family business. He turned out to be a diligent and devoted worker, and ever since he started working, the revenue grew. Peter chose to redesign the place, began to sell new products and invested a lot in marketing. However, when he described his initiative and the business' benefits, he was quite forlorn because he did not receive any appreciation for his efforts.

When he turned for therapy, he smoked cannabis daily and abused MDMA and lysergic acid diethylamide (LSD) at parties. When he played professionally, Peter lived a sportive lifestyle and did not use alcohol or drugs. The dam has been breached following his retirement when he began to abuse cannabis with some friends and then alone. After a few months, he began to attend parties and abused MDMA and, on some trips abroad, experimented with LSD. In one of the times when he abused cannabis, his family saw that he was talking "*very strange*" and began to worry. The therapist asked if there were more similar experiences, and he replied that there were a few times when he abused cannabis or synthetic cannabinoids and felt very confused without any ability to understand what happens around him. The therapist said that it sounds like an experience of lack of control, and Peter answered very quickly that he: "*knows to stay in control even when he uses drugs*". The therapist asked if such experiences led him to turn to therapy, and Peter answered positively, saying that he was anxious since he did not know when such an experience would end. Hearing this answer, the therapist tried to ask a few more questions to understand if the patient experienced brief psychotic episodes, but Peter answered elusively.

The therapist felt Peter's shame and concealment about such experiences and decided to leave this issue for now. He decided to provide information on the association between cannabis and anxiety and psychotic states. Peter's comments included many of the prevalent answers heard among cannabis abusers: "*it is not dangerous*", "*look what is happening around. Everyone is smoking weed*", "*I know when to stop*". Peter's therapist said that peter and individuals who had the same experiences differ from other individuals because of family genetics and because there is evidence that the drug abuse led to a deterioration in his mental condition. The therapist added that he understood that Peter's friends abuse drugs, but he should be cautious when he hangs with them. Peter answered that he learned from his unpleasant experiences and that he can handle anxiety states. The therapist looked at him, concerned, and said that he worries about him.

Establishment of empathic matrix and vicarious introspection

Peter said a few times that he does not want to use drugs throughout his whole life. He explained that he is a young man without many commitments, and cannabis use is a means for relaxation from the hard work at the end of the day. A relevant question that arises at such situations is: *"so you are actually saying that you have difficulties in calming yourself or relaxing?"*. Some patients with narcissistic disorders immediately revolt when they hear this question because it implies on their imperfection, and the therapist can continue and explore this issue. However, Peter's attitude was completely different since he said that he uses cannabis because of its growing social legitimacy. In such situations, arises a question about the therapy's aim because the patient does not see either cannabis abuse or its consequences as a problem. Peter turned to therapy due to a general feeling of distress and negated any harmful consequences of cannabis abuse.

In many mental health facilities, the answer is clear because when non-psychotic individuals with mental disorders and active drug abuse turn for treatment, they are told that they cannot receive treatment as long as they abuse drugs. Sometimes, they are referred to dual diagnosis facilities when they feel unbelonging because other patients have schizophrenia and other psychotic disorders. Peter was like many other cannabis abusers who functioned quite well toward outside, but in therapy reported on lack of futility and meaninglessness.

In my opinion, the first stage in the therapy of such patients should include the establishment of an empathic matrix in which the therapist begins to locate himself as a selfobject. In this context, Kogan (2008) notes that there is no human existence without the presence of another person who presents oneself as a responsible presence and constitutes a matrix for the coming to being of the self. In the therapy of drug abusers, the provision of information about the consequences of drug abuse and sayings that drug abuse risks the patient with an authentic concern create a clear, responsive and living presence of a new selfobject in the patient's life.

Psychoeducation about the effects of drug abuse is conceived as a component of cognitive-behavioral treatment (CBT) for drug abusers, and counselors who work within the motivational interviewing approach use it for eliciting motivation for change. I believe that psychoeducation is part of the second stage of the treatment of drug abusers. This stage consists mainly of questioning the patient about the various drugs he abused, understanding his expectations before the abuse and his feelings following it. When the therapist wants to receive information about the patient's drug abuse history, he should place himself in the patient's place to understand his experiences and use vicarious introspection (Kohut, 1984), as the leading line of the investigation. One of the main characteristics of a therapist who works within the self psychology school of thought and treats drug abusers is non-judgmentalism and understanding that drugs induce pleasant experiences. Such therapist does not try to frighten the patients with slogans about drugs and provides psychoeducation according to the patient's knowledge level. The therapist holds in mind that drug abuse only indicates the patient's distress and on his repeated attempts to cure the defects in his selfhood.

The vicarious introspection is directed toward understanding the patient's mental condition before the beginning of the drug abuse, recognizing the selfobjects in the past and present, the way of the drug abuse, the expectations before abuse of drug of any class and certainly the setting. Vicarious introspection and empathy serve for data gathering and for the systematic ordering of the data, with the aid of a particular conceptual framework (Bacal & Carlton, 2010; Kohut, 1981). This approach enables the therapist to understand the drug's role in the patient's mental life, and especially what selfobject needs tries the patient repetitively to provide.

In this case, cannabis abuse has begun after Peter's retirement and helped him to cope with disappointment, frustration, anger and emptiness. The rituality involved in preparing a joint at the end of the day and the smoking allowed him an encounter with himself without any accompanied anxiety or any negative emotions. Nevertheless, after a while, the same drug which provided a temporary cohesiveness led to an intensification of fragmentation anxiety.

A month after the beginning of therapy, Peter said that occasionally he uses cocaine and MDMA. These drugs are associated with parties and night clubs and with the will to feel elation and excitement. He added that sometimes he snorts cocaine when he is in night clubs with friends and when he wants "*to make a move*" on a beautiful girl and then stopped talking. The therapist remained silent with him for a minute and then asked him if cocaine gives him self-confidence to hit on girls. Peter answered positively and added that in the last months, he is more reluctant than before when it comes to starting conversations with girls and that he fears rejection. The therapist asked him if he had such fears when he played basketball, and Peter answered negatively. He replied that he was more self-confident when he played basketball and used to brag that he was a professional athlete when he met girls at parties. In this context, Ulman and Paul (2006) note that drugs provide false grandiosity and arrogance, which elevates self-value and simultaneously allows avoidance of intense shame.

Because of the high price of cocaine and after cannabis abuse failed him and caused unpleasant experiences, MDMA became his favorite drug. The setting of the party and this drug's effect made people around him look more loving and happier. Individuals who use MDMA report on such experiences (Leneghan, 2013), and perhaps this drug provided a merger experience with selfobjects and, simultaneously, helped to create an environment with living and responding selfobjects.

Drugs as building blocks of compensatory structures

The vicarious introspection allowed the therapist to receive essential data on Peter's drug abuse and his sense of defectiveness before turning to therapy. The fragmentation anxiety intensified after he stopped playing professional basketball and led to disintegration of mental structures. The fragmentation anxiety includes loss of sense of self and estrangement from body and mind and breakup of the sense of continuity in time (Kohut, 1977b). Peter used different drugs and especially cannabis for creating certain cohesion, and in a recent empirical study among medical cannabis users, cannabis was found effective in dissipating fragmentation anxiety (Kamal, Kamal, & Lantela, 2018).

The idea that drug abuse constitutes unsuccessful attempts to cure the central defects of the self-structure and that drugs are the substitution for selfobjects appear in self psychology conceptualizations of addiction for years (Kohut, 1977a; Ulman & Paul, 2006). Van Schoor (1992) notes that recurrent drug abuse constitutes a compensation attempt on lack of missing structures, and in my opinion, drugs constitute building blocks of the compensatory structure and defensive structures.

In Kohut's (1977b) developmental theory, beneficent experiences with selfobjects assist in the development of the bipolar self, which is a superordinate configuration. The bipolar self is composed of two poles – the grandiose pole, which relates to ambitions and the idealized parental imago, which refers to ideals. Peter recalled his mother encouraging him to turn to sports from an early age and that she had even escorted him to a few games. It looked that his parents did notice his athletic skills, and his development as a professional player helped in the establishment of the grandiose pole. Peter received constant mirroring from his family, friends and the audience. The appreciation and admiration that he received during the years constituted a prolonged empathic resonance that allowed the development of healthy grandiosity and especially the establishment of an identity of a professional athlete. Nevertheless, other developmental needs were not provided, and Peter did not remember any memory of his parents playing with him or talking to him about his life. He explained that because of the father's lasting addiction, his mother was busy getting money to pay bills and to sustain the family during hard times.

After five months in therapy, he recalled how, as a teenager, he used to peep at the girls' locker rooms and that he had sexual experiences at a young age. He said that he became a subject of jealousy from his friends when he bragged on his successes, and perhaps besides the satisfaction of exhibition-istic-grandiose tensions, these sexual behaviors were also an oedipal victory over the father. In the grandiose pole, a compensatory structure with rel-atively stable secondary structures was established because of prolonged mirroring of grandiosity. However, outbursts of archaic exhibitionism oc-curred when he bragged before his friends on sexual experiences, or when during games, he would dribble and did not pass the ball to his teammates to show the crowd his unique skills.

Consequently, the personality structure was composed of a primary struc-tural defect in the grandiose pole, whereas the other pole has not been suc-cessfully developed because of the absence of an idealized parental imago. The father's addiction was accompanied with many absences and Peter saw him either when he was suffering withdrawal symptoms or under drug influ-ence. In such states, there are not any opportunities for a merger with a sig-nificant figure and internalization of ideals and values. In some cases, there is an identification with the father's behavior. Meaning, like in families of traumatized individuals, there is also a trans-generational transmission of addiction and, sometimes, therapists, during their professional career, meet not only the abusing parents but also the abusing children.

Kohut (1977b) notes that compensatory structure creates functional re-habilitation of the self by making up for the weakness in one pole of the self through the strengthening of the other pole. He adds that a weakness in the area of ambitions and exhibitionism is compensated for by the self-value provided by the pursuit of ideals and vice versa (Kohut, 1977b). In this case, the family's dedication and the parents' will that Peter will grow to be pro-fessional player contributed to a success experience and endowed him also a sense of belongingness to a sort of family (team) where the members (play-ers) wear the same uniform, support each other and share the same values.

During Peter's professional career, many of his selfobject needs were pro-vided, and he achieved a solid feeling of coherence. His athletic abilities and self-efficacy were an exit ticket from poverty and enabled the experience of independence and omnipotence without any need for selfobjects. The ending of the career was a significant narcissistic fault because professional sports gave him a sense of meaning and consisted of a barrier before the outbreak of fragmentation anxiety. In such states, there is a fall from grace, as the love of the crowd, the excitement and the adrenalin rushes are all gone at once, and a pervasive feeling of emptiness threatens the self-structure. In the absence of self-soothing capabilities and soothing selfobjects, drugs were conceived as selfobjects that can repair the self's defects. At the emo-tional absence of empathic selfobjects, transmuting internalization could not occur, and Peter could not internalize the parents' comforting abilities.

Cannabis abuse provided calmness and mental equilibrium while MDMA gave the excitement and the love that he received during a merger with the audience in basketball matches.

When there is either a disturbance in the flow or a disconnection of the empathic matrix, there is an experience of an empathic failure. The failure raises rage at different severity levels and when it is tolerable, a compensatory structure, which provides self-soothing through a thought, speaking or a song, is created by the self (Hominer, n.d.; Kulka, 2005). When the failure is intolerable for many reasons, the self cannot create a compensatory structure and the result is a defensive structure that manifests in either relinquishing the matrix or withdrawal (Hominer, n.d.; Kohut, 1977b, 1984).

Some of the criteria for cannabis use disorder include greater use of cannabis than intended, unsuccessful attempts to cut down or control the use and strong desire to use the drug (APA, 2013). Such phenomenon indicate that the drug has become a significant selfobject with which the patient tries to establish an empathic matrix. The growing amount of time the individual spends in obtaining drugs and functional impairment in different life areas imply that the individual is desperate, at least temporarily from creating a significant relationship with other people. Hominer (n.d.) notes that compensatory structure patches the hole in the self–selfobject matrix and saves a place for renewing the relationship. In my opinion, in some cases, drug abuse also signifies a patching attempt in the empathic matrix with selfobjects, and drugs assist in building a compensatory structure.

Drugs are the building blocks or the bricks in the different structures that are required to create a certain cohesiveness of the self. In this case, self-cannabis and self-MDMA matrixes provided self-soothing and excitement and merger (audience love), respectively. I believe that a defensive structure is created in cases of traumatic experiences, which elicit powerlessness and when the fragmentation anxiety is unbearable. Since an individual cannot exist without any matrix or any selfobject, there is compulsive attempt to establish a matrix with a drug, which is conceived as the desired selfobject that can provide the essential selfobject needs. In peter's case, compensatory structures were created following his retirement, but underneath was a yearning for human touch, and therefore, he turned to therapy.

After about six months of therapy, Peter said that he feels emotionally better ("*I feel much better. I don't know why, but I know that the fact that I'm arriving here contributes to it*"). He said that he started to abuse cannabis once in two or three weeks and began to talk more openly about himself. He reported that he works many hours in the family business and sees himself as the future manager of the place. It looked that his charismatic abilities assisted him in remarketing the coffee house and that he received healthy mirroring for his abilities from customers and suppliers. Despite the success, he felt that his father and his brothers do not appreciate him. Peter was discouraged and felt that he was not paid enough, although he rarely had a day off. Many times, he reported that his requests for a raise ended in anger outbursts from both sides.

After eight months of therapy, the positive feedbacks to his healthy grandiosity made him contemplate about academic studies. In one of the sessions, he reported on a fantasy in which he sees himself as a successful businessman, but this fantasy was accompanied with shame because he had many doubts concerning his learning abilities. Kohut's (1971) idea of vertical split relates to the existence, side by side of different structures of goals, attitudes and moral and aesthetic values. Siegel (1996) notes that the vertical split is a personality sector that is split off from the central sector by a defence of disavowal, which allows to hold ideas and engage in acts that are in variance with those held by the central personality sector.

In Peter's case, the splitted-off personality part was ashamed, lacking self-confidence, demanding mirroring for archaic grandiosity and yearning for a merger. This personality part appeared during family disputes with a renewed hope for the fulfillment of the selfobject needs, but the family drama was repeated all over again. When Peter talked about the disputes with his family, he noted that he is quite sure that his mother loves his brothers more than she loves him. The therapist said that he feels Peter's frustration and disappointment, but also his hope that the dispute will end, and his family members will say to him that they love him. Peter shed a tear and said that he is very doubtful if such an event will indeed happen because his family members are self-centered.

After a year in therapy, Peter thought of completing matriculation exams and registering for an entrepreneurship course. He began to play basketball with his friends on his free time but still abused drugs. After an additional three months, he reported that he stopped buying cannabis and abused it only once a month when his friends offered him. He did not give up the MDMA abuse and said that it's a *"way of discharge that enables him to have fun in parties"*.

"Experience-near" mode of observation

Additional significant issue concerned Peter's late arrivals. The therapy took place at the evening since he worked from the early morning hours. Already in the first meetings, Peter arrived a few minutes late, and the therapist tried to examine if this behavior reflects resistance. Peter assured the therapist that this behavior characterizes him from an early age. In the first meetings, while waiting, the therapist considered ending the treatment. On the one hand, he appreciated Peter's efforts and his willingness to arrive to therapy, but on the other hand, the idle sitting and the uncertainty whether the patient would be late this time in five or ten minutes raised anger.

In one of those times, the therapist started to think that perhaps he demands of the patient too much and that he is not empathic enough. He thought that ending the treatment would be an additional failure experience for a patient who could not almost persist in any setting in his life. He recalled that Peter grew up in a chaotic house where his selfobjects needs were not fully provided, and therefore, he did not have the opportunity to learn about responsibility. One of the therapist's contemplations was that maybe Peter strives for an omnipotent control over him as part of a merger transference, in which the therapist is experienced as an extension of the self (Kohut, 1971). He wondered again if ending therapy would not be an additional empathic failure that would hurt Peter's self, or perhaps Peter is afraid that further discovery of his inner world will lead to traumatization and therefore the late arrivals. Finally, the therapist wondered where in fact passes the line that distinguishes between empathic failure and traumatic failure?

When Peter arrived ten minutes late, he apologized as usual. The therapist asked him if he was also late for his team's games. Peter smiled and said that he had always appeared a few minutes before the beginning and played because he was one of the best players in the team. The therapist said that when he played professionally, players who were late used to sit on the bench the entire game and did not play. He added that Peter sees himself as a future businessman, but he should know that the workers constantly look up to the manager for personal example, and probably so does his employees in the coffee house. Peter looked quite surprised and did not say a word. Following this conversation, Peter was rarely late and, after a while, said that he commented one of his employees when he was late.

The continuing establishment of an empathic matrix in therapy allows the development of transferences, and in this case, the patient felt a certain twinship with the therapist. Such transference could take place because of the therapist's self-disclosure about his own active participation in professional sports. In twinship transference, the patient experiences the therapist as very similar or identical to himself, and thereby enhancing the patient's feeling of being understood and valued (Kohut, 1984). The therapist's choice not to end therapy but to become a selfobject by emphasizing values, such as personal responsibility, is an example of a process that can contribute to the cohesiveness of the self.

Hominer (n.d.) notes the difficulty of staying "experience-near" and adds that it is much easier to provide interpretations and explanations than to enter the patient's inner world and try endlessly to understand his experience. In my opinion, the decisions neither to confront the patient harshly nor to interpret the patient's acts as an oedipal struggle with the father and the usage of examples from the patient's world constitute attempts to remain "experience-near". Geist (2008) suggests that connectedness is a process in which both therapists and their patients experience each other as a deeply felt presence in each other's life. He notes that this is the unarticulated foundation upon which the self-structure is built (Geist, 2008).

Narcissistic fault, tragedy and restoration

As treatment progressed, Peter was ready to disclose more covert and embarrassing experiences. He reported an incident in which he took MDMA and thought people at a party look at him strangely. Peter mentioned similar experiences following cannabis abuse. In the beginning, he liked to abuse cannabis because it gave him a sense of harmony and relaxation, and when he smoked with his friends, he became more talkative and shared some deliberations about life.

Consequently, his friends nicknamed him *"the philosopher"*. However, after a few months of cannabis abuse, Peter smoked a joint with his friends and started thinking that he is worthless, and that other people can see that he is worthless. His friends noticed that he is confused and withdrawn and took care of him. Peter refused to see a psychiatrist and added that once in a year, he has a *"bad trip probably because of the bad quality of the MDMA or the cannabis"*.

Such incidents raise questions about the containment boundaries of psychotherapy of drug abusers. The continuing drug abuse during therapy also raises a relevant question to this period: does any drug abuse implies mental pathology, or is it just a recreational activity? There are probably many societal answers, but for therapists, the answer lies in the consequences of drug abuse and parameters, such as the patient's mental distress and his functioning level. Peter did not differ from other functioning individuals who used MDMA during parties at weekends. However, the drug abuse has begun following the cessation of Peter's professional career, and perhaps it was a repetitive attempt to cope or, more accurately, to heal a basic narcissistic fault.

According to Kulka (2005), Kohut's ideas signal a transition from Freud's guilty individual who struggles with unconscious conflicts toward a tragic man who yearns for the rehabilitation of the self from its fracture. In my opinion, Peter has been experiencing a few tragedies. First, the career termination disrupted the constant mirroring of his grandiosity. He said that following his retirement, he felt as he had plunged into a pit of despair and depression because all his life, he had trained to be a professional basketball player when suddenly all his qualities seemed irrelevant. Second, the patching attempt of the self, meaning the drug abuse, has failed and led to feelings of powerlessness. The "nourishment substances", which once made him feel better and decreased his anxiety level, have been revealed as toxic substances, which only enhanced the fragmentation experience.

Third, during therapy, Peter achieved, to some extent, rehabilitation of the self when he had managed a coffee house and cultivated a new dream of becoming a successful businessman. However, next to the high ambitions, which included academic studies and management of big companies, there were also feelings of shame, inferiority and many doubts about his ability to achieve such goals. The gap between his current condition and his longings reflects the tragic existence of an individual who feels a lack of authenticity in his life. This gap also appeared in his romantic life when he had incidental sexual relations but yearned for a close and intimate relationship.

The narcissistic fault in the self-structure enhances the patient's fragmentation anxiety, and in therapy, both the patient and therapist can look at the issues that nourish it. For example, after quite a long time in therapy, Peter answered positively to the repetitive question does he dream. When the therapist asked him about the content, Peter looked quite reluctant but finally said that he had dreamt that he is with some friends in a place that looks like a bathroom, and everybody is hugging and dancing. Next, he saw himself holding a friend and many friends having fun. The associations to the dream included a locker room of a sport's team after winning a match, but also a recent party when he used MDMA. At this party, he felt confused and inferior in comparison to his friends, and he was sure that everyone stares at him.

After reporting these associations, he seemed more reluctant to continue. The therapist did not mirror Peter's behavior but asked him about any sexual attraction toward one of his friends who appeared in the dream. It seemed that this question lowered a shame curtain because Peter was discouraged from talking about his dreams in the next months. The threatening interpretation, which was embodied in the therapist's question, probably scared the patient, and his subsequent saying that many individuals have dreams in which they find themselves in intimate situations with friends still left the patient withdrawn.

This dream reminds Carl Abraham's article about alcoholism. Abraham (1908/1979) relied on observations of men in pubs and noted that alcohol use enables the release of inhibitions, which causes the rise of latent homosexual impulses to the conscious. Dream content and associations of sweaty, not fully dressed men in situations of drive discharge will probably lead analysts and therapists working within the drive school of thought to conduct a clinical investigation that leads toward latent homosexuality. The dream indeed implies on issues of sexuality and manhood, but also on self-value issues and fears of an individual to meet his selfhood.

In my opinion, the dream implies the enormous yearning for a merger with an all-powerful idealized object that can provide help, protection and comfort. According to Kohut (1977b), when dealing with a traumatic state during an analysis of individuals with narcissistic personality disorder, the therapist should not actively supply the patient with rationalizations associated with oedipal psychopathology, but rather support the crumbling self by explaining the events that triggered the threatening dissolution.

About two months following this incident, Peter felt prouder of himself after completing an entrepreneurship course and thinking of a new project. He started to date women but still sporadically abused cannabis and MDMA. Much of the therapeutic work at this stage included helping Peter to tolerate grief and sadness associated with his childhood and the sportive career termination. The contents of the next sessions dealt with his family relations over the years and especially now when he has become the major figure who runs the family business. Peter felt exploited by the father who owned the business. He appreciated his father for recovering from drug addiction and running a business, but he often noted that his father always saw himself as a manager and not as a worker.

Peter also criticized his brothers for not working as hard as he does. He used to open the coffee house early in the morning to order products and, sometimes, to serve the customers. He felt bitterness, and every attempt to talk with his family about his employment terms ended in a verbal and aggressive argument. The subsequent sessions dealt with this issue, and in the next months, he succeeded in creating more convenient working hours and started learning for completion of matriculation examinations. He also started to talk about being the first family member who applies to college. However, he still felt exploited by his family members who spent less time in the coffee house, and when they appeared, they criticized him. In one of the loud arguments, Peter shouted at his father that if he is so unsatisfied with his work, he can fire him.

PETER: "My father annoyed me again".

THERAPIST: "You argued again about work?"

PETER: "He thinks that he knows everything and argues for no reason. When I say something, it turns out that I was right. He will never admit it".

THERAPIST: "You feel appreciated by your father?"

PETER: "Are you kidding me?! He won't say any good word. Some regular customers and suppliers say to him directly that I'm a better businessman than him. I hear from him mere criticism".

THERAPIST: "You work quite a time at the coffee house and sometimes you worked together with your father. Did you hear compliments from him?

PETER: "What, compliments? Only criticism! Yesterday I had enough and there were curses".

THERAPIST: "Curses?"

PETER: "Yes, yesterday I had enough. I cursed him and he cursed me back".

THERAPIST: "This conversation between you. A conversation between a father and a son sounds extremely unpleasant".

PETER: "It happens regularly between us".

THERAPIST: "I hear in your words that you experience your father's sayings not as criticism but rather as a humiliation and that you expect after all these years to hear compliments. But the compliments do not arrive, and therefore there is much frustration and aggression towards him".

PETER KEPT QUIET FOR A MINUTE AND THEN SAID: "I had enough. I work my butt off. I told him to fire me if he has the guts for it!"

THERAPIST: "I hear the skepticism in your voice".

PETER: "He won't do it. He knows damn well that no one will work as hard as I do. All my brothers work for only a few hours. They do not want to sell the business. It is very convenient for everyone that a reliable family member is present at the business all day".

THERAPIST: "So you actually protest against your father knowing that he cannot do a thing in this situation?"

PETER: "Yes. Definitely".

THERAPIST: "You feel victorious over him in this situation?"

PETER: "I never thought about it this way. But, yes, I surpassed him".

AFTER A SILENT PAUSE, THE THERAPIST SAID: "I think that your anger is not associated only with the family business but mainly with the past. I hear in your anger a saying towards your father that was not it enough that you were not next to me or supported me during childhood, and now you dare to criticize me instead of thanking me and acknowledging the good work I'm doing. Like he has no right to say the things he says to you".

PETER: "He indeed has no right! The family was almost torn apart because of his addiction. The authorities confiscated almost everything in our house. I saw syringes as a child! How much crying and suffering all these years?!"

THERAPIST: "You know Peter, in the last minutes when I am listening to you, I hear a child who asks all these years his father to see him, to understand what he's going through and mostly will be proud of him and tell him how much special he is".

Peter became silent and his eyes became red.

THERAPIST: "I see and hear the pain of a child who held inside much frustration and anger towards his father for many years. This child was afraid to show himself and was protected by a part of you that did not want the child to be hurt again. But this child appeared more often here in therapy and outside therapy and discovered many exciting things about himself and his abilities".

Kohut (1972) coined the term narcissistic rage to describe a condition in which an individual with vulnerable self-structure feels that his self-worth is threatened or injured and responds with anger, resentment and vengeance. Narcissistic rage stems from shame and dejection and is characterized by *"need for revenge, for righting a wrong, for undoing a hurt by whatever means, and a deeply anchored, unrelenting compulsion in the pursuit of all these aims"*

(Kohut, 1972, p. 638). Other clinicians and theorists have also suggested that individuals with narcissistic vulnerability exhibit rage, which is instigated by rejection that opens childhood wounds or events that contradict one's sense of uniqueness (Kernberg, 1975; Millon, 1997).

This sad vignette illustrates how narcissistic rage is accumulated throughout years of selfobjects needs frustration and nourished by the father's unavailability for merger and his inability to mirror Peter's grandiosity in the present. The renewed meeting between the recovered father and the son created opportunities for responding to Peter's narcissistic needs and perhaps providing a corrective experience for the entire family. In the new situation, proper responses of the father could help establish alternative structures to the archaic narcissistic structures. During the therapy, Peter understood that the family's traumatic history has influenced on all its members. He noted that he is sure that many of his brothers' behaviors, such as impulsivity, chasing money, buying solely expensive brand name products (clothes, watches, cars) and bragging about personal wealth, are all consequences of the fact that they also did not have a normal childhood. Although he had many disputes with his brothers, he always appreciated them because they started working at a young age and helped the mother. Peter raised the option of family therapy a few times, but the family members declined the idea. In this respect, every family member was a tragic man who lived estranged from other family members and carried his emotional scars silently.

In his therapeutic interventions, the therapist tried to present himself as a sustainable selfobject who sees, feels, listens and responds to the patient's experience. A main aim of therapy was to create an analytic matrix with flowing empathic resonance that allows a feeling of cohesion and assists in establishing mental structures. The therapist's ability to stay in an empathic stance that identifies the patient's selfobject needs, signals to splitted-off personality parts to appear, to be seen without fear of frustration, to receive acknowledgment and to move toward integration. In my opinion, such significant interventions pave the way to interpretations that clarify the patient's behavior in relation to his past, and allow recognition of additional elements of his selfhood that were dejected and ashamed. Such interventions help in dissolving the disavowal, which separates between personality parts and allows the vulnerable narcissism to appear without danger of traumatization.

Psychotherapy of drug abusers with narcissistic disorders may begin with a complaint that is not related to drug abuse because of the fear that the splitted-off elements will reappear and suffer re-traumatization. Praising the patient for drug abstinence of days and weeks or emphasizing his success in daily tasks constitutes mirroring of healthy grandiosity and encourages transference relations Patients will adhere to treatment if they conceive the therapist as a living and caring presence that provides empathic resonance even when the patient relapses sometimes.

Concluding remarks

According to self psychology conceptualizations, drugs either provide different functions that the abuser's self-structures cannot provide or they constitute as selfobjects who provide emotional needs. In my opinion, cannabis addiction (as well as gaming disorder and pathological buying) perhaps more than any other drug addiction consists of a solution for alienation and loneliness of an entire generation that suffers from imminent loneliness and has difficulties in creating empathic matrices with living selfobjects. In a few studies among cannabis abusers, impaired social and occupational functioning was found next to high prevalence of social anxiety (Buckner, Schmidt, Bobadilla, & Taylor, 2006; Mass, Bardong Kindl & Dahme, 2001). Additional studies among this population found intrinsic loneliness feelings and low self-value (Buckner et al., 2006; Dorard, Bungener, Corcos, & Berthoz, 2014; Mass et al., 2001).

Kulka (2005) notes that the flowing and the plentiful availability of empathic relation abolishes the tragedy of the individual. The creation of an empathic matrix and the continuing availability of empathic relating along therapy are vital in psychodynamic treatment of drug abusers. This therapeutic task is not simple because of the many complexities that characterize narcissistic disturbances, such as rigid defences, demandingness, entitlement or blaming the therapist for the patient's flaws. The treatment of this population stretches the barriers of the therapist's empathic relating and raises questions about the essences of empathic failures and optimal frustrations.

As illustrated in the clinical material, patients may continue abusing drugs during therapy. The chronic emptiness that patients experiences and their frustrating reality nourish the drug abuse and harden the therapeutic work. Relapses may occur during the treatment, especially when the disavowal dissolves, and new self-elements appear. These relapses will decrease as more self-elements are integrated into the personality and as a sense of cohesion in space and time increases. Consequently, the patient will feel that he lives an authentic life and actualizes the nuclear program of the self. However, sometimes, therapists meet patients with heavily damaged self-structures who abuse drugs for many years and cannot keep a job or create and maintain social ties. The selfobject needs of such patients cannot be provided solely during individual psychotherapy, mainly because of the high necessity for constantly available selfobjects, and lack of basic self-regulation skills required for relapse prevention. Attending Narcotics Anonymous meetings is an option for such patients, and, in the next chapter, I will explain why 12-step fellowships provide much of these patients' selfobject needs.

References

Abraham, K. (1908/1979). The psychological relations between sexuality and alcoholism. In *Selected papers on psychoanalysis* (pp. 80–90). Brunner/Mazel. (Original published in 1908).

Adamowicz, P. (2016). Fatal intoxication with synthetic cannabinoid MDMB-CHMICA. *Forensic Science International, 261*, e5–e10.

American Psychiatric Association. (2013). *Diagnostic and statistical manual of mental disorders* (5th Ed.). Author.

Bacal, H. A., & Carlton, L. (2010). Kohut's last words on analytic cure and how we hear them now: A view from specificity theory. *International Journal of Psychoanalytic Self Psychology, 5*(2), 132–143.

Bagot, K. S., Milin, R., & Kaminer, Y. (2015). Adolescent initiation of cannabis use and early-onset psychosis. *Substance Abuse, 36*(4), 524–533.

Barrigón, M. L., Gurpegui, M., Ruiz-Veguilla, M., Diaz, F. J., Anguita, M., Sarramea, F., & Cervilla, J. (2010). Temporal relationship of first-episode non-affective psychosis with cannabis use: A clinical verification of an epidemiological hypothesis. *Journal of Psychiatric Research, 44*(7), 413–420.

Becker, H. S. (1963). *Outsiders: Studies in the sociology of deviance.* Macmillan.

Bruno, A., Quattrone, D., Scimeca, G., Cicciarelli, C., Romeo, V. M., Pandolfo, G., Zoccali, R. A., & Muscatello, M. R. (2014). Unraveling exercise addiction: the role of narcissism and self-esteem. *Journal of Addiction, 2014*, 987841.

Buckner, J. D., Schmidt, N. B., Bobadilla, L., & Taylor, J. (2006). Social anxiety and problematic cannabis use: Evaluating the moderating role of stress reactivity and perceived coping. *Behaviour Research and Therapy, 44*(7), 1007–1015.

Budney, A. J., & Hughes, J. R. (2006). The cannabis withdrawal syndrome. *Current Opinion in Psychiatry, 19*(3), 233–238.

Bush, D. M., & Woodwell, D. A. (2014, October 16). Update: Drug-related emergency department visits involving synthetic cannabinoids. The CBHSQ Report, Substance Abuse and Mental Health Services Administration. Retrieved from http://www. samhsa.gov/data/sites/default/files/SR-1378/SR1378.pdf

Carter, R. R., Johnson, S. M., Exline, J. J., Post, S. G., & Pagano, M. E. (2012). Addiction and "generation me": Narcissistic and prosocial behaviors of adolescents with substance dependency disorder in comparison to normative adolescents. *Alcoholism Treatment Quarterly, 30*(2), 163–178.

Davis, F., & Munoz, L. (1968). Heads and freaks: Patterns and meanings of drug use among hippies. *Journal of Health and Social Behavior, 9*(2), 156–164.

Dorard, G., Bungener, C., Corcos, M., & Berthoz, S. (2014). Estime de soi, coping, soutien social perçu et dépendance au cannabis chez l'adolescent et le jeune adulte [Self-esteem, coping, perceived social support and substance use in young adults with a cannabis dependence disorder]. *L'Encephale, 40*(3), 255–262.

Flanagan, L. M. (2002). The theory of self psychology. In J. Berzoff, L. M. Flanagan, & P. Hertz, (Eds.), *Inside out and outside in: Psychodynamic clinical theory and practice in contemporary multicultural contexts* (pp. 173–198). Rowman & Littlefield Publishers.

Geist, R. (2008). Connectedness, permeable boundaries, and the development of the self: Therapeutic implications. *International Journal of Psychoanalytic Self Psychology, 3*(2), 129–152.

Gorelick, D. A., Levin, K. H., Copersino, M. L., Heishman, S. J., Liu, F., Boggs, D. L., & Kelly, D. L. (2012). Diagnostic criteria for cannabis withdrawal syndrome. *Drug and Alcohol Dependence, 123*(1–3), 141–147.

Hagman, G. (1995). A psychoanalyst in methadonia. *Journal of Substance Abuse, 12*(3), 167–179.

Hall, W. (2015). What has research over the past two decades revealed about the adverse health effects of recreational cannabis use? *Addiction, 110*(1), 19–35.

Hominer, D. (n.d.). The structural self and its characteristics according to Kohut. Retrieved July 7, 2020, from http://www.self-psy.co.il/. (in Hebrew).

Hudson, S., & Ramsey, J. (2011). The emergence and analysis of synthetic cannabinoids. *Drug Testing and Analyses, 3*(7–8), 466–478.

Iversen, L. (2003). Cannabis and the brain. *Brain, 126*(6), 1252–1270.

Jacobus, J., & Tapert, S. F. (2014). Effects of cannabis on the adolescent brain. *Current Pharmaceutical Design, 20*(13), 2186–2193.

Jenkins, J., & Zunguze, S. (1998). The relationship of family structure to adolescent drug use, peer affiliation, and perception of peer acceptance of drug use. *Adolescence, 33*(132), 811–822.

Kamal, B. S., Kamal, F., & Lantela, D. E. (2018). Cannabis and the anxiety of fragmentation – A systems approach for finding an anxiolytic Cannabis chemotype. *Frontiers in Neuroscience, 12*, 730.

Kernberg, O. F. (1975). *Borderline conditions and pathological narcissism.* Jason Aronson.

Kohut, H. (1959). Introspection, empathy, and psychoanalysis: An examination of the relationship between mode of observation and theory. *Journal of the American Psychoanalytic Association, 7*(3), 459–483.

Kohut, H. (1971). *The analysis of the self.* International Universities Press.

Kohut, H. (1972). Thoughts on narcissism and narcissistic rage. *The Psychoanalytic Study of the Child, 27*, 360–400.

Kohut, H. (1977a). Preface. In D. Blaine & D. A. Julius (Eds.), *Psychodynamics of drug dependence.* Research Monograph 12 (pp. vii–ix). National Institute on Drug Abuse.

Kohut, H. (1977b). *The restoration of the self.* International Universities Press.

Kohut, H. (1981). On empathy. In P. Ornstein (Ed.), *The search for the self: Selected writings of Heinz Kohut, 1978–1981* (Vol. 4, pp. 525–535). International Universities Press.

Kohut, H. (1984). *How does analysis cure?* University of Chicago Press.

Kulka, R. (2005). Between tragic and compassion. An introductory essay. In H. Kohut (Ed.), *How does analysis cure?* (pp. 13–52). Am Oved Publishers. (In Hebrew).

Law, R., Schier, J., Martin, C., Chang, A., & Wolkin, A. (2015). Increase in reported adverse health effects related to synthetic cannabinoid se — United States, January–May 2015. *Morbidity and Mortality Weekly Report (MMWR), 64*(22), 618–619.

Leneghan, S. (2013). The varieties of ecstasy experience: A phenomenological ethnography. *Journal of Psychoactive Drugs, 45*(4), 347–354.

Levin, J. D. (1987). *Treatment of alcoholism and other addictions: A self-psychology approach.* Jason Aronson.

Mass, R., Bardong, C., Kindl, K., & Dahme, B. (2001). Relationship between cannabis use, schizotypal traits, and cognitive function in healthy subjects. *Psychopathology, 34*(4), 209–214.

Mensen, V. T., Vreeker, A., Nordgren, J., Atkinson, A., de la Torre, R., Farré, M., Ramaekers, J. G., & Brunt, T. M. (2019). Psychopathological symptoms associated with synthetic cannabinoid use: a comparison with natural cannabis. *Psychopharmacology, 236*(9), 2677–2685.

Millon, T. (1997). DSM narcissistic personality disorder: Historical reflections and future directions. In E. F. Ronningstam (Ed.), *Disorders of narcissism: Diagnostic, clinical, and empirical implications* (pp. 75–101). American Psychiatric Association.

Moore, T. H., Zammit, S., Lingford-Hughes, A., Barnes, T. R., Jones, P. B., Burke, M., Lewis, G. (2007). Cannabis use and risk of psychotic or affective mental health outcomes: A systematic review. *The Lancet, 370*(9584), 319–328.

Mora, G. (2011). *Leaving the drug addict role and creating a recovering identity-variations by gender* (Master's thesis). Retrieved from https://scholarworks.edu.

Murray, R. M., Quigley, H., Quattrone, D., Englund, A., & Di Forti, M. (2016). Traditional marijuana, high-potency cannabis and synthetic cannabinoids: Increasing risk for psychosis. *World Psychiatry: Official Journal of the World Psychiatric Association, 15(3)*, 195–204.

Mustonen, A., Niemelä, S., Nordström, T., Murray, G. K., Mäki, P., Jääskeläinen, E., & Miettunen, J. (2018). Adolescent cannabis use, baseline prodromal symptoms and the risk of psychosis. *British Journal of Psychiatry, 212*(4), 227–233.

NASEM. (2017). *The health effects of cannabis and cannabinoids: The current state of evidence and recommendations for research.* National Academies Press for the National Academies of Sciences Engineering and Medicine.

Pertwee, R. G. (2008). The diverse CB1 and CB2 receptor pharmacology of three plant cannabinoids: Delta9-tetrahydrocannabinol, cannabidiol and delta9-tetrahydrocannabivarin. *British Journal of Pharmacology, 153*(2), 199–215.

Shevyrin, V., Melkozerov, V., Nevero, A., Eltsov, O., Shafran, Y., Morzherin, Y., & Lebedev, A. T. (2015). Identification and analytical characteristics of synthetic Cannabinoids with an indazole-3-carboxamide structure bearing a N-1-methoxy-carbonylalkyl group. *Analytical and Bioanalytical Chemistry, 407*(21), 6301–6315.

Siegel, A. M. (1996). *Heinz Kohut and the psychology of the self.* Routledge.

Solowij, N., Michie, P. T., & Fox, A. M. (1991). Effects of long-term cannabis use on selective attention: An event-related potential study. *Pharmacology, Biochemistry, and Behavior, 40*(3), 683–688.

Solowij, N., Stephens, R. S., Roffman, R. A., Babor, T., Kadden, R., Miller, M., Christiansen, K., McRee, B., Vendetti, J., & Marijuana Treatment Project Research Group (2002). Cognitive functioning of long-term heavy cannabis users seeking treatment. *Journal of the American Medical Association, 287*(9), 1123–1131.

Tait, R. J., Caldicott, D., Mountain, D., Hill, S. L., & Lenton, S. (2016). A systematic review of adverse events arising from the use of synthetic cannabinoids and their associated treatment. *Clinical Toxicology, 54*(1), 1–13.

Tolpin, M. (1996). Selfobjects in psychosis – The twinship compensation. *American Journal of Psychotherapy, 50*(2), 178–193.

Tolpin, M., & Kohut, H. (1980). The disorders of the self: The psychopathology of the first years of life. In S. I. Greenspan & G. H. Pollock (Eds.), *The course of Life* (pp. 425–442). NIMH.

Ulman, R. B., & Paul, H. (2006). *The self-psychology of addiction and its treatment: Narcissus in wonderland.* Routledge.

United Nations Office on Drugs and Crime. (2015). *World Drug Report 2015.* United Nations Publication, Sales No. E.15.XI.6.

Vandrey, R., Dunn, K. E., Fry, J. A., & Girling, E. R. (2012). A survey study to characterize use of Spice products (synthetic cannabinoids). *Drug and Alcohol Dependence, 120*(1–3), 238–241.

van Schoor, E. (1992). Pathological narcissism and addiction: A self-psychology perspective. *Psychoanalytic Psychotherapy*, *6*(3), 205–212.

Wesson D. R. (2011). Psychedelic drugs, hippie counterculture, speed and phenobarbital treatment of sedative-hypnotic dependence: a journey to the Haight Ashbury in the Sixties. *Journal of psychoactive drugs*, *43*(2), 153–164.

Winnicott, D. W. (1953). Transitional objects and transitional phenomena; a study of the first not-me possession. *The International Journal of Psychoanalysis*, *34*, 89–97.

Winstock, A. R., & Barratt, M. J. (2013). Synthetic cannabis: A comparison of patterns of use and effect profile with natural cannabis in a large global sample. *Drug and Alcohol Dependence*, *131*(1–2), 106–111.

World Health Organization. (2016). *The health and social effects of nonmedical cannabis use*. World Health Organization.

World Health Organization. (2018). *International classification of diseases for mortality and morbidity statistics* (11th Revision). Retrieved from https://icd.who.int/browse11/l-m/en.

Chapter 10

The 12-step program

"Our faith, strength and hope come from people sharing their recovery and from our relationship with the God of our own understanding".
(Narcotics Anonymous, 2008, p. 98)

The 12-step program is a general program of recovery from addictive disorders and compulsive behaviors. According to the APA Dictionary of Psychology (VandenBos, 2007), "working the 12-step program" includes admitting one's inability to control addictive or compulsive behavior, recognizing a higher or greater power that can give one strength, examining past errors with the help of an experienced member, making amends for these errors, learning to live a new lifestyle with a new set of behavioral norms and helping others that suffer from the same addictive or compulsive behaviors (VandenBos, 2007). This program contains a mixture of diverse philosophical and therapeutic approaches, such as pragmatism, existentialism, motivational interviewing, cognitive-behavioral treatment (CBT) and even psychoanalytic ideas.

Along with sharing certain similarities with the above-named therapeutic methods, the 12-step program also differs significantly from them, chiefly in its concern with the idea of God or a Higher Power. When therapists and laypeople hear these terms, they assume that this is a religious program. However, this is a misconception because the 12-step program is a spiritual program, which grew out of the experience of individuals who coped with addiction.

The growth of the 12-step program

The 12-step program grew out of the experience of two men who were struggling with alcoholism in the United States in the 1930s. Bill Wilson and Dr. Bob Smith are known in the 12-step program lore as "Bill W." and "Dr. Bob", respectively. Throughout his life, Bill W. was admitted to hospitals several times because of his alcoholism. During one of those admissions, he met a physician named Dr. William Silkworth, who assumed that alcoholism was a disease with physical and mental aspects. The physical aspect relates to an allergy to alcohol and an inability to stop drinking once the alcoholic has started. The psychological aspect relates to a psychological craving for alcohol and obsession with continuing to drink alcohol despite harmful consequents (Alcoholics Anonymous, 2001).

Actually, Dr. Silkworth had told Bill that alcoholics are not sinners or morally bad people, but ordinary people who suffer from a disease. This saying implanted hope in Bill, but he did not quit drinking, although he was told that further alcohol drinking would lead to death. In 1934, Bill met Ebby Thacher, an old school friend who also battled with alcoholism. Bill offered him a drink, but Thacher refused and explained his success in the adoption of the principals of the Oxford Group that was an evangelistic Christian group (Hartigan, 2001). He offered Bill W. to adopt the group's principal's, but the latter hesitated because he was not a religious person. Then, Thacher recommended him to choose his own conception of God (Alcoholics Anonymous, 2001).

Afterward, Bill was admitted in the fourth time to a New York hospital that treated alcoholics with belladonna, and it seems that under the influence of this substance, he experienced an experience he termed spiritual awakening (Dick, 2006; Pitman, 1988). Bill W. claimed that following this experience, he quit drinking alcohol until his death (Cheever, 2004). When he reported this experience to Dr. Silkworth, the latter said that he does not understand what had happened but advised him to embrace this experience (Alcoholics Anonymous, 2001; Cheever, 2004). Bill joined the Oxford Group where he met Dr. Bob. He told the physician about his experiences and the two began to work with other alcoholics in order to help them (Hartigan, 2001). Dr. Bob himself relapsed and drank alcohol in a medical conference he had attended. Bill came to his assistance, and according to the Alcoholics Anonymous (AA) literature (Alcoholics Anonymous, 2001), since this relapse, Dr. Bob did not drink alcohol until his death in 1950.

The main book of AA, the Big Book, had been written by Bill W. and included suggestions for activities that aim for spiritual awakening, entitled the twelve steps (Wilson, 1939). Later, Bill wrote the twelve traditions, which are valuable guidelines that assure the survival of the informal structure of the fellowship, the term for the group that practices and works the 12-step program (Alcoholics Anonymous, 2001). Over the years, the number of AA fellowships in the United States has grown, and drug abusers have started to join AA meetings. However, they did not find their place there because of a few reasons.

First, the course of alcoholism differs from the course of drug addiction, and the personal experiences of alcoholics differ from those of drug abusers. For example, alcohol is legal and relatively cheaper in comparison to heroin and cocaine, which are illicit drugs, and therefore, individuals who use these drugs usually have encounters with the law enforcement agencies. Second, according to AA's fifth tradition, the primary purpose of the group is to carry its message to the alcoholic who still suffers (Alcoholics Anonymous, 2001) and not all drug abusers who have attended AA meetings suffered from alcoholism. In addition, drug abusers who did not express a desire to quit drinking were not invited to closed AA meetings (Wilson, 1944).

In 1953, Jimmy Kinnon and few other drug abusers who attended AA meetings had established the first Narcotics Anonymous (NA) fellowship in California. This fellowship adopted the path to recovery suggested by AA's 12-step program. With the increase in the members' number, appeared the need for guidance, and in 1972, the general world services had been opened in Los Angeles. The basic purposes of the world services are communication, coordination, information and guidance for NA fellowships (Narcotics Anonymous, 2002). NA fellowships (groups) offer a recovery program for drug addiction when the only requirement for membership is the desire to stop using drugs. There is not any need for paying membership fees or pledging allegiance. The fellowships are open for people of any gender, race and religious orientation, as well as atheists.

Despite the declared openness to any individuals who desire to stop using drugs, in some NA fellowships, opioid maintenance treatment patients are not considered as "full members". Meaning, NA adheres to the total abstinence principle according to which a member must abstain from any substances, such as alcohol and drugs. Methadone maintenance patients are not considered "drug abstinent" although methadone maintenance treatment (MMT) is legal and legitimate treatment. Opioid maintenance treatment patients who attended NA groups report that in some fellowships, they can participate only by listening, whereas in others, they are even not allowed to participate because they are considered as 'drug addicts who still use drugs'.

The twelve steps of narcotics anonymous

Step One – *"We admitted we were powerless over addiction, that our lives had become unmanageable"*.

The first step includes several components, and it begins with an admission that the addicted individual cannot cope any longer with the addiction disease that harms his life (Narcotics Anonymous, 2008). The addicted individual also admits that his attempts to simultaneously control his addiction and live productive life have completely failed. The derivative of this failure is surrender, a critical term that constitutes an integral part of this step, and which is sometimes confused with giving up. Surrender means acceptance of the powerlessness in battling the addiction disease and understanding that recovery is a solution (Narcotics Anonymous, 1998).

In the 12-step program, addiction is considered a disease, but not a medical disease in the way that the medical model views the addiction disease (Volkow, Koob, & McLellan, 2016). The addiction disease has three aspects – physical, mental and spiritual (Narcotics Anonymous, 1998). The physical aspect relates to the bodily reaction that causes craving after every drug use and the inability to control over the amount of abuse. The mental aspect of the disease relates to the frequent obsessions about drugs and drug abuse, which is sometimes called in the fellowships as 'the greater aspect of the disease'.

The third aspect of the disease is self-centeredness and the belief of the addicted individual that the world revolves around him (Narcotics Anonymous, 1998). Self-centeredness includes selfishness, egotism and a constant occupation of the addicted individual in his needs, and his belief that his demands are the only ones worth consideration. The spiritual aspect of the addiction disease is evident in the addict's daily behavior when he tries to manipulate individuals and situations according to his own needs (Narcotics Anonymous, 1998). Therefore, the remedy to the addiction disease should also include a spiritual solution that appears in the second step.

Step Two – *"We came to believe that a Power greater than ourselves could restore us to sanity"*.

In the first step, there is an admission in the powerlessness of the addicted individual to cope or control the addiction disease. In the second step, the 12-step program offers the individual to accept external assistance. Family members, therapists, NA fellowships, sponsors and God are all examples for greater power. Members are encouraged to choose a power that is carrying, loving and especially could return them to sanity. In the 12-step program, the word insanity refers to the distorted world view of the addicted individual and his behaviors during the addiction period (Narcotics Anonymous, 1998). The belief of an addicted individual that he can stay drug abstinent without any help and the belief that addiction does not harm his functioning are examples for insane thinking.

Examples of insane behavior include deceiving family members, theft and use of violence to get drugs or money for buying drugs (Narcotics Anonymous, 1998). In recovery, members often use this term to explain how they could harm their closest people or risk their life for getting drugs. It should be noted that the meaning of the term insanity differs radically from the term reality testing, which is an excepted term in the mental health field that relates to the capacity to differentiate between internal and external reality and to maintain empathy with ordinary social criteria of reality (Kernberg, 1996).

Step Three – *"We made a decision to turn our will and our lives over to the care of God as we understood Him"*.

The central characteristic of this step is a decision (Narcotics Anonymous, 1998). The working of the first two steps with a sponsor gave hope and showed that there is a path for recovery. Now the addicted individual stands before a crossroad – to continue with the new recovery program or to return to his old lifestyle. At this point, the 12-step program suggests the addicted individual to turn his will and life over to the care of God or a Higher Power. Since the addicted individual's decisions in life brought disastrous consequences, the program suggests that God or any other spiritual entity may do a better job (Narcotics Anonymous, 2002).

There are two essential points in this step. First, turning the will and life over to the care of God as one understands Him does not mean to become a mindless robot (Narcotics Anonymous, 1998). On the contrary, the addicted individual is required to keep on with his commitment of drug abstinence and continue attending the meetings. Second, the concept of 'God as we understand Him' does not mean that this is a religious program. In the 12-step program, God or the Higher Power is loving, caring and interested in the member's recovery. The fellowship or the spiritual principles of the 12-step program can also be a Higher Power (Narcotics Anonymous, 1998). However, since a major pillar of the program is about developing a relationship with God or a Higher Power and communicating with him by prayer or other ways (Narcotics Anonymous, 1998), it can be understood that this program encourages addicted individuals to choose a spiritual entity that would help them in the path of recovery. The program neither coerces its members to adopt any religion, nor does it encourage religious conversion. People of any religion, as well as non-religious, atheists and Gnostics, can hold to their faith.

Step Four – "*We made a searching and fearless moral inventory of ourselves*".
Step four is a highly significant stage in the 12-step program, and it aims to find the blocks that prevent the addicted individual from acting from the will of god (Narcotics Anonymous, 1998). The essence of this step is conducting a moral and fearless inventory or self-examination in a few ways:

a   Writing life story – The member writes his life story and then reads it before the group as the group members only listen and do not comment.
b   Release from resentments – The member writes a list of resentments as this action helps him to let go of old anger that affects his life. Second, exploring the resentment helps to identify one's own expectations in his relationship with others. Third, this process helps to reveal repetitive patterns, which keep the member trapped in a cycle of anger and self-pity (Narcotics Anonymous, 1998). At the end of the process, the member should let go of his resentments and feel released.
c   Release from fears – The member is encouraged to write a list of his fears, the reason to each fear and what part of self-reliance has failed him.
d   Examining the harm done to others – The member is encouraged to make a list of the people he hurt (emotionally, physically) during his life.

The working of this step, as well as the others, is carried out with the guidance of a sponsor, who is a member with a broader experience whose primary responsibility is to help a newer member work the 12 steps (B., Hamilton, 1996). Every step in the 12-step program has its uniqueness, and the various steps differ in their significance to the various members. In my opinion, the fourth step is one of the most significant steps because it encourages brave and painful self-examination. The examination of resentments, fears and hurts is similar to a situation in which an individual stands wholly exposed in front of a mirror and looks at himself without turning his eyes away. Working the fourth step leads the individual to acknowledge his flaws, his character defects and his indecent habits. The self-criticism raises numerous questions about past life, the motives for decision making and, simultaneously, it raises disturbing questions about his present life.

Step Five – *"We admitted to God, to ourselves, and to another human being the exact nature of our wrong".*

Step five is not simply a reading of step four. The recurrent encounters with complex mental contents require a commitment to follow the path of recovery offered by the 12-step program. The work of this step also requires courage and honesty from individuals who usually tend to lie and avoid any self-examination. In this step, individuals who usually did not trust anyone, learn to trust another person and continue developing their relationship with God as they understand Him. The recurrent encounters with fears and resentments assist in identifying repetitive and maladaptive behavioral patterns as well as the reasons behind them (Narcotics Anonymous, 1998).

Step Six – *"We were entirely ready to have God remove all these defects of character".*

The sixth step deals with the member's readiness to relinquish maladaptive behavioral patterns and character deficits, which only lead to negative consequences. The working of the two previous steps helped the member to gain awareness about his character defects. Meaning, personality traits or behaviors, such as egotism, lying, self-pity, self-justification, dishonesty, envy, jealousy, procrastination, fear and greed.

The sixth step includes an admission that the member's way of living brought him only pain and degradation (Narcotics Anonymous, 1998). However, awareness of those character defects is not enough, and therefore, there is turning to God or a Higher Power that is considered the only entity that can remove the shortcomings (Narcotics Anonymous, 1998). The spiritual principals that stand in the basis of this step include willingness, faith, trust, commitment and perseverance and self-acceptance.

Step Seven – *"We humbly asked Him to remove our shortcomings".*

Steps five to seven are direct continuation of the fourth step that has begun in the identification of the character defects. The admission before another human being and a Higher Power, as well as the request to remove the member's shortcomings, indicates the member's readiness for a big personality change. Many addicted individuals are characterized by selfishness, impulsivity, lack of empathy and self-centeredness and the working through of the previous steps assists in developing humility.

Individuals choose rituals or specific personal routines to address their Higher Power in a request to remove their shortcomings. In the 12-step program, such practice is termed a prayer without any mentioning of any religion (Narcotics Anonymous, 1998). The seventh step also focuses on surrender because the member looks back on his journey from the first step and understands that the positive changes in his life had occurred only after he admitted his powerlessness. The spiritual principles that characterize this step are faith, humility, patience and trust.

Step Eight – *"We made a list of all persons we had harmed, and became willing to make amends to them all"*.

Until this point, the working through of the steps focused on personality changes and strengthening the relationship with God or any other Higher Power. The next steps deal with repairing the relationships with those whom the member had hurt purposefully with intent or by accident. The core of the eighth step is about identifying the damage the member has caused (Narcotics Anonymous, 1998). Specifically, the individual is instructed to prepare a list of whom he harmed, what was the harm and is he willing to make amends. This process should be carried out carefully because such actions may cause more harm.

Therefore, involving the sponsor in the steps work is significant in general and in this step in particular. The help of the sponsor is invaluable because resentments may appear during this process and influence on the willingness to continue to the ninth step. If individuals report that they had not hurt anyone during their lives, the 12-step program suggests more meticulous self-examination or simply tells the member that he is in denial (Narcotics Anonymous, 1998). The sponsor helps the member also to acknowledge the fact that one of the people who were hurt during the active addiction period is himself. The spiritual principles that stand at the base of this step include honesty, courage, willingness and compassion.

Step Nine – *"We made direct amends to such people wherever possible, except when to do so would injure them or others"*.

Acknowledging personal responsibility during the eighth step helps to continue to the ninth step and to meet the offended individuals. The amendments could take many forms, such as direct apology, financial amend or commitment to treat family members differently than in the past. Sometimes, the work of the ninth step is a continuous effort to repair damaged bonds. The sponsor can help in gaining perspective on the compatibility between the hurting and the amend. The view of an experienced member who also follows the same recovery path is important since members find themselves in complex dilemmas. A member who hesitates about telling his employer about embezzlement he made in the past and a member who thinks about confessing infidelity before one's partner are examples for such dilemmas.

In my opinion, this step is one of the most significant steps (next to the fourth) in the 12-step program because the member continues in his fearless and moral inventory and is willing to cope with highly disturbing emotional and interpersonal situations. Besides, this step, perhaps more than the other steps, symbolizes the member's request to restore his relations with society. Finally, the work of this step helps the individual to forgive himself and to develop self-love or self-care.

Step Ten – *"We continued to take personal inventory and when we were wrong promptly admitted it"*.

The work of the previous steps changed the member's life dramatically because self-centeredness turned its place to honesty and humbleness. However, the program emphasizes that even profound changes are not permanent and that the disease is chronic, progressive and fatal (Narcotics Anonymous, 2008). Therefore, the recovery work never ends, and the member is continuously required examining his behavior to make amends and to strengthen his relationship with his Higher Power. The tenth step is not about maintenance. It's about maintenance and progress because commitment to this recovery program demands self-discipline, honesty and integrity.

Step Eleven – *"We sought through prayer and meditation to improve our conscious contact with God as we understood Him, praying only for knowledge of His will for us and the power to carry that out"*.

This step encourages continuing and examining the relationship with God or with the Higher Power. Addicted individuals come to this program with previous conceptions or views about God that are influenced by their culture or by their experience with religious figures or religious establishments. Although NA fellowships do not have any approved or official spiritual path for recovery, the description of the Higher Power is quite clear. The Higher Power of this program is conceived as a spiritual entity that is loving, caring and is interested in the member's well-being (Narcotics Anonymous, 1998, 2008). In other words, according to the 12-step program, God or the Higher Power is not angry or punishing.

Every member is free to explore his spiritual path through prayer and meditation. Often NA members describe prayer as talking to God and meditation as listening to God (Narcotics Anonymous, 1998). The spiritual facet of the 12-step program is entwined with practical and active doing. Since life is dynamic and involves unpleasant encounters and transgressions, this work never ends. Daily writing, sharing experiences in the fellowship, consulting a sponsor, prayer and meditation are major elements in this spiritual path of recovery.

Step Twelve – *"Having had a spiritual awakening as a result of these steps, we tried to carry this message to addicts, and to practice these principles in all our affairs"*.

The program suggests spiritual awakening to those who will follow a spiritual path that includes being a member in a fellowship, conducting moral and fearless inventory, asking forgiveness and readiness to amend, consulting a sponsor, prayer and meditation (Narcotics Anonymous, 1998, 2008). Prominent expressions of this spiritual awakening are strong faith in God or a Higher Power and adoption of new moral code. The 12th step suggests to the member to carry on the message of the program's success and his own success to others. Carrying the message of recovery may include sharing personal experiences with a new member, sharing struggles and victories over substance abuse in rehab centers and in other various ways. The working through of the 12 steps does not end, and those who arrived at this point can work through the last three steps or start over from the first step.

The twelve traditions of NA

The 12 traditions provide guidelines for the members' behavior in the fellowships, the relations between the different fellowships, and the relations between the fellowships and the society (Narcotics Anonymous, 2008). The guidelines address issues of receiving donations, public relations and other contacts with external organizations and authorities. These are the basic rules for the management of the fellowships and adhering to them helps to focus on the recovery process and not to divert to other directions, which may jeopardize the continuing existence of the 12-step fellowships. The 12 traditions were written by Bill Wilson and appeared for the first time in the main book of AA (Wilson, 1939). Since then, they were adopted by various 12-step fellowships that help their members to recover from drug addiction and behavioral addictions.

Tradition One – *"Our common welfare should come first; personal recovery depends on N.A. unity"*.

The first tradition emphasizes unity as a vital condition for survival of the fellowship. If members decide to place personal desires before the group's favor, they might jeopardize the continuance of the group, and therefore, this tradition directs the members remembering that in crises, they should set differences aside and work for the common good (Narcotics Anonymous, 2008).

Tradition Two – *"For our group purpose there is but one ultimate authority — a loving God as He may express Himself in our group conscience. Our leaders are but trusted servants; they do not govern".*

Since many members are strong-willed, self-centered and charismatic people, this tradition reminds all members and especially the leaders that God is the Higher Power in this program. This tradition warns members that direction and manipulation will fail, so there is no point to try and gain control and exploit other members. The fellowships have secretaries, treasurers and representatives and not presidents, masters or directors. An important sentence that relates to this tradition is: "in Narcotics Anonymous, we are concerned with protecting ourselves from ourselves" (Narcotics Anonymous, 2008, p. 64).

Tradition Three – *"The only requirement for membership is a desire to stop using".*

The 12-step program grew out of the experience of drug addicts who understood that any attempts to force drug abstinence are destined for failure. Addicts can come freely and openly to meetings, whenever and wherever they choose and leave just as freely (Narcotics Anonymous, 2008).

Tradition Four – *"Each group should be autonomous except in matters affecting other groups or NA as a whole".*

A NA group is any group that meets regularly and continuously for the purpose of recovery and follows 12 steps and 12 traditions of NA. Each group is self-governed and is not subjected to any external influence. The groups have freedom except when their actions affect other NA groups (Narcotics Anonymous, 2008).

Tradition Five – *"Each group has but one primary purpose—to carry the message to the addict who still suffers".*

According to this tradition, NA is not a social club, a place to make money or to receive education or medical help. The primary purpose is to spread a message of recovery to addicts who still suffer. Each member indeed strives for drug abstinence and recovery, but the therapeutic value of one addict helping another is without parallel, and every member should remember it (Narcotics Anonymous, 2008).

Tradition Six – *"An NA group ought never endorse, finance, or lend the NA name to any related facility or outside enterprise, lest problems of money, property or prestige divert us from our primary purpose".*

Dealing with sanctions, approvals or recommendations diverts NA groups from its primary purpose, and therefore, the groups should avoid any suggestions for endorsement. Although 12-step groups also exist in hospitals, drug recovery houses, probation offices or other facilities, NA groups would not finance those facilities or allow them to use their name. This tradition forbids receiving any financing or property because it may divert the groups from the spiritual path (Narcotics Anonymous, 2008).

Tradition Seven – *"Every NA group ought to be fully self-supporting, declining outside contributions"*.

This tradition continues the previous one and guides declining any outside funding, endowments, loans or gifts. Money has always been a problem for addicts who stole it, begged for it or worked for it in order to finance drugs. In recovery, money continues to be a problem, and therefore, groups are not allowed to deal with financial issues, except raising money from group members for rent or any other services which further the primary purpose (Narcotics Anonymous, 2008).

Tradition Eight – *"Narcotics Anonymous should remain forever nonprofessional, but our service centers may employ special workers"*.

Twelve-step programs do not have any staff members, such as physicians, criminologists, psychologists, social workers, nurses, lawyers or counselors. The basis of this program is the recommendation that one addict helping another is the most effective way of recovery (Narcotics Anonymous, 2008). Service centers may employ workers, such as telephone receptionists or secretaries, for providing service for members and newcomers, but these workers do not have tenure or any special status. All the members, even the most experienced, have equal status, and they are "forever nonprofessional" (Narcotics Anonymous, 2008, p. 73).

Tradition Nine – *"NA, as such, ought never be organized, but we may create service boards or committees directly responsible to those they serve"*.

This tradition relates to the way that NA fellowships function. Service boards and committees neither control nor manage the fellowships and they exist only for serving the needs of the fellowship. A loving God, as he may express himself in the collective conscience of the group membership (group conscience), is the ultimate authority (Narcotics Anonymous, 2008, p. 73).

Tradition Ten – *"Narcotics Anonymous has no opinion on outside issues; hence the NA name ought never be drawn into public controversy"*.

NA has no opinion on political, economic or sociocultural issues (Narcotics Anonymous, 2008). Involvement in external issues, no matter how important they are, would jeopardize the survival of the groups, and the tenth tradition specifically helps to protect the reputation of NA as a unique and goal-directed organization.

Tradition Eleven – *"Our public relations policy is based on attraction rather than promotion; we need always maintain personal anonymity at the level of press, radio, and films"*.

This is one of the few traditions that regularizes the relationship with the external world (Narcotics Anonymous, 2008). It guides how to conduct NA efforts at the public level, and it emphasizes that this unique spiritual path of recovery speaks for itself without any need for public relations. Members practice personal anonymity to protect the membership and the reputation of NA (Narcotics Anonymous, 2008).

Tradition Twelve – *"Anonymity is the spiritual foundation of all our Traditions, ever reminding us to place principles before personalities"*.

The last tradition reminds members that the spiritual foundation is more important than any group or individual. Meaning that this tradition reminds new as well as old members that character defects may harm recovery and that the spiritual principles of the 12-step program stand before any personal desire or interest (Narcotics Anonymous, 2008).

Useful tools of the 12-step program

The 12-step program offers a vast array of tools for helping members to cope with cravings and stressful life situations. The implementation of these tools helps to develop self-efficacy and promotes recovery.

1   The serenity prayer – "God grant me the serenity to accept the things I cannot change; courage to change the things I can; and wisdom to know the difference". Probably, the most identified tool with this program, the serenity prayer, instructs the member to examine his behavior and identify situations in which he acts in a maladaptive manner and continually fails. One of the most prevalent misconceptions about the serenity prayer is that it emphasizes radical acceptance of any difficulty in life. On the contrary, in this prayer, the member asks for virtues, such as willingness to face fears and fortitude, which is related to courage. Serenity relates to a state of inner peace following recognizing the inability to change uncomfortable or negative situations. Wisdom relates to the ability to distinguish between changeable and unchangeable situations. The serenity prayer indeed encourages acceptance, but at the same time, it instructs the member to stop repeating the same mistakes. The turning to God is a plea of help for receiving the necessary wisdom for distinguishing between changeable and not changeable situations.
2   The fellowship – The program offers its members a social group in which they could feel acceptance and belongingness. There are meetings almost every day of the week, and such setting offers a holding environment for individuals who cope with loneliness and emptiness. Besides, a member can always call other members for help when he copes with craving. The mutual help is an essential element in this recovery program.

3   Sponsor – A sponsor is an experienced member of the fellowship whose primary responsibility is to help a newer member work the 12 steps (B., Hamilton, 1996). Sponsors do many things, such as providing guidance, eliciting motivation, explaining 12-step terminology, helping in the process of self-examination (step four), confront the member when it is appropriate and introducing the member to other members (B., Hamilton, 1996).
4   Use of slogans – The 12-step program has many slogans that assist newcomers and old members in daily coping and implant hope, such as 'take what you want and leave the rest', 'time takes time', 'one day at a time'. The use of slogans helps in interrupting negative thoughts that may lead to relapses and help the member to stay in the present.
5   'Just for today' – During periods of drug abstinence, members promised themselves and others that they would not use drugs anymore. The experience shows that such promises are futile, and therefore, the program offers members to commit not using drugs just for one day. The saying 'just for today' relates to the member's commitment and the attempts to pass the present day without using drugs and with the assistance of the fellowship and the rest of the 12-step program's tools.
6   Daily writing – The member's daily writing about his life helps him to increase awareness of his behavior and his relations with others.
7   Exercising gratitude – Daily writing of gratitude helps in reducing the magnitude of negative feelings and starting to appreciate the positive things in life.
8   Relapse prevention strategies – The program instructs its members to stay away from any reminder that could trigger any desire to use. Raising awareness for risky situations is embodied in the slogan "people, places and things". Meaning, there is clear and unambiguous recommendation of avoiding any encounters with people who use drugs and avoiding any places associated with drug use or drug selling. Besides, the members should get rid of any things that are associated with drug abuse such as needles, syringes or rolling papers.
9   Personal stories – Members are encouraged to share personal stories of successful coping with craving and life's challenges. Such stories help newcomers in their recovery by learning from the experience of others who were in their place. Sharing a personal story in front of the group is an empowering experience, and the individual receives positive feedbacks.

The interfaces between the 12-step program and other approaches and philosophical traditions

A few philosophical traditions and therapeutic approaches and strategies are embodied in the 12-step program. For example, the 12-step program encourages its members to accept help from any greater power that can promote drug abstinence and do whatever it takes to avoid using drugs. This principle is based on pragmatism, a philosophical movement that began in the 19th century in the United States, and which is identified with scholars, such as Charles Sanders Pierce, John Dewey and William James. This approach emphasizes thinking or dealing with problems in a practical way rather than by using theoretical ideas or abstract principles (Kilpinen, 2009).

Another salient interface exists between the 12-step program and existentialism, a philosophical–cultural movement identified with philosophers, such as Kierkegaard, Nietzsche and writers, such as Sartre and Camus. Over the years, existentialist thinkers have emphasized issues of facing anxiety and pursuing authenticity (Bolea, 2014), and existential psychotherapists have written extensively on issues of freedom, death, isolation and meaninglessness (Frankl, 2006; Yalom, 1980). The 12-step program emphasizes the suffering of the addicted individual as a necessary condition for change (Chen, 2010) and encourages him to ask himself consistently if he lives an authentic life. Drug addiction distances the individual from his selfhood, and the 12-step program offers him a spiritual path for discovering authenticity. In recovery, the member also deals daily with the existential issues of choice, decision-making and responsibility.

Evident similarities exist between therapeutic principles and strategies of different psychotherapeutic methods and those of the 12-step program. In my opinion, the focus of the serenity prayer is in finding a balance between acceptance and change, and therefore, it corresponds with acceptance and commitment therapy (ACT). The two main purposes of ACT include acceptance of unpleasant internal experiences that cannot be changed and commitment to action based on personal values (for a broader review of the compatibilities between ACT and the 12-step program, see Wilson, Hayes, & Byrd, 2000).

Daily writing is usually associated with CBT when the patient is asked to run a diary of thoughts and emotions to assist both himself and the therapist in identifying maladaptive thinking patterns and ineffective behaviors (Cully & Teten, 2008). Daily writing is a vital component in the treatment of people who act impulsively and use drugs without much thinking about the consequences of their behavior.

Twelve-step fellowships serve as communities that support and reinforce recovery.

Attending meetings helps to cope with feelings of loneliness and isolation, and patients report that it is more comfortable talking to people who shared similar experiences. The membership in such fellowships facilitates socialization and learning, and Kaskutas (2009) notes that meetings attendance leads to learning of relapse prevention mechanisms because the 12-step program uses standard behavioral modification techniques. Members learn how to refuse when they are offered drugs, to have a plan of

action when confronted with risky situations and choosing alternative behaviors instead of drug abuse (Kaskutas, 2009). However, members relapse
because the addiction disease is chronic, progressive, fatal and not curable
(Narcotics Anonymous, 2008).

This program does not encourage relapses nor supports excusing relapses. On the contrary, the 12-step program encourages acceptance of
personal responsibility and using all the possible and rational means for
remaining drug abstinent (Narcotics Anonymous, 2008). Once a member
has relapsed, he should learn from his experience and renew the attempts
to remain drug abstinent. This idea corresponds with those of the wheel of
change, which is a transtheoretical model that explains change processes
(Prochaska, Norcross, & DiClemente, 2013). According to this model, relapse is an integral part of a change process, and therefore, recurrence of
undesired behaviors does not mean failure.

The spiritual origins of the 12-step program

Some of the practices of the program have interfaces with some spiritual
and religious ideas, practices and rituals. Major spiritual elements correspond with Christianity. First, the idea of loving god appears in both the
Old and the New Testaments, and it corresponds with the Greco-Christian
term Agape, which means unconditional love. This term is based on the
world view of the Christian tradition where God is the center of the universe and of all that happens in it (Wivestad, 2008). Second, a religious
practice appears in the fifth step when the member is suggested to admit
the exact nature of his wrongs before another human being. This practice
corresponds with the Sacrament of Penance, which is accepted in certain
Christian denominations.

Third, sharing personal stories of successful coping with drug craving en-
dows hope among the fellowship members. Such stories resemble Christian
mythology stories of saints and heroes fighting with dragons or other
mythical creatures. In both cases, an individual stands before a dreadful
challenge, which he overcomes with his faith in God or a Higher Power. As
Litfin (2014) notes, personal narratives constitute powerful instruments for
teaching, conveying information and forming character.

Besides Christianity, the spiritual path of the 12-step program was
profoundly influenced by William James's book (1961) "The Varieties of
Religious Experience". Bill W. was exposed to this book at Towns hospital
and adopted ideas, such as openness to unconventional spirituality and the
perception of God as beneficent and affirmative (Kurtz, 1990). Besides, the
acceptance and the insistence on a specific identity, such as a "sober alcoholic", stems from a conception that human duality is like a constitutional
disease (Kurtz, 1990). There is a quite evident similarity between this idea

and the idea of drug addiction as a chronic, not curable but treatable disease (Narcotics Anonymous, 2008).

Finally, conversion, a term which is associated with religiosity, constituted a significant element in the legacy of the 12-step program. At the Towns hospital, Bill W. experienced a flash of white light and an extraordinary sense of well-being that freed him from his alcoholism. At this period, he already had read James's (1961) book, which described detailed conversion experiences of recovering alcoholics. In addition, he heard from one of his friends at the Oxford Group that a famous psychiatrist named Carl Jung also thought that conversion is a solution for alcoholism (B., Dick, 2006). The idea of conversion was one of the tenants of this religious group (Clark, 1951), so it seems that Bill W. had heard this concept a few times during his attempts to quit drinking.

Ebby Thacher, the person who introduced the Oxford Group ideas to Bill W., had reported his conversion to Bill W., who followed his action. Bill accepted Christ and wrote that he had been born again there (B., Dick, 2006). However, it must be emphasized that in NA groups, the conversion, the experience of releasing the addicted individual from his craving following a surrender to a Higher Power, is conceived as a spiritual experience.

Psychodynamic conceptualizations of the 12-step program

Psychodynamic conceptualizations of the 12-step program can assist professionals working in this field in general, and therapists who work within the dynamic approach in particular to understand the interfaces between the different approaches and to provide integrative treatment. There is a small number of articles that present psychodynamic formulations of the program or discuss similarities between psychodynamic concepts and principles of the 12-step program. One of the few analysts who found interest in AA was Simmel (1948), who noted that the AA groups provide the required abilities to cope with dominant latent impulses. He hoped that the psychoanalytic establishment and AA would collaborate to treat alcoholism (Simmel, 1948), but it seems that the dialogue between these two approaches has not flourished.

Bean (1975) described elaborately how AA fellowships help in coping with denial, and others noted that the fellowships offer creative tools for self-regulation (Khantzian, 1981; Mack, 1981). Kass (2015) describes several interface points between a few psychoanalytic schools of thought and AA. Relating to ego psychology, he argues that attendance at the 12-step program meetings helps members replace primitive defence mechanisms in favor of advanced ones. When he discusses the object relations school of thought, he notes that the 12-step program provides a holding environment and the fellowship provides object consistency. Relating to Kohut's ideas, he notes that the program provides the selfobject needs of the addicted individual (Kass, 2015). In my opinion, the 12-step program offers the addicted individual to join a recovery journey, and in the next lines, I will present different dynamic conceptualizations of this journey.

Winnicottian conceptualization of the 12-step program

From a Winnicottian perspective, the 12-step program offers a journey from absolute dependence towards independence. The absolute dependence (drug addiction) is characterized by extreme self-centeredness often found among many drug abusers, and it reminds the infant's mental reality (Winnicott, 1960). During the journey towards independence, the addicted individual will examine the traits that compose his false self (step four), and the work of the next steps will assist him in changing the matrix of his internal and external object relations.

The 12-step program will offer a holding environment that reminds that of the good-enough mother (Winnicott, 1953). This environmental holding includes the possibility of daily meetings attendance, option to call other members in times of need and of course calling the sponsor who acts as a good-enough mother. The sponsor's and the group's handling of the member during the various steps and relapses reminds the mother's technique of holding the baby, which adds up to his first idea of the mother (Winnicott, 1964). The daily work that this program offers helps to relinquish magical omnipotence, self-centeredness and infantile aggression, and later, the development of the capacity for concern (Winnicott, 1963).

Winnicott (1963) coined this term to describe a developmental achievement, which relates to many life aspects and is achieved through good-enough mothering. The capacity for concern is associated with establishing a sense of self and equilibrium between destructive elements in drive-relationships to objects and other positive aspects of relating. A few times during this article, Winnicott (1963) emphasizes that this capacity is associated with taking and accepting responsibility, which is one of the personal qualities that the 12-step program encourages.

One of the prevailing misconceptions about the 12-step program is that it assists its members to avoid responsibility for their condition by adopting the saying that "drug addiction is a disease". In this context, one of the disturbing realizations that the 12-step program encourages its members to acknowledge is that "although we are not responsible for our disease, we are responsible for our recovery" (Narcotics Anonymous, 2008, p. 15). The desire to stop using drugs, and the commitment to total drug abstinence, requires personal responsibility in many ways. Staying away from drugs or drug-using friends, calling a NA member while experiencing craving and attending more meetings following relapse are a few examples.

The working through of the steps helps developing guilt associated with care and concern toward the influence of the individual's actions on the fellowship and the objects in his life. This capacity is embodied in the eighth and ninth steps and in the readiness to amend. Finally, in my opinion, members' reports of renewed aliveness and readiness to live an authentic life following step work correspond with the emergence of the true self (Winnicott, 1960).

Kleinian conceptualization of the 12-step program

From a Kleinian perspective, the 12-step program offers a recovery journey from the paranoid-schizoid position toward the depressive position. This program helps the addicted individual to leave internal and external reality composed of aggression, envy and greed and progress toward a lifestyle characterized with acceptance, self-examination and amends. In a certain sense, the addicted individual learns to cope with anxieties and desires through interactions with good objects (group members), and the daily self-examination helps in identifying self-regulation difficulties.

The fellowship is like a caring mother or a good and constant breast that the addicted individual never had, and mother's milk is the love and acceptance that the member accepts every time he appears to meetings. If the member had offended other members, they would address him assertively but not aggressively in a manner that will convey the message that the member is still loved and accepted. The member will not be destroyed by bad objects and will not be able to destroy them since the external reality is not persecutory. Meaning, the other members had moved toward the depressive position and they will not retaliate or hold a grudge against a member who misbehaved in the group or relapsed. On the contrary, they understand that this member needs much help to move from the schizoid-paranoid position.

Steps eight and nine have many similarities to the Kleinian reparation because the member deals with issues of hope, a desire for revenge, concern for the object and asking for forgiveness. The last two steps focus on strengthening the conscious connection to god and carrying the message to others. In my opinion, these two steps focus on internal and external work, which helps to arrive beyond reparation and toward the third place. The third place is a repairing position, which is characterized by searching the good, achieving personal meaning, a feeling of release and happiness (Dorban, 2004). The third place is a place of spiritual awakening, which includes establishing inner nuclei of wholeness and compassion toward the self and the world.

The third place is a state of mind of letting go, meaning, stop worrying and contemplating about things that cannot be changed, and stop feeling persecuted by inner objects. The similarity of this idea to the serenity prayer is quite evident. This is a mental place that includes remission of guilt after reparation and penance. According to Dorban (2004), this is the ability to hold the center and to dive into deep anxieties without drowning in them.

A common principle to both conceptualizations is that movement between both the different positions and the steps is associated with mental health. In the Kleinian theory, both the infant and the adult move constantly between the different positions (Hinshelwood, 1991), and in the 12-step program, after the completion of the 12th step, the member continues his journey by returning to the first step where he reencounters his powerlessness and self-centeredness. In the fourth step, he reexamines the role of aggression in his life, and in the eighth and the ninth steps, he deals again with issues of guilt, loss, damage and reparation. The continuous work of the steps helps in forming an integrated internal world and developing more compassion toward objects as well as toward the self.

Self psychology conceptualization of the 12-step program

From a self psychology perspective, the 12-step program provides many of the necessary conditions for the establishment of a cohesive self-structure. The fellowship provides selfobject needs when the members of the fellowship are the selfobjects. The unconditional acceptance of the group is embodied in the saying: "the newcomer is the most important person at any meeting" (Narcotics Anonymous, 2008, p. 9), and many members finally find a place in which they can start discovering their selfhood. The personal development is possible mostly because of the quite constant presence of selfobjects in the member's life. In contrast to other people in his life, the selfobjects in the fellowship will not fail or disappoint the new member when he needs help because of their high availability.

The opportunity to attend daily meetings and to call a sponsor contributes to the development of tolerance ability of optimal frustration. In such way, members can start to develop new coping skills with drug craving and with stressful situations. The constant mirroring, which members receive when they appear to meetings or report on successful coping with craving, assists in facilitating healthy grandiosity. For example, when a member shares a personal story of such a success and receives positive feedbacks, mental structures are created through processes of transmuting internalizations.

"In some ways, a sponsor is like a good friend, a wise teacher, a private tutor, a favorite uncle, a seasoned mentor, an experienced guide, and that older brother or sister we always wanted" (B., Hamilton, 1996). The relationship with the sponsor corresponds with the healthy need to form an idealized image of significant other and enables the new member to merge with an idealized figure in times of stress. This empathic matrix allows developing self-soothing capabilities and emotional regulation, and to practice these skills in the world outside the group.

Membership in the 12-step fellowships also allows development on the alter ego–connectedness axis. The intimate and emotional interactions with other members during step work and sharing personal stories are significant experiences for individuals who rarely trust others and feel isolated. Constant attendance helps the member to feel twinship toward the fellowship and to begin developing a feeling of belongingness and identity. Meaning, the member is not an anonymous drug addict, but a member in a specific community that helps him to become a functioning and productive individual in the society.

The 12-step program clearly corresponds with self psychology because it offers a transformation of the self. Drug addiction involves isolation, cruelty, violence, estrangement and inauthenticity, and such experiences lead to fragmentation of the self and finally to admission in powerlessness. The fragmentation of the self is a threatening experience (Kohut, 1971), but only following fragmentation, a restoration of the self is possible. Step work enables the reconstruction of the self along the three axes of development, as the selfobject needs are provided quite constantly.

The 12th step deals with spiritual awakening, but actually, this step describes a personality transformation. Such a transformation is possible only after almost total fragmentation of the previous self and the establishment of a new and cohesive self and a new identity. A member who completed the 12th step is not an individual who feels constant guilt over hurting close people in the past, nor is he a tragic person who is looking for meaning. A member who completed the 12th step is an individual with a positive and stable self-value who acquired self-regulation skills. It is a person who writes and practices meditation daily and inspires to strengthen his connection with his Higher Power. In my opinion, in the last two steps, there is a movement toward melting in the cosmic narcissism space, as the transformation of the self leads to compassionate view of the world, which is not a peak experience but an active approach to life, which includes an in-depth insight toward reality (Kohut, 1966).

Criticism of the 12-step program

There are professionals in the addictions and mental health fields who consider this program as simplistic in comparison to more complicated theories of human behavior. Wurmser (1985) considered twelve-step groups as simplistic yet necessary solution because they provide an external substitute for a damaged superego. He added that one of the therapy's aims is assisting the patient developing mental agencies (Wurmser, 1985).

Dodes supports individual treatment for drug abuse and addiction over other treatment modalities, such as twelve-step programs for a few reasons. He notes that the central concept of a "higher power" consists of a search for an idealized object and an omnipotent transitional object, "whose powers are utilized in exchange for the loss of power entailed in giving up the drug" (Dodes, 1990, p. 417). In therapy, the analyst may also be perceived as an idealized narcissistic object or as a target of merger, and so the patient regains a sense of control which he previously had while he abused drugs. The continuous attendance at twelve-step groups may help the patient to regain a sense of control, but he will not be able to internalize the function of the idealized object. Prolonged analytic work which includes interpretation of the unconscious processes underlying the addiction can lead to insight and personal growth (Dodes, 1990).

Dodes and Dodes (2015) raise important questions about the effectiveness of the 12-step program and criticize treatment centers that rely on its principles without studying their own treatment outcomes. In their polemical book, Dodes & Dodes (2015) analyze dozens of studies about Alcoholics Anonymous and other twelve-step groups and emphasizes that they rest on the flimsiest of scientific evidence.

Interestingly, Dodes's idea that helplessness lies at the basis of addiction corresponds with the first step of the program he criticizes. The first step in the twelve-step program holds that: "We admitted we were powerless over our addiction, that our lives had become unmanageable" (Narcotics Anonymous, 1998). This step includes an admission that the addiction is more powerful than the individual and that he does not control his life. Further work on this step includes recognizing the times the individual acts out of powerlessness and either abuses drugs or is he involved in other self-defeating behavior.

In my opinion, the 12-step program is being presented in a simple and clear language, and it offers drug addicts a path for recovery, which includes substantial work. Daily writing, daily literature reading, attending meetings and working with a sponsor are all components of intensive and demanding recovery method. Actually, the working of the 12 steps is actually a process of working through. The 12-step program does not deal with interpretations and transference relations, but it does help members in recognizing and overcoming resistances, coping with the compulsion to repeat drug abuse and gaining insight. All of which are processes related to Freud's concept of working through (Sedler, 1983).

Another point of criticism concerns the term God as we understand Him. The words God, religion and spirituality often raise inconvenience among analysts trained in different psychoanalytic schools of thought (Aron, 2004). A significant reason for such resistance stems from Freud's view of God and religion. Freud thought that the representation of God stems from the image of the father, when God serves as the ideal father figure that assists in coping with life's difficulties (Freud, 1927/1961). Furthermore, Freud hoped that in the future, science would replace religion and rationality will replace belief in God (O'Neill & Akhtar, 2009). Consequently, unlike other issues, belief in God or a Higher Power remains outside the analytic training, supervision and the therapy room.

Lewis Aron, a leading analyst, (2004) noted that issues concerning God and religion remained taboo among analysts for years. He addedd that his belief influenced his values and his analytic work, but any mentioning of God in front of colleagues was not welcomed. It should be noted that the 12-step program is a recovery program with spiritual elements and not a religious program with religious elements. In this context, it is essential distinguishing between religion and spirituality. Bienefeld and Yager (2007) note that religion is an organized system of beliefs, practices and rituals, which is usually shared with others, although everyone creates their version. Spirituality relates to the individual's attempt to make sense of his world beyond the tangible and temporal and to a strive for connection with the transcendent and transpersonal elements of human existence (Bienefeld & Yager, 2007).

The efficacy of NA – empirical evidence

In large surveys in NA, AA and CA (Cocaine Anonymous) organizations, members were asked to report on drug and alcohol abuse. About one third of the participants reported on abstinence periods, which ranged between one year to five years, when the median length of abstinence reported by AA and NA members was higher than five years (Alcoholics Anonymous, 2008; Cocaine Anonymous, 2011; Narcotics Anonymous, 2010). The average meeting attendance of the respondents was two to four meetings per week, and these findings suggest that longer-term abstinence is associated with relatively regular meeting attendance (Alcoholics Anonymous, 2008; Cocaine Anonymous, 2011; Narcotics Anonymous, 2010).

However, these findings rely solely on self-report, and there are not any other objective measures like drug urine tests. In a few empirical studies, AA and NA participation was associated with higher likelihood of abstinence, prolonged periods up to 16 years, improved psychosocial functioning and higher levels of self-efficacy (Humphreys et al., 2004; Kaskutas, 2009; Krentzman et al., 2010; Moos & Moos, 2006; Owen et al., 2003). Over the years, the philosophy of the 12-step program entered official addiction treatment facilities, and there is an empirical support for reduction in drug abuse rates following attendance and involvement in 12-step groups (Timko & DeBenedetti, 2007; Weiss et al., 2005). Constant attendance of three times a week and more was associated with reduced rates of drug abuse (Humphreys & Moos, 2001, 2007), and in another study among NA members, reduced drug abuse rates had been found (Toumbourou, Hamilton, U'Ren, Stevens-Jones, & Storey, 2002).

These studies provide empirical support for the beneficial effect of the 12-step program, but it is hard to understand the nature of the relationship from correlational studies. In three studies, using cross-lagged analyses of longitudinal data or structural equation modeling, reductions in drug and alcohol abuse were associated with 12-step involvement and were not attributed to any potential third variable (Connors, Tonigan, Miller, & Project MATCH Research Group, 2001; McKellar, Stewart, & Humphreys, 2003; Weiss et al., 2005). In this context, one of the famous sayings of NA is: "We have learned from our group experience that those who keep coming to our meetings regularly stay clean" (Narcotics Anonymous, 2008, p. 9).

Besides, the increased involvement in 12-step groups serves as a significant support source, which leads to decreased utilization of mental health and drug abuse treatment services and associated costs (Humphreys & Moos, 2001, 2007).

Concluding remarks

The 12-step program is a recovery program that grew out of the experience of addicted individuals, who came to the conclusion that the mutual help of members is the most efficient way to remain drug abstinent. However, therapeutic principles and strategies that are used in other treatment methods for the treatment of mental disorders and malaises are used in the program to promote and maintain behavioral and personality changes. Over the years, there has been significant growth in the number of 12-step organizations, and today, there are fellowships that help to cope with behavioral addictions, such as gambling, sex and gaming.

References

Alcoholics Anonymous. (2001). *Alcoholics Anonymous: The story of how many thousands of men and women recovered from alcoholism* (4th Ed.). Alcoholics Anonymous World Services.

Alcoholics Anonymous. (2008). *Alcoholics Anonymous 2007 membership survey.* Retrieved from http:// aa.org/pdf/products/p-48_07survey.pdf

Aron, L. (2004). God's influence on my psychoanalytic vision and values. *Psychoanalytic Psychology, 21*(3), 442–451.

B., Dick. (2006). *The conversion of Bill W.: More on the creator's role in early A.A.* Paradise Research Publications, Inc.

B., Hamilton. (1996). *Twelve-step sponsorship: How it works.* Hazelden.

Bean, M. H. (1975). Alcoholics Anonymous: AA. *Psychiatric Annals, 5,* 3–64.

Bienefeld, D., & Yager, J. (2007). Issues of spirituality and religion in psychotherapy supervision. *Israeli Journal of Psychiatry and Related Sciences, 44*(3), 178–186.

Bolea, Ş. (2014). What is existentialism? A revision of contemporary definitions. *Studia UBB. Philosophia, 59*(2), 63–72.

Cheever, S. (2004). *My name is Bill: Bill Wilson-his life and the creation of Alcoholics Anonymous.* Simon and Schuster.

Chen, G. (2010). The meaning of suffering in drug addiction and recovery from the perspective of existentialism, Buddhism and the 12-Step program. *Journal of Psychoactive Drugs, 42*(3), 363–375.

Clark, W. H. (1951). *The Oxford group: Its history and significance.* Bookman Associates.

Cocaine Anonymous. (2011). *What is Cocaine Anonymous?* Cocaine Anonymous World Services.

Connors, G. J., Tonigan, J. S., Miller, W. R., & Project MATCH Research Group. (2001). A longitudinal model of intake symptomatology, AA participation and outcome: Retrospective study of the Project MATCH outpatient and aftercare samples. *Journal of Studies on Alcohol, 62*(6), 817–825.

Cully, J. A., & Teten, A. L. (2008). *A therapist's guide to brief cognitive behavioral therapy.* Department of Veterans Affairs South Central MIRECC.

Dorban, S. (2004). Reparation – The third place? *Sihot – Dialogue: Israel Journal of Psychotherapy, 19*(1), 59–65. (in Hebrew).

Frankl, V. (2006). *Man's search for meaning.* Beacon Press. (Original work published 1946).

Freud, S. (1927/1961). The future of an illusion. In J. Strachey (Ed. & Trans.), *The standard edition of the complete psychological works of Sigmund Freud* (Vol. 21, pp. 1–56). Hogarth Press, (Original work published 1927).

Hartigan, F. (2001). *Bill W.: A biography of Alcoholics Anonymous cofounder Bill Wilson.* St. Martin's Griffin.

Hinshelwood. R. D. (1991). *A dictionary of Kleinian thought.* Free Association Books.

Humphreys, K., & Moos, R. (2001). Can encouraging substance abuse patients to participate in self-help groups reduce demand for health care? *Alcoholism: Clinical and Experimental Research, 25*(5), 711–716.

Humphreys, K., & Moos, R. H. (2007). Encouraging posttreatment self-help group involvement to reduce demand for continuing care services: Two-year clinical and utilization outcomes. *Alcoholism: Clinical & Experimental Research, 31*(1), 64–68.

Humphreys, K., Wing, S., McCarty, D., Chappel, J., Gallant, L., Haberle, B., & Weiss R. (2004). Self-help organizations for alcohol and drug problems: Toward evidence-based practice and policy. *Journal of Substance Abuse Treatment, 26*(3), 151–158.

James, W. (1961). *The varieties of religious experience.* Collier Books. (Original work published 1902).

Kaskutas, L. A. (2009). Alcoholics Anonymous effectiveness: Faith meets science. *Journal of Addictive Diseases, 28*(2), 145–157.

Kass, N. (2015). *The philosophies and practices of Alcoholics Anonymous from a psychodynamic perspective.* (doctoral dissertation). University of Pennsylvania, PA.

Kernberg, O. F. (1996). A psychoanalytic theory of personality disorders. In J. F. Clarkin & M. F. Lenzenweger (Eds.), *Major theories of personality disorder,* (pp. 106–140). Guilford Press.

Khantzian, E. J. (1981). Some treatment implications of the ego and self-disturbances in alcoholism. In M. H. Bean & N. E. Zinberg (Eds.), *Dynamic approaches to the understanding and treatment of alcoholism* (pp. 163–188). Free Press.

Kilpinen, E. (2009). Pragmatism as a philosophy of action. In S. Pihlström & H. Rydenfelt (Eds.), *Pragmatist perspectives* (pp. 163–179). Philosophical Society of Finland.

Kohut, H. (1966). Forms and transformations of narcissism. *Journal of the American Psychoanalytic Association, 14*(2), 243–272.

Kohut, H. (1971). *The analysis of the self.* International Universities Press.

Krentzman, A. R., Robinson, E. A., Moore, B. C., Kelly, J. F., Laudet, A. B., White, W. L., Strobbe, S. (2010). How Alcoholics Anonymous (AA) and Narcotics Anonymous (NA) work: Cross-disciplinary perspectives. *Alcohol Treatment Quarterly, 29*(1), 75–84.

Kurtz, E. (1990). *The spirituality of William James: A lesson from Alcoholics Anonymous.* Paper presented at the American Psychological Association 98th Annual Conference, Boston, MA, USA.

Litfin, B. M. (2014). *Early Christian martyr stories: An evangelical introduction with new translations.* Baker Academic.

Mack, J. E. (1981). Alcoholism, A.A., and the governance of the self. In M. H. Bean & N. E. Zinberg (Eds.), *Dynamic approaches to the understanding and treatment of alcoholism* (pp. 128–162). Free Press.

McKellar, J., Stewart, E., & Humphreys, K. (2003). Alcoholics Anonymous involvement and positive alcohol related outcomes: Consequence, or just a correlate? A prospective 2-year study of 2,319 alcohol dependent men. *Journal of Consulting and Clinical Psychology, 71*(2), 302–308.

Moos, R. H., & Moos, B. S. (2006). Participation in treatment and alcoholics anonymous: A 16-year follow-up of initially untreated individuals. *Journal of Clinical Psychology, 62*(6), 735–750.

Narcotics Anonymous. (1998). *Narcotics Anonymous step working guides.* Narcotics Anonymous World Services.

Narcotics Anonymous. (2002). *A guide to local services in Narcotics Anonymous.* Narcotics Anonymous World Services.

Narcotics Anonymous. (2008). *Narcotics Anonymous* (6th Ed.). Narcotics Anonymous World Services.

Narcotics Anonymous. (2010). *2009 membership survey.* Retrieved from http://www.na.org/admin/ include/spaw2/uploads/pdf/NA_membership_survey.pdf

O'Neill, M. K., & Akhtar, S. (2009). *On Freud's 'the future of an illusion'.* Karnac Books.

Owen, P. L., Slaymaker, V., Tonigan, J. S., McCrady, B. S., Epstein, E. E., Kaskutas, L. A., & Miller, W. R. (2003). Participation in alcoholics anonymous: Intended and unintended change mechanisms. *Alcoholism: Clinical and Experimental Research, 27*(3), 524–532.

Pitman, B. (1988). *AA: The way it began.* Glen Abbey Books.

Prochaska, J. O., Norcross, J. C., & DiClemente, C. C. (2013). Applying the stages of change. *Psychotherapy in Australia, 19*(2), 10–15.

Sedler, M. J. (1983). Freud's concept of working through. *The Psychoanalytic Quarterly, 52*(1), 73–98.

Simmel, E. (1948). Alcoholism and addiction. *The Psychoanalytic Quarterly, 17*, 6–31.

Timko, C., & DeBenedetti, A. (2007). A randomized controlled trial of intensive referral to 12-step self-help groups: One-year outcomes. *Drug and Alcohol Dependence, 90*(2–3), 270–279.

Toumbourou, J. W., Hamilton, M., U'Ren, A., Stevens-Jones, P., & Storey, G. (2002). Narcotics Anonymous participation and changes in substance use and social support. *Journal of Substance Abuse Treatment, 23*(1), 61–66.

VandenBos, G. R. (2007). *APA dictionary of psychology.* American Psychological Association.

Volkow, N. D., Koob, G. F., & McLellan, T. A. (2016). Neurobiologic advances from the brain disease model of addiction. *New England Journal of Medicine, 374*(4), 363–371.

Weiss, R. D., Griffin, M. L., Gallop, R. J., Najavits, L. M., Frank, A., Crits-Christoph, P., & Luborsky, L. (2005). The effect of 12-step self-help group attendance and participation on drug use outcomes among cocaine dependent patients. *Drug and Alcohol Dependence, 77*(2), 177–184.

Wilson, B. (1939). *Alcoholics Anonymous.* Works Publishing Co.

Wilson, B. (1944). *The fellowship of Alcoholics Anonymous.* College and University Press, 1945.

Wilson, K. G., Hayes, S. C., & Byrd, M. (2000). Exploring compatibilities between Acceptance and Commitment Therapy and 12-Step treatment for substance abuse. *Journal of Rational-Emotive and Cognitive-Behavior Therapy, 18*(4), 209–234.

Winnicott, D. W. (1953). Transitional objects and transitional phenomena. *International Journal of Psychoanalysis, 34,* 89–97.

Winnicott, D. W. (1960). Ego distortion in terms of true and false self. In *The maturational processes and the facilitating environment* (pp. 140–152). The Hogarth Press and the Institute of Psycho-Analysis, 1965.

Winnicott, D. W. (1963). The development of the capacity for concern. *Bulletin of the Menninger Clinic, 27,* 167–176.

Winnicott, D. W. (1964). *The child, the family and the outside world.* Penguin Books.

Wivestad, S. M. (2008). The educational challenges of agape and phronesis. *Journal of Philosophy of Education, 42*(2), 307–324.

Yalom, I. D. (1980). *Existential psychotherapy.* Basic Books.

Index